VISUAL QUICKSTART GUIDE

SEARCH ENGINES

FOR THE WORLD WIDE WEB, 3rd Edition

Alfred and Emily Glossbrenner

 Peachpit Press

Visual QuickStart Guide
Search Engines for the World Wide Web, 3rd Edition
Alfred and Emily Glossbrenner

Peachpit Press

1249 Eighth Street, Berkeley, CA 94710
510/524-2178 · 800/283-9444 · 510/524-2221 (fax)

Find us on the World Wide Web at http://www.peachpit.com

Peachpit Press is a division of Addison Wesley Longman

Editors: Nancy Davis, Whitney Walker, Becky Morgan
Production coordinators: Lisa Brazieal, Connie Jeung-Mills
Compositor: Owen Wolfson
Indexer: Emily Glossbrenner
Cover design: The Visual Group

ISBN 0-201-73401-X

9 8 7 6 5 4 3 2 1

Printed and bound in the United States of America

 Printed on recycled paper

About the Authors

Alfred and Emily Glossbrenner are the authors of more than 60 books with combined sales of well over one million copies. They have been alerting people to the power and possibilities of online information since 1982—long before there was a World Wide Web. Their uncanny knack for explaining complex subjects in a way that anyone can understand, combined with their conversational style, has earned them praise from publications as diverse as *MacWorld*, *Forbes*, and *The New York Times*.

What information do you want to find today? The Glossbrenners will show you how to do it. Recently, they put their search skills to work to write *About the Author: The Passionate Reader's Guide to the Authors You Love, Including Things You Never Knew, Juicy Bits You'll Want to Know, and Hundreds of Ideas for What to Read Next* (Harcourt, 2000).

Packed with fascinating details about 125 popular novelists, plus lots of other book-related information—like how to find out-of-print books online, where to go for reading-group resources, what books have been featured on Oprah's Book Club and other major book lists—*About the Author* simply could not have been written without the Web.

The Glossbrenners live and work in a 200-year-old farmhouse on the Delaware River in Bucks County, Pennsylvania. You can write to them at gloss@gloss.com, or visit them on the Web at www.trulyuseful.com.

Praise from Readers and Critics

Here's a sampling of what readers and critics have said about earlier editions of *Search Engines for the World Wide Web: Visual QuickStart Guide.*

"[This book] is exactly what Web guides should be—concise, easily referenced, informative, and appropriate for all levels of expertise. If you have ever had the problems that most surfers experience when conducting a search—dredging up 100,000-plus hits on AltaVista, finding coffee pages when searching for Java, or pulling up the dreaded goose egg—you need to have this book close at hand."

—The Editors of Amazon.com

"I immediately liked *Search Engines for the World Wide Web....* It's a small book, nicely organized, well written, and full of illustrations that make learning easier."

—Danny Sullivan, "Search Engine Report" Newsletter

"[The Glossbrenners' book] goes a long way toward bringing search newcomers, and even those who have been exploring the Net for awhile, to a higher skill level.... Those who read the book from cover to cover will feel they have 'been there' in all the nooks and crannies of each site before even going online to try them out."

—Wallys W. Conhaim, *Link-Up*

"If you've been stumped, overwhelmed, or just plain frustrated with your Internet searching, pick up this book and find the answers you've been looking for."

—*The Naked PC*

"This great little book covers all the major search engines Web users deal with every day.... There is information to get technophobes comfortable with the basics as well as advanced techniques that will help professional researchers and librarians. Highly recommended."

—Thom Gillespie, *Library Journal*

"At last, thanks to the lucid writing of the Glossbrenners and the ingenious format of Peachpit's *Visual QuickStart Guide* series, we have a work of reference that is clear, comprehensive, and concise.... With the Glossbrenners' new book in hand, you'll gain speed, confidence, and skills for searching the Web and finding precisely what you need."

—Michael Pastore, review for YouthTopia Web Site

"This [book] won me over in the first paragraph of the introduction: 'If you're like us, the fascination of *browsing* the Web wore off a long time ago. We want to sign on, get the information we need, sign off, and go about our business and our lives.'

"Hey, that's me.... This *QuickStart Guide* is easy to read without being condescending—perfect for beginners and advanced users alike."

—Krissy Harris, *Los Angeles Times*

"I just want to congratulate you on your excellent book, *Search Engines for the World Wide Web.* I thoroughly enjoyed it and will use it in my reference and training work."

—Margaret Smyth, Central Library, North York, Ontario, Canada

"The organization and design of this book are splendid.... The reader quickly learns how search engines work, and the importance of keywords. Useful tips are plentiful. The brief chapter on Basic Search Tools is helpful enough to have you slam your fist into your keyboard and exclaim, 'Why didn't someone tell me this stuff in the first place?' Ditto for the Seven Habits of Highly Effective Web Searchers....

"Perhaps my favorite part of [the book] is Appendix A, the Quick Reference pages, where all the important search engine commands are presented in alphabetical order by search engine name. This book is a winner for everyone who spends more than two minutes per month on the Web, with practical information at an affordable price."

—John Nemerovski, Book Bytes Reviewer, *My Mac Magazine*

"*Search Engines for the World Wide Web* shows readers the fastest and most efficient ways to find what they need with the least frustration. With easy-to-follow, step-by-step instructions accompanied by dozens of useful illustrations, [it] makes learning about search engines as quick and efficient as possible.

"[This book] is essential reading for the novice and has much to offer the experienced Internet information researcher as well.... It's also highly recommended for any Internet and World Wide Web information provider [who wants to] enhance and maximize accessibility and 'presence awareness' among Internet and Web users."

—The Computer Shelf, `alt.books.reviews`

"I would think that almost every library using the Internet would want at least one copy! We have had to rely on magazine articles and the Help sections at each search engine Web site in order to understand the rules for searching with each engine. [This] book will make it much easier to understand how to construct search strategies, since the information is all in one place."

—Richard Strauss, Branch Manager, Bucks County Free Library, Langhorne, PA

"[A] concise, thorough, readable guide.... Highly recommended."

—Windweaver Online Bookstore

TABLE OF CONTENTS

INTRODUCTION

Late in the year 2000, the Internet passed the two billion mark—two billion Web pages, that is, all accessible via the World Wide Web. And with an estimated seven million new pages being created every day, it's entirely possible that as you read this, the Net may be approaching three, four, or even five billion total pages.

So how in blazes does anyone *find* anything? That's the million-dollar question. If you're like us, the fascination of "browsing the Web"—clicking on links to go aimlessly hither and yon—wore off years ago. We want to sign on, get the information we need, sign off, and go about our business and our lives.

Fortunately, some excellent tools are available on the Net to help you do just that. Dozens of them, in fact. They're called *search engines*, and, not surprisingly, the best of them consistently rank among the most popular sites on the Internet.

But the proliferation of search sites has created a new problem and a whole new set of questions. With so many search engines out there competing for our attention (one popular Internet directory currently lists 3,569), how do we find out what the really good ones are? Does it make any difference which one we choose? Will a search for, say, digital camera product reviews or Ally McBeal episode guide produce the same results whether we use AltaVista or Google or Yahoo?

How to Get the Most Out of This Book

This book will answer all of these questions and more. And like all the books in the *Visual QuickStart* series, it's designed to do so with a minimum of technical jargon and extraneous information. You'll find lots of step-by-step instructions and specific examples for using search engines in general, and the very best ones in particular.

In writing the book, we've made just a few basic assumptions about you:

◆ You understand the fundamentals of working with a computer, such as how to use a mouse and how to choose menu commands.

◆ You have access to the Internet—either through an Internet Service Provider (ISP) like AT&T WorldNet or EarthLink, or an online service like America Online (AOL) or Microsoft Network (MSN)—and you know how to sign onto the Net.

◆ You have some experience using a Web browser program like Microsoft Internet Explorer or Netscape Navigator to visit Web sites, and now you're ready to learn how to do more than just "surf the Net."

If you're not quite up to speed on one or more of these fronts, you may want to hold off on this book for the time being.

Instead, if you have a personal computer running Windows, check your favorite bookstore or local library for *The Little PC Book* by Larry Magid. If you have a Macintosh, look for *The Little Mac Book* or *The Little iMac Book*, both by Robin Williams. Published by Peachpit Press, all three of these books include chapters specifically aimed at people who are venturing onto the Internet for the very first time.

For in-depth coverage of Internet Explorer, try Steve Schwartz's *Internet Explorer 5: Visual QuickStart Guide*, also published by Peachpit Press and available in both Windows and Macintosh versions.

Once you're comfortable using your computer and Web browser software—and you've spent some time exploring Web sites on your own—the information presented in *this* book will make a lot more sense.

Companion Web Site

For book updates, links to search engine resources, and other goodies, visit the companion Web site for this book at www.peachpit.com/vqs/search.

How the Book Is Organized

The chapters in *Search Engines for the World Wide Web* are organized into four major parts, followed by four appendices. Here's what's covered in each one:

Part 1: Search Basics

In this part of the book we introduce you to the concept of search engines and how they work. You'll also learn about *keywords*—how to choose the right ones and the various methods of combining them for more effective searches. We round things out with some specific tips and techniques for using any search engine.

You should read the four chapters in this part of the book from start to finish, since each chapter builds on the information presented in the ones before. Also, you'll need this basic grounding in online searching to get the most out of the chapters on specific search engines in Parts 2, 3, and 4.

Part 2:
The Big Six Search Engines

Here you'll find chapters on six of the best and most powerful search engines available today. You can read these chapters in any order. If you're somewhat familiar with one of the search engines covered here, you might start with that one and then branch out from there to learn about two or three others.

By the time you're finished reading about a particular search engine, you'll know its strengths and weaknesses and how to use the major features to create effective queries. Best of all, whenever you need a refresher, you can consult the Quick Reference guide included in each chapter.

Part 3: Other General-Purpose Search Engines

The Big Six search engines aren't the only game in town, of course. In this part of the book, we'll introduce you to four additional general-purpose search engines. You may very well be using one of these sites as your "portal" to the Internet—the place you visit first whenever you go online. But are you using the site's search features to maximum advantage? If you're not sure, read the relevant chapter in this part of the book, and refer to the Quick Reference guide for search rules and examples.

Part 4:
Specialized Search Engines

Next we present some alternatives to the all-purpose "Swiss Army Knife" approach of the search engines covered in Parts 2 and 3. Just as cooks and carpenters need special tools from time to time, so too do Web searchers. This part of the book introduces you to some of the best of these special tools and helps you understand when to use them for faster, more efficient searches.

Appendix A:
Search Engines Quick Reference

This is a collection of all the Quick Reference guides from throughout the book, organized alphabetically by search engine. Our thought is that when you're online and need a quick reminder of, say, the HotBot or Northern Light search rules, you may find it more convenient to turn to this appendix instead of going back to the individual search engine chapter.

Appendix B: Internet Domains and Country Codes

The information presented here will help you take advantage of power-searching techniques like zeroing in on a specific *type* of organization (based on the Internet domain designation in its Web address), or locating sites that originate in a particular country.

Appendix C: Usenet Newsgroup Hierarchies

This appendix explains how newsgroups are named and gives you the information you need to limit your queries to specific newsgroups, a feature offered by some search engines.

Appendix D: Web Searcher's Toolkit

In this part of the book, we'll tell you about a handful of Windows and Macintosh programs that we've found to be especially useful for getting the most out of the Internet. All of the programs are public domain or shareware, or they are offered in free demo versions, so that you can "try before you buy." We'll explain what each of these programs is designed to do and tell you how to get them.

HOW THE BOOK IS ORGANIZED

PART 1

SEARCH BASICS

Search Basics

If you're new to online searching, we suggest that you read the four chapters in this part of the book from start to finish. With this information under your belt, you'll get a lot more out of the specific search engine chapters in Parts 2, 3, and 4.

Chapter 1, **Search Engines and How They Work**, brings you up to speed fast on what search engines are all about and how they accomplish the mammoth task of collecting information from Web sites around the world.

Chapter 2, **Unique Keywords**, lays out specific steps for choosing the best search terms for your Web searches. Coming up with the right keywords is the essence of effective searching, and this chapter will show you how to do just that.

Chapter 3, **Basic Search Tools**, builds on the keyword concept by showing you how to enter and combine search terms. Each search engine has its own way of doing things, but the basic concepts are similar from one search engine to the next. Once you know the basics, you'll be well equipped to deal with almost any search engine.

Chapter 4, **Tips and Techniques**, lays out the "Seven Habits of Highly Effective Web Searchers," offers advice on customizing your Web browser, and presents some tried-and-true techniques for making your online sessions easier and more productive.

SEARCH ENGINES AND HOW THEY WORK

Listening to television news shows and reading the daily paper, you could easily get the impression that the Internet and the World Wide Web hold the answers to virtually any question you could possibly ask. Sign on to your favorite search engine, tap a few keys, and all the world's knowledge is there for the taking. It couldn't be simpler.

But ask anyone who has actually tried to use a search engine to answer a specific question or track down a particular fact or figure and you're likely to hear a far different story: "I can't find *anything* on the Net." Or "The search engine I used turned up so *much* information, most of it totally useless, that I gave up."

The problem is at least twofold. First, the Internet is so vast and so lacking in organization that even longtime, experienced searchers express great frustration in using it for finding information.

Second, most people who use search engines don't really understand what they are and don't bother to learn how to take full advantage of their unique information-finding features. Falling prey to the hype, perhaps, they simply type one or two words into a search form and are then unpleasantly surprised when they are presented with thousands (or even millions) of Web pages.

The current state of search engines can be compared to a phone book that is updated irregularly, is biased toward listing more popular information, and has most of the pages ripped out.

—Steve Lawrence and Lee Giles, authors of a widely publicized 1999 study of search engines for the NEC Research Institute

The Perils of
Internet Searching

One of our favorite descriptions of what it's like to search the Internet is offered by Clifford Stoll, veteran searcher and author of *Silicon Snake Oil* and *The Cuckoo's Egg*. By way of background, and to help you appreciate Mr. Stoll's formidable research skills, we should mention that *The Cuckoo's Egg* recounts how he used the Net to track down the notorious "Hanover Hacker"—a trail that also led to a KGB-backed spy ring. That was in the late 1980s, before most of the world had even heard of the Internet.

But despite his considerable research background and demonstrated ability to find information, here's how Mr. Stoll once described the Internet and his struggle to locate the answer to a specific question:

What the Internet hucksters won't tell you is that the Internet is an ocean of unedited data, without any pretense of completeness. Lacking editors, reviewers, or critics, the Internet has become a wasteland of unfiltered data. You don't know what to ignore and what's worth reading.

Logged onto the World Wide Web, I hunt for the date of the Battle of Trafalgar. Hundreds of files show up, and it takes 15 minutes to unravel them—one's a biography written by an eighth grader, the second is a computer game that doesn't work, and the third is an image of a London monument. None answers my question...

Figure 1.1 Google emphasizes *searching*—rather than browsing the Web by topic.

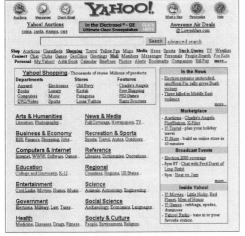

Figure 1.2 Yahoo's home page gives you two ways to look for information. You can type a query in the search form or click on one of 14 subject areas and work your way through the site's comprehensive topic directory.

Search Engines to the Rescue

It's not likely that the Internet will become less chaotic any time soon. In fact, it's a virtual certainty that it won't. After all, unlike America Online (AOL) and Microsoft Network (MSN), no one is "in charge" of the Internet. Once you understand and accept that, you'll be better able to deal with the chaos—and perhaps more forgiving when you can't find what you're looking for.

That said, let's move on to what you *can* do something about—developing a better understanding of search engines and how to use them to make sense out of the Internet's "ocean of unedited data."

Search engines defined

A s*earch engine* is a tool that lets you explore databases containing the text from hundreds of millions of Web pages. When the search engine software finds pages that match your search request (often referred to as *hits)*, it presents them to you with brief descriptions and clickable links to take you there.

Google (**Figure 1.1**) and other leading search engines focus primarily on providing a powerful search capability and offering the largest possible database of Web pages. But in order to compete with Yahoo (**Figure 1.2**)—the most popular site on the Net—they also give you the option of using a multi-level *topic directory* to browse a much smaller collection of Web pages for information on a given subject.

Topic directories are prepared by human beings, who spend their days visiting, selecting, and classifying Web sites based on content. Yahoo maintains its own staff of "Yahoo Surfers" to perform this function and is widely considered to be the premier topic directory on the Net. Most of the other leading search engines rely on either LookSmart (`www.looksmart.com`) or the Open Directory Project (`dmoz.org`) for their topic directories.

The Big Six Search Engines

Of all the search sites available today, several are especially impressive: AltaVista, Google, HotBot, Lycos, Northern Light, and Yahoo. What sets them apart and earns them the distinction of being included in what we call the "Big Six" search engines?

◆ They've been around for two or more years.

◆ Their creators know the Net and the Web and have designed their sites and the underlying software with the primary goal of making searching as easy as possible.

◆ They all offer exceptionally large searchable databases, excellent help information, powerful search tools, and an overall "look and feel" that's conducive to searching.

Of course, like virtually all search engines these days, they also carry advertising of one form or another (**Figure 1.3**). That's how they finance their operations and avoid having to charge subscription fees for the use of their services.

Some have begun offering *portal features* like free e-mail, news, chat, stock quotes, and weather reports (**Figure 1.4**)—stuff that's completely unrelated to searching but presumably helps attract visitors (and thus advertisers). The idea is to get you to think of the site not just as a place to search but as your *portal to the Internet*—the first place you visit whenever you go online.

Fortunately, in the case of the Big Six, the advertising and ancillary features interfere very little (if at all) with your ability to search effectively. Thus, we strongly recommend that you get to know at least a couple of these sites and choose one as your primary search engine.

Figure 1.3 Advertising messages and corporate sponsorships, like this one for Network Solutions, are common on search engine sites.

Figure 1.4 Extra features like news, weather, stock quotes, chat, and so forth get equal billing with searching at many search engine sites. Lycos is no exception.

If you already have a favorite Internet portal (AOL, Excite, MSN, and Netscape all have large followings), consider making one of the Big Six your *backup* search site—the place you go for a "second opinion" when you can't find exactly what you're looking for using your portal site's search feature.

✔ Tip

■ One good way to quickly size up a search engine or portal is to look at its search tips and help information. Sites that are serious about searching will offer clear, detailed instructions for new and advanced users.

Where to find the Big Six

We'll have much more to say about each of the Big Six search engines in Part 2 of this book, but if you'd like to visit them now, here's where to find them:

AltaVista	www.altavista.com
Google	www.google.com
HotBot	www.hotbot.com
Lycos	www.lycos.com
Northern Light	www.northernlight.com
Yahoo	www.yahoo.com

✔ Tips

- The official address or URL (Uniform Resource Locator) for any Web site always begins with `http://`. However, with the latest versions of Web browsers like Microsoft Internet Explorer (IE) and Netscape Navigator, you don't have to include this portion of the address.

- You can often even omit the www and com portions of a Web address (**Figure 1.5**). It doesn't work for multi-word names separated by periods, but try it with any of the addresses in our search engine list.

  Just type the search engine name (`altavista`, `google`, `hotbot`, etc.) in your Web browser's Address or Location box and then hit Enter (or Ctrl Enter if you're using IE for Windows).

- For Web addresses ending in anything other than com (`edu`, `gov`, `net`, `org`, etc.), it's a good idea to type the complete address, like `www.whitehouse.gov`. IE and Netscape are working on enhancements to their methods of dealing with partial Web addresses, but both currently make the assumption that if you type, say, `whitehouse`, you're looking for `www.whitehouse.com`, which happens to be a pornography site instead of the official Web site for the home of U.S. presidents.

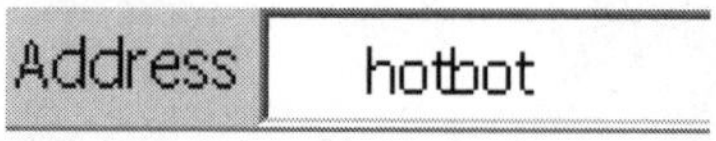

Figure 1.5 HotBot's official address is `http://www.hotbot.com`. But with the latest versions of Microsoft Internet Explorer and Netscape Navigator, you can just type `hotbot`.

Figure 1.6 Scooter is the spider responsible for building AltaVista's database of Web pages.

Figure 1.7 Here's a typical search engine submission form. Northern Light and other search engines try to make it as easy as possible for people to alert them to new sites.

How Search Engines Work

Search engines are designed to make it as easy as possible for you to find what you want on the Internet. But with hundreds of millions of Web pages stored on computers all over the world—and more being added all the time—how can search engines possibly collect them all? And what do they do with the information once they get it?

Spiders and indexes

Search engines do their data gathering by deploying robot programs called *spiders* or *crawlers*. Some even have names and personalities, like "Scooter," the AltaVista spider (**Figure 1.6**). Scooter and other such programs are designed to track down Web pages, follow the links they contain, and add any new information they encounter to a master database or *index*.

You don't really need to know the specifics. The key point to understand is that each search engine has its own way of doing things. Some have programmed their spiders or crawlers to search for only the *titles* of Web pages and the first few lines of text. Others snare every single word, ignoring only the graphics, video, sound, and other multimedia files.

The spiders' work is supplemented with information supplied directly to the search engines by professional and amateur Web developers. With millions of new Web pages being created every day, search engines welcome this kind of help and make it easy for anyone to suggest a site by simply clicking on a link on the home page and completing a simple form (**Figure 1.7**).

continues on next page

It may take weeks or even months for a form to be processed using these free submission services, however. So some search engines have begun offering "express service" to customers willing to pay a fee for having a Web site added to the database within a couple of days. Others are experimenting with charging customers to have their Web pages visited more frequently by the search engine's spider program.

These services go by different names, but they're often referred to generically as *paid-inclusion* or *pay-for-submission* services. As they begin to catch on, such services should help to improve the freshness and comprehensiveness of search engine databases.

✔ Tips

- Yahoo currently charges $199 for adding a commercial Web site to its topic directory within 48 hours. (The free service can take as long as six months.)

- Inktomi, the search engine that powers HotBot and a number of other leading search sites, charges $6 to $20 per page for a one-year subscription. (The more pages you submit, the lower the cost per page.) The service promises inclusion in the database within two days and a return visit by the Inktomi spider every 48 hours.

- Don't confuse paid-inclusion and pay-for-submission services with the more controversial *pay-for-placement*, which guarantees preferential treatment in search engine rankings. The GoTo search engine (www.goto.com) pioneered the concept of pay-for-placement. Instead of charging a set fee for inclusion in its database, GoTo allows Web site owners to bid on search terms that are relevant to their sites. The higher the bid, the higher that Web site appears in the search results (**Figure 1.8**).

Figure 1.8 With GoTo's pay-for-placement approach to presenting search results, these Web sites paid the most for the keyword *travel* and therefore get the top three slots.

```
<META NAME="KeyWords" CONTENT="free, free, free, free, free, free, free, free,
money, money, money, money, money, money, money, money, money, money, money, sex,
sex, sex, sex, sex, sex, sex, sex, sex, sex, sex, sex, sex, sex, sex, sex, sex, sex, sex, sex,
web, pages, Mall, online, shopping, shop, mall, malls, store, stores, birthday, christmas,
holiday, gift, gifts, art, collectibles, automotive, books, clothing, computers, electronics,
food, beverage, restaurant, health, fitness, housewares, money, finance, bank, music,
professional services, real estate, specialty shops, sports, recreation, toys, games, travel">
```

Figure 1.9 One technique for spamdexing or spoofing is to insert a block of text like this in the Web page. The words may or may not have anything to do with the actual content of the page.

Table 1.1

How Much of the Web Is Indexed?

Search Engine	Number of Web Pages Indexed	Percentage of Web Pages Indexed
Google	1.2 billion	57%
Netscape Search (powered by Google)	1.2 billion	57%
Yahoo (powered by Google)	1.2 billion	57%
Lycos (powered by FAST)	575 million	27%
HotBot (powered by Inktomi GEN3)	500 million	24%
AltaVista	350 million	17%
Northern Light	330 million	16%
Excite	250 million	12%
AOL Search (powered by Inktomi)	110 million	5%
MSN Search (powered by Inktomi)	110 million	5%

Note: The percentage figures have been calculated based on search engine sizes reported by Search Engine Watch (www.searchenginewatch.com) as of January 2001 and an estimate that the World Wide Web contains 2.1 billion pages.

Relevancy formulas

Every search engine uses a different method for calculating *relevancy*—how well a particular Web page matches your search request. As mentioned above, at GoTo, the method is quite straightforward: the higher the bid, the higher a site's ranking.

For most search engines, however, the relevancy formulas are a closely guarded secret. And they are constantly being changed in an effort to stay one step ahead of crafty Web developers, some of whom engage in a practice called *spamdexing* or *spoofing*—doctoring a Web page to fool search engines into putting it high on the list of search results.

One of the most common tricks is to load a Web page with words—like *free* or *money* or *sex*—that may or may not have anything to do with the site (**Figure 1.9**). The Web page may even be designed so that the words are hidden from view when you look at the page with your browser.

A search engine can respond to tactics like this by rewriting its software, changing the relevancy formula to give a *lower* ranking to pages with a lot of repeated words.

How good are the spiders?

The beauty of spiders and crawlers is that they operate around the clock. But some take longer than others to make their rounds. And, with one exception, even the best of them have located and indexed less than a third of the estimated 2.1 billion pages that are out there. (See **Table 1.1** for a comparison of several of the leading engines.)

That's why you may be successful finding a specific Web site using one search engine but not another. It's also a good reason to get into the habit of trying the same search on multiple engines.

continues on next page

At this writing, Google holds the record for the largest database—some 1.2 billion pages. (The Google database is used by both Netscape Search and Yahoo for their Web results.) FAST (the search engine that powers Lycos) is second, with 575 million pages. And Inktomi's GEN3 database (the one used by HotBot) is a close third, with 500 million pages.

But remember, even though Google is more than twice as big as FAST and Inktomi, there are still close to a *billion* Web pages that it doesn't cover. You can count on the fact that a large percentage of those Web pages *have* been found by and included in the databases of one or more of the other leading search engines.

✔ Tips

- Keep in mind that when you use a search engine to "search the Web," what you are actually searching is that particular site's database of information, collected by a spider program and supplemented with entries submitted by site creators. Each search engine you use will produce a different set of results, because each creates and maintains its own database.

- When you explore a subject using a search engine's topic directory, you're likely to get far fewer hits. But the sites you find will all have been selected and classified by human beings.

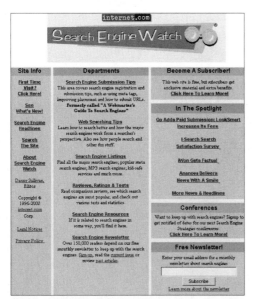

Figure 1.10 The Search Engine Watch Web site at www.searchenginewatch.com is the definitive online source for information about search engines and how they operate.

More Information for Webmasters and Others

Many search engines provide basic information about how their spiders operate—what they search for, how many sites they visit in a day, how often the master database is updated, and so forth. You may have to dig a bit to find it, but it's probably there.

Start by checking the search engine's home page for an About link. Or try the search tips and help information, usually accessible via a Help link on or near the search form.

For even more detail, look for the site's instructions to Webmasters on how to submit a URL to the search engine. To learn more about the AltaVista spider, database, and indexing methods, for example, go to the AltaVista home page (www.altavista.com) and click on Submit a Site and then on How AltaVista Works.

Resources for Webmasters

If you're responsible for designing Web pages and making sure that people can find them on the Internet, you'll definitely want to track down the information provided by each of the major engines on how their spiders operate and how their indexes are developed. But you'll also want to pay a visit to one of the Net's premier resources for Webmasters:

Search Engine Watch. This Web site (**Figure 1.10**) is hands down the best source of information we've encountered on how search engines work. Created several years ago by Internet consultant and journalist Danny Sullivan, Search Engine Watch is now owned by Internet.com (www.internet.com). But Mr. Sullivan continues to maintain the site, which is located at www.searchenginewatch.com.

continues on next page

Among its many offerings is a section called "Search Engine Submission Tips," with all the latest information on how to design a site for maximum visibility by the major engines. For people who are simply curious about search engine technology, there's a wealth of interesting information—facts and figures about search engine sizes, comparative reviews and ratings, tutorials, a glossary, and more.

✔ Tips

- If you don't see what you want on the Search Engine Watch home page, try using the site's search feature.

- Search Engine Watch publishes a twice-monthly newsletter issued via e-mail. You can sign up for free, but regular readers are encouraged to pay $79 for an annual subscription ($49 for six months), which helps to support the site and entitles you to additional reports and information not available to the general public.

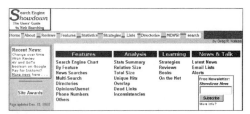

Figure 1.11 Search Engine Showdown at www.searchengineshowdown.com is aimed at *users* of search engines, rather than Webmasters.

Figure 1.12 The Web Search site at websearch.about.com is a good place to look for beginner's guides and tutorials on search engines.

Figure 1.13 Pandia (www.pandia.com) is another excellent source of beginner's guides, tutorials, and search tools.

Other great resources

Search Engine Watch is aimed largely, though not exclusively, at Webmasters. If you're primarily interested in learning about search engines so that you can become a more effective *searcher*, we recommend these sites:

Search Engine Showdown. Created and maintained by researcher and writer Greg R. Notess, this award-winning site (**Figure 1.11**) compares and evaluates search engines from a user's perspective. Check here for regularly updated feature lists, detailed reviews, and performance reports. The site is located at www.searchengineshowdown.com.

Web Search. This site (**Figure 1.12**), hosted by Web consultant Chris Sherman, is a good source of search tips, tutorials, and feature articles. One of the About.com subject guides, it's located at websearch.about.com.

Pandia Search Central. Named after a Greek goddess of light and enlightenment, the Pandia Web site (www.pandia.com) is beautifully designed and full of great information (**Figure 1.13**). Its creators, Per and Susanne Koch, who happen to live in Norway, are dedicated to helping Internet users become more effective searchers. They have produced a truly remarkable resource for doing just that.

2

UNIQUE KEYWORDS

The biggest challenge with any type of online searching is choosing the right search terms or *keywords*. This goes double for Web searching because, when you use tools like AltaVista, Google, Lycos, and other search engines, what you are typically searching is the *full text* of Web pages collected automatically by spider or crawler programs.

That sounds great in theory. But ask any librarian or professional searcher—anyone who makes a living using high-powered, high-cost databases like DIALOG, Dow Jones/News Retrieval, and LEXIS-NEXIS—about full-text searching. What they'll tell you is that it's actually the most difficult type of searching in the online world.

To help you understand why, we'll take a look in this chapter at another type of database searching that most everyone is familiar with—using the electronic card catalog at the local library. Then, with that as background, we'll show you how to meet the challenge of full-text searching by choosing the right keywords for your Web searches.

The Challenge of Full-Text Searching

Traditional databases like the electronic card catalog at your local library let you do *field searches*. If you're interested in the writer Kurt Vonnegut, for example, you can search for Vonnegut in the database's *author* field to produce a list of his books. Click on a title and all the relevant information about that book will be presented in familiar, card-catalog format (**Figure 2.1**).

If, on the other hand, you're looking for Kurt Vonnegut's biography or other information *about* him, you can search for his name in the *subject* field. Or maybe what you really want is a recent magazine article that features Kurt Vonnegut, in which case you'd use the periodicals database instead of the one for the library's collection of books.

Web search engine databases, in contrast, make no distinction among the various types of information available about Kurt Vonnegut. Do a search on his name and you'll get a hodge-podge of Web sites, many of them personal home pages created by Vonnegut fans (**Figure 2.2**).

Web page field searches

Field searching with Web search engines, if it's available at all, is limited to fields having to do with the Web page itself—its title, Web address or URL (Uniform Resource Locator), the date the page was created, and so forth—not the information *on* the page.

Searching these Web page fields can be quite useful, but it doesn't come close to matching the precision and sophistication of traditional database field searching. Which brings us back to our original point: To be an effective Web searcher you'll need to get quite good at coming up with the *right* keywords.

```
Records 1 through 1 of 103 returned.

Author:          Vonnegut, Kurt.
Title:           Cat's cradle.
Edition:         [1st ed.]
Published:       New York, Holt, Rinehart and Winston [1963]
Description:     233 p. 22 cm.
LC Call No.:     PZ4.V948 Cat
Subjects:        Humorous stories. gsafd
                 Science fiction. gsafd
                 Satire. gsafd
Control No.:     63010930 /L/r952
```

Figure 2.1 Search for author Kurt Vonnegut at your local library and you'll get information like this for each of his books.

Top 10 Displayed: Full Description | Show Titles Only | View by URL

- KURT VONNEGUT: The most comprehensive Vonnegut site in the cosmos
  URL: http://www.duke.edu/~crh4/vonnegut/vonnegut.html

- Kurt Vonnegut Index
  URL: http://www.duke.edu/~crh4/kv/

- Marek Vit's Kurt Vonnegut Corner
  URL: http://www.geocities.com/Hollywood/4953/vonn.html
  Excite Directory Match: Kurt Vonnegut

- Kurt Vonnegut -- Home Page
  URL: http://www.vonnegut.com/
  Excite Directory Match: Kurt Vonnegut

- Kurt Vonnegut
  URL: http://www.levity.com/corduroy/vonnegut.htm
  Excite Directory Match: Kurt Vonnegut

- Books by Kurt Vonnegut
  URL: http://www.a-ten.com/books/vonnegut/

- Untitled
  URL: http://sunsite.unc.edu/brian/vonnegut.html

- Kurt Vonnegut - Quotes, Bokonon, and more
  URL: http://acad.fandm.edu/~al_burgman/vonnegut/vonnegut.html
  Excite Directory Match: Kurt Vonnegut

- Stories, Listed by Author
  URL: http://www.best.com/~contento/s224.html

- Kurt Vonnegut Essay Collection
  URL: http://www.geocities.com/Hollywood/4953/kv_essays.html
  Excite Directory Match: Theory for 20th Century Literature

`Next >>`

Figure 2.2 Search the Web for Kurt Vonnegut and there's no telling what you'll come up with, as these results show.

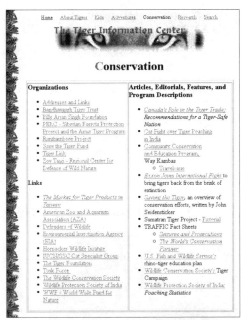

Figure 2.3 Searching for a unique phrase like Bengal tiger is more likely to produce a site like this near the top of your search results list than would a search for the far more common tigers.

Choosing the Right Keywords

Learning to come up with the most effective keywords for your Web searches will take time and practice. Don't be surprised or disappointed if you're not successful every time. After all, even the best online searchers find Web searching to be quite a challenge.

We don't pretend to have all the answers ourselves, but here are some points to keep in mind that can help you improve your Web searching success rate.

To get the best search results:

1. **Use the most unique keyword you can think of**. Take the time to think about the words that will almost certainly appear on the kind of Web page you have in mind. Then pick the most unique or unusual word from that list.

    If you're looking for information about efforts to save tiger populations in Asia, for example, don't use tigers as your search term. You'll be swamped with Web pages about the Detroit Tigers, the Princeton Tigers, and every other sports team that uses the word *tigers* in its name.

    Instead, try searching for a particular tiger species that you know to be on the endangered list—Bengal tiger or Sumatran tiger or Siberian tiger. (With some search engines, you'll need to enclose the words in quotation marks to let them know you're doing a *phrase search*: "Bengal tiger".) Chances are, you'll find sites like the one in **Figure 2.3** near the top of the list.

continues on next page

2. **Make it a multi-step process**.
Don't assume that you'll find what you
want on the first try. Take your best shot.
Then review the first couple of pages of
results, paying particular attention to the
sites that contain the *kind* of information
you want. What unique words appear on
those pages? Make a few notes and then
do another search using those words.

You might even try changing the *order*
in which you type your keywords in the
search form's text box. Some search
engines give more weight to the first word
in your query than to those that appear
second or third, on the assumption that
you will typically put your most important search word first.

Consequently, a search for endangered
tiger species might very well produce
different results than a search for tiger
endangered species.

3. **Narrow the field by searching just your
previous results**. If your chosen keyword
returns relatively good information but
too much to review comfortably, try a
second search of just those results. This
is sometimes referred to as *set searching*.

Most of the leading search engines make
set searching quite easy by providing an
option on the search results page that
allows you to "Search within these results"
(**Figures 2.4** and **2.5**). But even if the search
engine doesn't provide this option, you can
accomplish essentially the same thing by
simply adding another keyword to your
search request and submitting it again.

4. **Look for your keyword in the Web
page title**. Often the best search strategy
is to look first for your unique keyword
in the *titles* of Web pages. All the Big Six
search engines allow you to search Web
page titles, but the rules for doing so vary
slightly depending on which search engine
you're using.

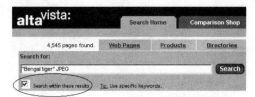

Figure 2.4 Set searching is easy with AltaVista. Once
you've located sites offering information about
Bengal tigers, for example, you can look for JPEG
images of Bengal tigers by doing a second search of
just those results.

View, Copy or Download *Bengal Tiger*

Figure 2.5 Here's the JPEG image we found
using AltaVista's set-searching option.

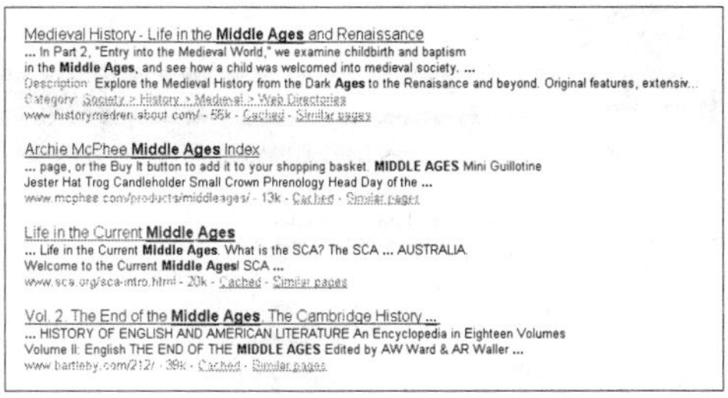

Medieval History - Life in the **Middle Ages** and Renaissance
... In Part 2, "Entry into the Medieval World," we examine childbirth and baptism
in the **Middle Ages**, and see how a child was welcomed into medieval society. ...
Description: Explore the Medieval History from the Dark **Ages** to the Renaissance and beyond. Original features, extensiv...
Category: Society > History > Medieval > Web Directories
www.historymedren.about.com/ - 55k - Cached - Similar pages

Archie McPhee **Middle Ages** Index
... page, or the Buy It button to add it to your shopping basket. MIDDLE AGES Mini Guillotine
Jester Hat Trog Candleholder Small Crown Phrenology Head Day of the ...
www.mcphee.com/products/middleages/ - 13k - Cached - Similar pages

Life in the Current **Middle Ages**
... Life in the Current **Middle Ages**. What is the SCA? The SCA ... AUSTRALIA.
Welcome to the Current **Middle Ages**! SCA ...
www.sca.org/sca-intro.html - 20k - Cached - Similar pages

Vol. 2 The End of the **Middle Ages** The Cambridge History ...
... HISTORY OF ENGLISH AND AMERICAN LITERATURE An Encyclopedia in Eighteen Volumes
Volume II. English THE END OF THE MIDDLE AGES Edited by AW Ward & AR Waller ...
www.bartleby.com/212/ - 36k - Cached - Similar pages

Figure 2.6 Notice that the phrase *Middle Ages* appears in all the Web page titles shown here. That's because we specified that we wanted to search for title:"Middle Ages".

With AltaVista, HotBot, Lycos, and Northern Light, you can put a title: field-search term right in your query. For example, if you're looking for information about marriage customs in the Middle Ages, start with a search of Web pages that have the words *Middle Ages* in the title, like this: title:"Middle Ages" (**Figure 2.6**). Then do a second search of just those results, looking for "marriage customs".

With Google, follow the same steps, but instead of title:, use the search term allintitle:"Middle Ages".

With Yahoo, use t:"Middle Ages" to find the phrase *Middle Ages* in topic categories and Web page titles.

Notice that in each of these examples, there is no space between the colon and the phrase that we are searching for.

5. **Find out if case counts**. It's important to know whether the search engine you're using pays attention to uppercase and lowercase letters in your keywords. Will a search for Java, the Sun Microsystems program, also find sites that refer to the program as JAVA?

   Some search engines ignore case completely. But with others (AltaVista and HotBot, for example), if you use *any* uppercase letters, the search engine will assume you want to look for only that combination of upper- and lowercase.

   Consequently, for the broadest possible search, it's usually a good idea to use all lowercase letters for your queries.

continues on next page

CHOOSING THE RIGHT KEYWORDS

6. Use initial caps to search for proper names. As we've said, it's usually a good idea to put your queries in lower-case because that gives you the broadest possible search. The keyword java will find references to *java*, *Java*, *JAVA*, and even *jaVa*.

But when you're looking for a person's name, a geographical location, a book or movie title, or anything else that you might reasonably expect to be presented with initial caps, by all means type your query that way. Doing so will greatly reduce the number of *false drops*, pages that contain the words in your query but are completely off the mark.

7. Check your spelling. If you've used the best keyword you can think of and the search engine comes back with the message "No results found" or some such, check your spelling before you do anything else.

Nine times out of ten, the reason a search engine comes up empty-handed is because of a spelling or typing error (**Figure 2.7**). At least, that's been our experience.

✔ Tip

■ The Quick Reference guides in Parts 2, 3, and 4 of this book (and repeated in Appendix A) are a good place to look for specifics on field searching and case-sensitive searching with different search engines.

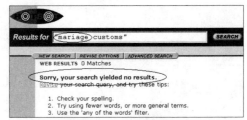

Figure 2.7 Spelling errors—typing mariage instead of marriage, for example—are virtually certain to stump the search engine and produce a "No results found" message.

BASIC SEARCH TOOLS

As we've said before, choosing the right keywords is the essence of effective searching. It's especially important for *Web* searching, because there's so much information out there—some of it worthwhile, much of it totally useless—and there's no single company or organization responsible for organizing and making sense of it.

But coming up with good, unique keywords is actually just half the battle. You also need to know how to *enter and combine* keywords, taking advantage of the basic search tools offered by the major search engines. Your success rate will improve dramatically once you learn what these tools are and when and how to use them.

Specific procedures vary from one search engine to the next, of course. In fact, some search engines have a different set of instructions depending on whether you're using their simple or advanced versions. But certain general concepts apply across the board. That's what we'll cover here.

Once you have this basic understanding of the tools that are available, you'll be better equipped to deal with just about any search engine you encounter on the Web. The chapters in Parts 2, 3, and 4 will fill in the details for some of the best of them.

Search Tools at a Glance

Here are the basic search tools you'll read about in this chapter:

- ◆ Plain-English Searches
- ◆ AND Searches
- ◆ OR Searches
- ◆ NOT Searches
- ◆ NEAR Searches
- ◆ Nested Searches
- ◆ Wildcards
- ◆ Stopwords

Searching in Plain English

For new Web searchers, one of the best tools going is *plain-English* or *natural-language* searching. Most of the leading search engines have developed techniques that are amazingly good at finding what you want based on a simple question—especially if the question includes at least one unique keyword or phrase.

One problem with plain-English searches like the one shown in **Figure 3.1** is that they typically produce a very large number of hits. But as long as the information you're looking for shows up at or near the top of the list (**Figure 3.2**), it doesn't really matter.

Another problem you're likely to encounter when you type your first plain-English search is fitting it into the tiny search box that's provided by many search engines. Don't be misled into thinking that you're limited to typing a very short question. The box in Figure 3.1 may look small, but at most search sites, you can actually type as long a question as you like. The first part will simply scroll out of view on the left-hand side of the box.

Figure 3.1 Plain-English searches like this often produce excellent results. Many search engines encourage you to simply "ask a question."

Figure 3.2 The question posed in Figure 3.1 identified more than two million sites, but the first two look extremely promising, so who cares?

Figure 3.3 The Ask Jeeves Web site at www.ask.com specializes in providing high-quality answers to plain-English questions.

✔ Tips

- Except for Yahoo, all of the Big Six search engines do a pretty good job of handling plain-English searches. But if you really like this method of looking for information on the Web, be sure to try Ask Jeeves (www.ask.com). Its Web database is very small and carefully selected by a staff of researchers. And unlike the Big Six, when you "ask Jeeves" a question (**Figure 3.3**), he'll attempt to provide you with the best *single* answer—rather than every possible match in the database.

- Word order and phrasing can make a big difference with plain-English searches. If you don't find what you're looking for with a direct question, try rephrasing your query, putting the most unusual word or phrase first:

  Query 1: What companies offer "parental control software"?

  Query 2: "parental control software" companies

  Think of it as a two-step process. The direct-question approach of Query 1 may not work. But it will help you clarify your search request and zero in on the most unusual term, which you can place first in Query 2.

Searching for Multiple Words and Phrases

The most important thing to find out about any search engine is how to look for *multiple* words and phrases. Plain-English queries are great, and they can probably handle many of your search requirements. But sometimes you need more precision than you can get from a plain-English search.

Here are the features to look for:

◆ **AND Search**. How do you tell the search engine that you want to find Web sites that include references to Keyword A *and* Keyword B?

◆ **OR Search**. How do you specify that it's not necessary for *both* keywords to appear in the results, as long as one *or* the other is present?

◆ **NOT Search**. How do you look for one keyword while specifically *excluding* another?

◆ **NEAR Search**. How do you find two words or phrases in close *proximity* to one another?

The technical term for this type of searching is *Boolean* searching, and AND, OR, NOT, and NEAR are among the traditional *Boolean operators*.

Over the next few pages, we'll explain how you can do AND, OR, NOT, and NEAR searches with the leading search engines. We'll also show you how to use parentheses to combine words and phrases into more complex queries.

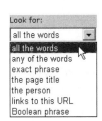

Figure 3.4 AND searches can sometimes be done by simply choosing all the words from a menu like this one.

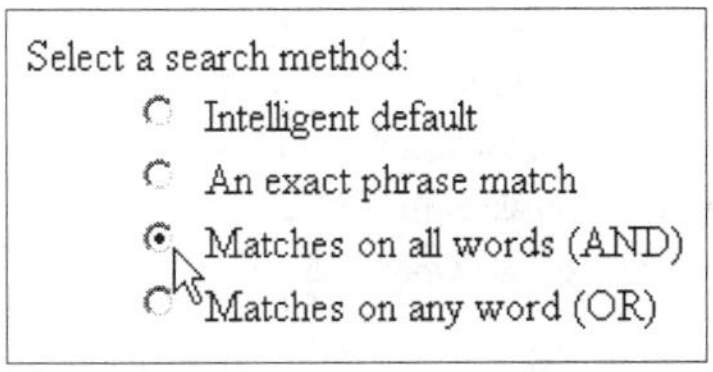

Select a search method:

   ○ Intelligent default

   ○ An exact phrase match

   ● Matches on all words (AND)

   ○ Matches on any word (OR)

Figure 3.5 Some search engines let you specify an AND search by clicking on a radio button.

Common Methods for Doing AND Searches

◆ Search for Monet AND Renoir

◆ Search for +Monet +Renoir

◆ Search for Monet Renoir and select the all the words option

AND Searches

Searching for two or more keywords—both of which *must* appear in the results—is an excellent strategy for doing precise searches and greatly reducing the number of search results you have to consider. Some search engines offer more than one method for doing AND searches, so you can choose the one you like best.

The most common way to tell a search engine that you want to do an AND search is to put a plus sign in front of each word or phrase that *must* appear in the results: +Renaissance +sculpture.

Other search engines require that you actually use the Boolean operator AND to combine words or phrases: needlepoint AND supplies, for example, to look for references to both terms. You may even be required to use full caps for AND. To avoid having to remember whether or not full caps are necessary, it's a good idea to get into the habit of using full caps all the time for AND.

Some search engines make AND searching extremely easy by offering it as a menu option or radio button. You simply type two or more unique keywords or phrases and then choose all the words from a drop-down menu (**Figure 3.4**) or click on the radio button with a similar label (**Figure 3.5**).

✔ Tips

■ You'll find that some search engines default to doing an AND search, while others default to doing an OR search. HotBot, for example, assumes that you want to do an AND search unless you tell it differently. AltaVista, on the other hand, defaults to OR searching.

■ Whenever you do an AND search, it's a good idea to put the most unusual search term first. That's because some search engines pay attention to word order and factor it into their relevancy rankings.

OR Searches

OR searches cast a much broader net than AND searches and may result in a very large number of hits for you to consider. They make good sense, though, when there's more than one way that the person, object, or thing you're looking for might be referred to in a Web page or other document. If you're doing research on the Clinton presidency, for example, you'd want to look for references to *President Clinton* or *Bill Clinton* or *William Jefferson Clinton*.

Some search engines do an OR search by default. In other words, if you type several words or phrases, leaving a space between each one, the search engine assumes that you want to find references to *any one* of them: "President Clinton" "Bill Clinton" "William Jefferson Clinton".

Other search engines require that you actually type the word OR between the words or phrases: Greenspan OR "Federal Reserve Chairman". Full caps may or may not be required for the word OR, but it's a good habit to get into.

Finally, some search engines offer OR searching as a menu option or radio button. You type your search words and phrases and then choose the option labeled any of the words or some such (as opposed to all the words). See **Figures 3.6** and **3.7** for examples.

Figure 3.6 Choosing *any of the words* from a menu like this is the way you tell some search engines to do an OR search.

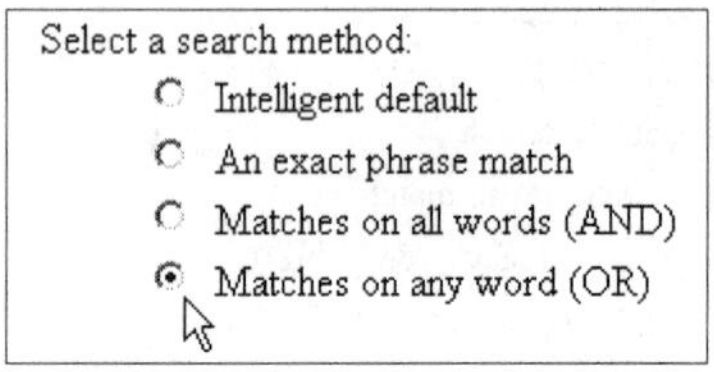

Figure 3.7 Here's another approach to OR searching. Just click on a radio button to indicate that the search engine should look for any of the words you've typed in the search form.

> ## Common Methods for Doing OR Searches
>
> ◆ Search for UPS U.P.S.
>
> ◆ Search for UPS OR U.P.S.
>
> ◆ Search for UPS U.P.S. and select any of the words option

OR SEARCHES

Those six pandemonium-mad Pythons are back with their craziest adventure ever!

These naughty Britons offer the usual tasteful sketches involving favorite bodily parts and functions, the wonders of war, the miracle of birth and a special preview of what is waiting for us in Heaven.

Figure 3.8 A NOT search like python -monty or python NOT monty can help you avoid information like this and find snakes instead.

NOT Searches

Here's the example you'll come across again and again to illustrate when to use a NOT search: You're looking for information on snakes and key in a search for python. Much to your dismay, your search results are dominated by Web pages aimed at devoted Monty Python fans (**Figure 3.8**). What to do?

The answer, of course, is to *exclude* Monty Python pages with a NOT search. Usually that means putting a minus sign in front of the word you want to avoid: python -monty. (Notice that there's no space between the minus sign and the word that's being excluded.)

Some search engines allow (or require) the use of the word NOT (or AND NOT) to exclude a word: python NOT monty or python AND NOT monty.

✔ Tips

- NOT can be a very powerful operator. But it also makes it quite easy to unwittingly throw the baby out with the bath water. Suppose the definitive Web site on pythons—"The Master Python Page"— happens to have been created by someone named Monty Shields. The NOT search in our example could very well prevent you from ever finding it.

- By all means learn to use NOT searches. Just be aware of the potential for inadvertently excluding good material.

Common Methods for Doing NOT Searches

- Search for python -monty

- Search for python NOT monty

- Search for python AND NOT monty

NEAR Searches

Sometimes you're not just interested in finding multiple keywords that are *mentioned* in the same document. You want to be able to specify that they appear in *close proximity* to one another. That's what NEAR searching is all about.

AltaVista is one of the few search engines that offers NEAR searching. And it's only available as part of the Advanced and Power Search capabilities, not on the main AltaVista search form. The format is: `Constitution NEAR "Electoral College"`.

See **Figures 3.9** and **3.10** for an example of NEAR searching with AltaVista.

✔ Tip

- Just how near is NEAR? AltaVista defines it to mean that the terms must appear within 10 words of each other.

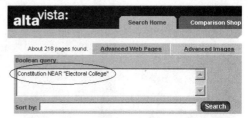

Figure 3.9 With AltaVista, you can do a NEAR search like this to find references to the word *Constitution* within 10 words of the phrase *Electoral College*.

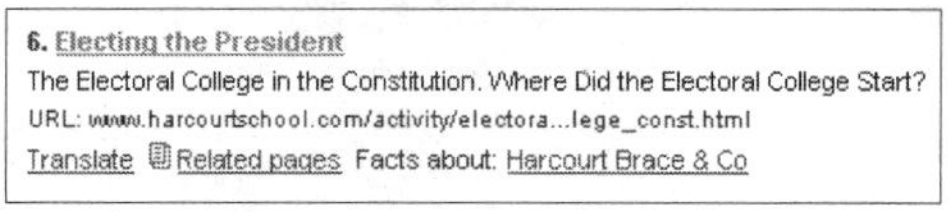

---

6. Electing the President
The Electoral College in the Constitution. Where Did the Electoral College Start?
URL: www.harcourtschool.com/activity/electora...lege_const.html
Translate Related pages Facts about: Harcourt Brace & Co

Figure 3.10 Among the first six sites found by the NEAR search in Figure 3.9 was this one, which looks like it might be right on the money.

NEAR Searches

- ◆ Use **AltaVista** (Advanced Search and Power Search only)

- ◆ Search for `Japan NEAR climate` to find the two terms within **10 words** of each other.

Figure 3.11 It doesn't take a complicated nested search to find the Web site for the Pro Football Hall of Fame in Canton, Ohio.

Parentheses and Nested Searches

Some search engines allow you to create more complex queries by grouping AND, OR, NOT, and NEAR statements using parentheses. For example, you could use a search like Canton NEAR (Ohio OR OH) to find any reference to Canton, Ohio, whether the state name is spelled out in full or abbreviated.

You can even create what are called *nested searches,* which can get quite complex, with one search statement "nested" within another: Canton NEAR ((Ohio OR OH) AND ("Pro Football" NEAR "Hall of Fame")).

Our advice is to use parentheses in your searches sparingly, and only when you really need them. Complex nested searches are fine for the professionals. But for most search tasks, and especially for new online searchers, they're not worth the mental NEAR ((energy OR effort) AND aggravation)!

You'll be far better off concentrating on coming up with good, unique keywords and sticking to simple combinations like AND, OR, NOT (and possibly NEAR) searches. Canton AND "Pro Football" AND "Hall of Fame", for example, is much more straightforward (and less error-prone) than the complex nested search presented above, and will very likely lead you to a page like the one shown in **Figure 3.11.**

Tips for Using Parentheses and Nested Searches

◆ Use parentheses sparingly if at all.

◆ Unique keywords combined with AND, OR, NOT, and NEAR often work just as well and are less error-prone.

◆ Complex nested searches are best left to the professionals.

Using Wildcards

Searching with *wildcards*—sometimes referred to as *truncation*—means using a special character, typically an asterisk, to indicate that you want to look for variations on a particular word, like medic* to find references to *medical, medicine, medicinal,* and *medication.*

Rules differ from one search engine to the next, but most require that you use at least three other characters along with the asterisk. And it's usually a good idea to also include at least one other unique keyword in your query (**Figure 3.12**). Otherwise, your search may take painfully long and return too many hits to be truly useful.

✔ Tips

■ Some search engines allow you to place wildcard characters in the middle (or even at the beginning) of a word.

■ You may also be given a choice between two different wildcard symbols, depending on whether you want to search for *multiple* characters or a *single* character.

■ For specifics on using wildcards with a particular search engine, see the Quick Reference guides in Parts 2, 3, and 4 of this book.

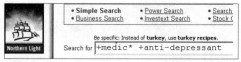

Figure 3.12 A wildcard search is likely to be excruciatingly slow unless you include at least one other term in your search request, as shown here.

Tips for Using Wildcards

◆ Use wildcards to look for spelling variations and alternate word endings.

◆ The wildcard character is usually (but not always) an asterisk: medic*.

◆ Use at least three letters along with the wildcard character.

◆ For best and fastest results, combine the wildcard search term with at least one other unique keyword.

Figure 3.13 The Google search engine tells you exactly what words have been ignored from your query, in this case *who* and *to*.

Figure 3.14 A Lycos search for "to be or not to be" finds Hamlet's soliloquy, even though the phrase is composed entirely of common stopwords. The secret is to enclose the words in quotes.

Dealing with Stopwords

You may come across the term *stopwords* at search engine sites, often in the help information or search tips. Stopwords are words that search engines ignore because they are too common, or because they are reserved for some special purpose.

The list varies from one search engine to the next, but it typically includes words like *a, an, any, the, to, with, from, for, of, that, who,* and the Boolean operators AND, OR, NOT, and NEAR. We're not aware of any major search engine that publishes its complete list. But Google does the next best thing—it tells you if it has ignored one or more of the words in your query (**Figure 3.13**).

Should you need to use a stopword as part of a search, you can sometimes signal the search engine *not* to ignore it by setting it off in double quotes: `Portland NEAR "OR"`.

Some (though not all) search engines also pay attention to stopwords that are included as part of a phrase: `"The Man Who Came to Dinner"` or `"to be or not to be"` (**Figure 3.14**). Of the Big Six search engines, AltaVista, Lycos, Northern Light, and Yahoo all do a pretty good job of recognizing and acting on stopwords that are included in phrases.

✔ Tips

- Most major search engines offer all of the basic tools described in this chapter. But keep in mind that the specifics vary from one to the next. In some cases, there's even a different set of rules depending on whether you're using the search engine's simple or advanced search form.

- The chapters in Parts 2, 3, and 4 of this book will introduce you to many of the specifics. Be sure to also check the search tips and help sections for any search engine you decide to use on a regular basis to learn about new features that may have been added.

Stopword Tips

- Every search engine ignores certain very common words (*stopwords*) like *the, to, with,* the Boolean operators, etc.

- To look for words that might be confused with Boolean operators, put them in double quotes: `Portland NEAR "OR"`.

- Some search engines will recognize stopwords that are included in phrases enclosed in double quotes: `"to be or not to be"`.

TIPS AND TECHNIQUES

So far we've covered search engines and how they work, the importance of choosing unique keywords, and the basic search tools offered by most search engines on the World Wide Web. We'll wrap up this part of the book with some specific tips and techniques that will help you get the most out of the time you spend online—no matter what search engine you decide to use on a regular basis.

We'll start with what we call "The Seven Habits of Highly Effective Web Searchers." Then we'll offer suggestions for customizing your Web browser so that you can access your favorite search tools automatically. We'll conclude with some advice on keyboard shortcuts and other timesavers.

The Seven Habits at a Glance

1. Develop the Internet habit.
2. Use the best tool for the job.
3. Read the instructions.
4. Choose unique keywords.
5. Use multiple search engines.
6. Consider the source.
7. Know when to look elsewhere.

The Seven Habits of Highly Effective Web Searchers

We're not professional searchers, but we've logged a lot of hours over the years searching the Internet and other online systems. We have a pretty good idea of what works and what doesn't. Here are our recommendations for effective Web searching, organized into seven steps or "habits" that can make you a better searcher.

1. Develop the Internet habit.

When you have a question about anything—and we mean *anything*—your first step in nearly every case should be to check the Net. The answer may lie deep within a company-sponsored Web site, or in a newsgroup posting from two years ago, or among the millions of listings in a white or yellow pages directory, or somewhere else. But with the right search tool and search strategy, chances are you can find it.

2. Use the best tool for the job.

For day-to-day searching, you can't go too far wrong with any of the Big Six search engines (AltaVista, Google, HotBot, etc.). Don't forget, though, that each has its strong points—summarized in a sidebar on page 37 and covered in more detail in Part 2 of this book—that you'll want to consider when choosing the one to use for a particular job.

Keep in mind, too, that as good as these search engines are, they're not the best tools for every job. For example, some search engines give you the option of searching Usenet newsgroups as well as the Web. But to take full advantage of newsgroups, the best tool is Deja (www.deja.com), a search engine designed and optimized for newsgroup searches (**Figure 4.1**).

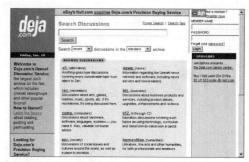

Figure 4.1 Deja (www.deja.com) is the ideal tool for searching newsgroups. No other site even comes close.

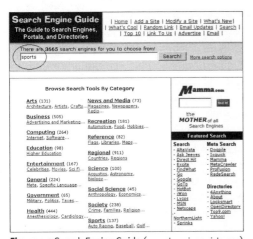

Figure 4.2 Search Engine Guide (searchengineguide.com) is a great place to look for special-purpose search engines. Browse by category or use the search feature, as we've done here to look for sports-related search engines.

Most general-purpose search engines that offer a newsgroup search feature use Deja to "power" it. But they typically provide only a *subset* of the search capabilities you'll find at the Deja site.

Part 4 of this book will introduce you to Deja and some of our other favorite special-purpose search engines, like Topica (`www.topica.com`) for locating Internet mailing lists and the Argus Clearinghouse (`www.clearinghouse.net`) for finding subject guides to the Net.

To track down other special-purpose engines using a searchable directory, visit Search Engine Guide at `searchengineguide.com` (**Figure 4.2**).

Big Six Search Engines and What They Do Best

◆ **AltaVista** is a good choice for finding obscure facts and figures. It's one of the few search engines to offer full Boolean and case-sensitive searching, as well as a variety of field-search options to help target a search.

◆ **Google** covers more of the Net than any other search engine. When thoroughness counts, be sure to check Google. Its method of ranking Web sites based on *link popularity* (the more links to a particular site, the higher its ranking) works especially well for general searches.

◆ **HotBot** makes it exceptionally easy to search for multimedia files and to locate Web sites by geography. If you want the power of AltaVista with a much simpler interface, go with HotBot.

◆ **Lycos** is another good choice for doing multimedia searches. Use it as well for finding phrases containing common stopwords (for example, "to be or not to be"). Unlike some search engines, Lycos won't ignore stopwords in phrases.

◆ **Northern Light** lets you simultaneously search both the Web and a "special collection" database of articles, transcripts, and other documents not readily accessible on the Net.

◆ **Yahoo** has the best, most detailed Web directory, making it an excellent choice for exploring a subject to find out what's available on the Net.

✔ Tip

- Usenet newsgroups (or *newsgroups* for short) are freewheeling "global conversations" on virtually every subject imaginable. They've been around far longer than the World Wide Web and are an excellent source of advice, personal opinions, and commentary. Think of them as expanding your circle of acquaintances when you're looking for things like recipes, travel tips, software fixes or workarounds—you name it.

3. Read the instructions.

No two search engines work exactly the same way, so it pays to read the online help and search tips provided at the site. For example, some search engines default to doing an AND search—type several words in the search box and the engine will assume you want to find *all* of them in your search results. Other search engines take the same request and by default perform an OR search—returning pages that contain any one of the words but not necessarily all of them.

At a minimum, you need to learn how to do AND, OR, and phrase searches at any site you're going to use on a regular basis. Another important point to zero in on is *case-sensitivity*—whether the search engine recognizes and acts upon uppercase and lowercase letters in your search request. Some search engines offer case-sensitive searching, others ignore case completely.

4. Choose unique keywords.

Before launching a search, take the time to think about what unique words or phrases are likely to appear in the information you want to find and try them first. To locate sites devoted to impressionist painters, for example, you might try Monet AND Renoir AND Degas. That's sure to produce better results than a search for impressionists or painters.

Figure 4.3 A few words of a poem enclosed in double quotes are often all it takes to locate the complete work, as shown here.

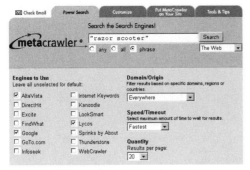

Figure 4.4 With MetaCrawler and other metasearch services, you can direct your query to multiple search engines—in this case AltaVista, Google, and Lycos.

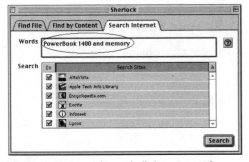

Figure 4.5 Mac users have a built-in metasearch capability called Sherlock. Type a word or phrase in the Words text box as shown here, select the engines you want to query, and click on Search.

What about the complete text of a famous quotation, literary work, or even a joke you heard at the office? Try a phrase search on some small portion that you remember: "tiger tiger burning bright" to locate the William Blake poem (**Figure 4.3**). Or "man walks into a bar" for that joke you'd like to add to your repertoire.

5. Use multiple search engines.

Every search engine has its own way of doing things and none of them covers *everything*. In fact, as you may recall from our discussion of spiders in Chapter 1, even Google—which currently holds bragging rights to the largest database of Web pages—has yet to find and index more than 40 percent of the Web. So when thoroughness counts, you should plan on using several search engines.

✔ Tips

- You can automatically submit a query to multiple search engines using what are called *metasearch* services. MetaCrawler (www.metacrawler.com) is one of the oldest and most popular (**Figure 4.4**). Others with large followings include Dogpile (www.dogpile.com), InFind (infind.com), ProFusion (www.profusion.com), and CNET Search.com (www.search.com). The idea has caught on with many professional and casual searchers, who find that it can be a real timesaver.

- Macintosh users running Mac OS 8.5 and later versions have a *built-in* metasearch capability. Part of the operating system's Sherlock application, the Internet Search tab lets you specify a word or phrase as well as the sites you want to search (**Figure 4.5**).

continues on next page

- The major drawback to using a metasearch service (or the Mac's Sherlock metasearch feature) is that it takes your query and reduces it to its *simplest* form—stripping out quotation marks, for example, and any other punctuation and search terms that can't be handled by *all* the engines on the metasearch service's list.

  That may or may not be a problem, depending on the nature of your search. But it's not the same—and won't produce the same results—as going yourself to, say, three different search engines and crafting a query for each one that follows the prescribed format and takes advantage of each engine's unique search features.

- We've also found metasearch engines to be more prone to timeouts than regular search engines. And they typically return only a small number of results (10-50) from any given search engine.

6. Consider the source.

Just because it's on the Net doesn't mean the information is either accurate or true. After all, virtually anyone can "publish" anything on the Internet and the World Wide Web. So be skeptical at all times.

If the information is on a Web site, try to determine:

- What person or organization created the information?

- What's the motivation behind it?

- When was the material last updated?

The same goes for newsgroup postings, where unscrupulous marketers sometimes plant positive comments about their own products and negative ones about their competitors'—making it appear as though the comments were made by actual users of the products.

Multiple Search vs. Metasearch

It might take a bit more time to visit two or three search engines and conduct separate queries at each one. But you're likely to get better results in the long run.

Metasearch engines and the Mac's Sherlock feature have several major limitations:

- Phrase and Boolean searching are generally not available.

- Most return only 10-50 hits from any given search engine.

- They are highly subject to timeouts.

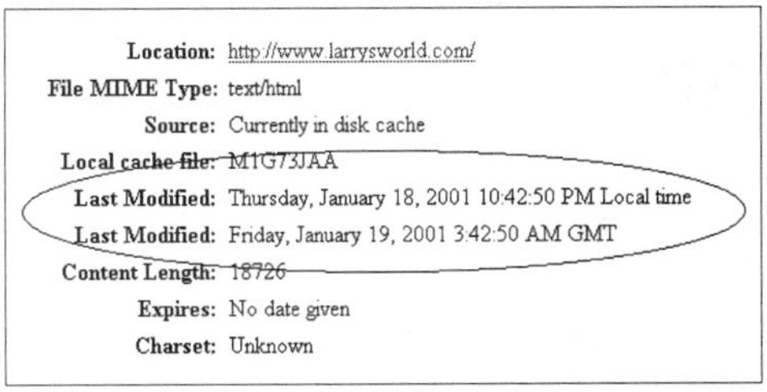

```
        Location:  http://www.larrysworld.com/
  File MIME Type:  text/html
          Source:  Currently in disk cache
 Local cache file: M1G73JAA
   Last Modified:  Thursday, January 18, 2001 10:42:50 PM Local time
   Last Modified:  Friday, January 19, 2001 3:42:50 AM GMT
  Content Length:  18726
         Expires:  No date given
         Charset:  Unknown
```

Figure 4.6 You can use Netscape's Page Info feature to find out when a Web page was last modified.

✔ Tips

■ Many Web sites include an About Us or Company Info link that you can click on to get more information about the company behind the site.

■ Netscape's Page Info feature can sometimes help in determining the currency of a specific Web page. Click on View and then on Page Info. The resulting screen (**Figure 4.6**) will often include the date the Web page was last modified. (Microsoft Internet Explorer doesn't currently offer a Page Info feature.)

7. Know when to look elsewhere.

Don't assume that the Internet contains the sum total of human knowledge. The Net will always surprise you, both with the information that it *does* contain and with its lack of information on some specific topic.

Part of being a good online searcher is knowing when to stop. The information you want may or may not be available online. And if it *is* online, it may be buried so deep that it's not worth the time and trouble to locate it.

Your efforts may be better spent getting the information, fact, figure, or whatever you need using conventional printed reference works: almanacs, dictionaries, encyclopedias, and so forth. Start with the reference section at your local library, or ask the reference librarian for help.

Avoiding Search Rage

Based on the results of a survey reported in a recent issue of Danny Sullivan's "Search Engine Report" newsletter, it takes about 12 minutes for the average person to start feeling anger and frustration at not finding what they are looking for on the Net. Consequently, Sullivan recommends that you follow the "10-minute rule."

If you haven't found what you're looking for in 10 minutes, says Sullivan, it's time to try more traditional alternatives—like contacting your local librarian, or picking up the telephone and calling directory assistance to get the phone number of a company that might be able to help you.

✔ Tips

■ For really tough search assignments, your best bet may be to find a recognized expert on the subject. Start by consulting the "Sources and Experts" list compiled by news researcher Kitty Bennett of the *St. Petersburg Times*. It's available at www.ibiblio.org/slanews/internet/ experts.html.

■ You might also consider hiring a professional searcher (or *information broker*, as they are known in the trade). For recommendations, contact the Association of Independent Information Professionals. Their Web site at www.aiip.org (**Figure 4.7**) includes information about the organization's member-referral program.

■ To learn more about becoming a professional searcher yourself, check your local library or favorite out-of-print book source for *The Information Broker's Handbook: Third Edition* by Sue Rugge and Alfred Glossbrenner. Although it's no longer in print, this book is still considered by information professionals to be the definitive work on the subject.

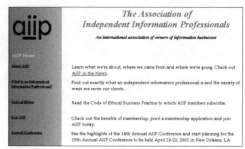

Figure 4.7 To hire a professional searcher, visit the AIIP Web site (www.aiip.org) and look for information about their member referral program.

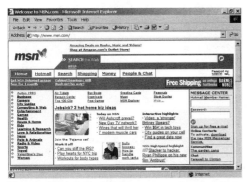

Figure 4.8 This is the MSN home page, the place that Microsoft hopes Internet Explorer users will begin all their online sessions.

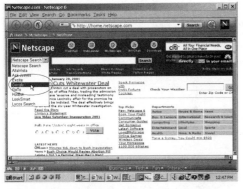

Figure 4.9 Netscape's home page includes a drop-down menu that lets you choose the search engine you use for your queries. The default is Netscape Search, but we've chosen Google instead.

Figure 4.10 Once you've customized your Web browser with your preferred home-page location, clicking on the Home button will take you there instantly.

Customizing Your Web Browser

When you install Microsoft Internet Explorer (IE), it will be set up so that whenever you go online, you'll be taken automatically to the Microsoft Network (MSN) home page at www.msn.com (**Figure 4.8**). Similarly, when you install Netscape Navigator, it assumes that you want to begin all of your online sessions at the Netscape home page, located on the Web at home.netscape.com (**Figure 4.9**).

We prefer, instead, to have our Web browser take us directly to our favorite search engine. After all, when we go online, it's usually to search for something. And even though both MSN and Netscape offer a selection of search tools on their home pages, neither site offers the range of features that you'll have access to if you go directly to one of the Big Six search engines.

That being the case, we've customized our Web browser so that the search engine we use most often comes up automatically when we sign on. We can also get to it quickly at any time by clicking on our browser's Home button (**Figure 4.10**). The other Big Six search engines are all included in our IE Favorites and Netscape Bookmarks lists, so that we can easily consult them when we need a "second opinion."

If you'd like to customize your Web browser so that it's optimized for searching, here are the steps to follow.

To make your favorite search engine appear automatically:

◆ **Internet Explorer 5 (Windows Users)**. Click on Tools and then choose Internet Options. In the home page Address box, type the complete Web address (including http://) of your favorite search engine. Then click on OK.

Note: If you are running an older version of IE for Windows, click on View (instead of Tools) to change your default home page.

◆ **Internet Explorer 5 (Macintosh Users)**. Click on Edit and then choose Preferences. Then click on Browser Display in the list on the left side of the screen. In the home page Address box, type the complete Web address (including http://) of your favorite search engine and click on OK.

Note: If you're running IE 4.5 for Mac, the link to choose from the list on the Preferences page is Home/Search (instead of Browser Display).

◆ **Netscape 4 and 6 (Windows and Mac Users)**. Click on Edit and then choose Preferences. On the Navigator page, make sure the Home Page radio button is selected. In the Location box, type the complete Web address (including http://) of your favorite search engine. Then click on OK.

Complete Web Addresses for Big Six Search Engines

◆ AltaVista
http://www.altavista.com

◆ Google
http://www.google.com

◆ HotBot
http://www.hotbot.com

◆ Lycos
http://www.lycos.com

◆ Northern Light
http://www.northernlight.com

◆ Yahoo
http://www.yahoo.com

To add other search engines to your Favorites or Bookmarks:

◆ With Microsoft Internet Explorer, go to the search engine site, click on Favorites, and then choose the option for adding a page to your Favorites.

Or use the keyboard shortcut [Ctrl][D] if you're a Windows user, [⌘][D] on the Macintosh.

◆ With Netscape Navigator, go to the search engine site, click on Bookmarks, and then choose Add Bookmark (if you're using Netscape 4) or Add Current Page (Netscape 6).

Or use the keyboard shortcut [Ctrl][D] (Windows) or [⌘][D] (Macintosh).

✔ Tip

■ Once you've set your browser's default home page location as described here, that's the site that will greet you whenever you sign on. It's also the one you'll be taken to when you click on your browser's Home button or select the menu option that tells the browser you want to "Go Home."

Keyboard Shortcuts and Other Timesavers

Customizing your Web browser so that it starts up automatically with your favorite search engine is one way to save time and get the ball rolling faster when you need to search for information on the Net. Now let's take at look at some other techniques for making your online sessions easier and more productive.

Keyboard shortcuts

Searching for menu commands can be a nuisance with any application, Web browsers included. We find that it's often faster and easier to perform common tasks with a couple of keystrokes. These keyboard shortcuts (**Table 4.1**) for Windows and Macintosh systems work with both Microsoft Internet Explorer and Netscape Navigator.

Making short work of Web addresses

We've mentioned this shortcut before but it bears repeating here: With the latest versions of Microsoft Internet Explorer (IE) and Netscape Navigator, you don't have to type http:// in your browser's Address or Location box to get to a Web site. You can even leave out www and com to access your favorite search engine—or any site that begins and ends with those letters.

For example, to go to the Google Web site (http://www.google.com), just type google in your browser's Address or Location box (**Figure 4.11**) and press Enter (Ctrl Enter if you're using IE for Windows).

Figure 4.11 With Internet Explorer and Netscape Navigator, you don't have to type http://www or com to get to Google's Web site. Just google is enough.

Table 4.1

Keyboard Shortcuts

TASK	WINDOWS	MACINTOSH
Go to the next Web page.	Alt ←	⌘ [
Go to the previous Web page.	Alt →	⌘]
Add current Web page to Bookmarks/Favorites.	Ctrl D	⌘ D
Organize Bookmarks/Favorites.	Ctrl B	⌘ B
Copy highlighted text from a Web page.	Ctrl C	⌘ C
Paste highlighted text from a Web page.	Ctrl V	⌘ V
Find text on a Web page.	Ctrl F	⌘ F
Print current Web page.	Ctrl P	⌘ P
Open History folder.	Ctrl H	⌘ H
Open new Web page.	Ctrl L	⌘ L
Open new Browser window.	Ctrl N	⌘ N

Figure 4.12 Locating the word *muggles* on this Harry Potter Web page is a snap (or a click!) with your browser's Find feature.

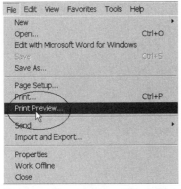

Figure 4.13 If your browser offers a Print Preview feature, it will be on the File menu. You can save time and paper by using Print Preview to selectively print just the pages you need from a multi-page Web page.

More Timesavers and Productivity Tools

In this section we focus on shortcuts and timesavers that are built into IE and Netscape. For recommendations on Web browser add-ons and other productivity-enhancing tools that you might want to add to your "Web searcher's toolkit," see Appendix D.

Searching for text in Web pages

Search engines often return pages that are loaded with text, and it's not immediately clear that the information you want is there. To avoid the time and trouble of scrolling and reading through page after page, let your Web browser's Find feature do the work for you.

With IE and older versions of Netscape (prior to Version 6), the Find feature is located on the Edit menu. With Netscape 6, it's on the Search menu. Alternatively, with both IE and Netscape, you can access the Find feature by using the keyboard shortcut Ctrl F (⌘ F on the Mac).

When the Find dialog box appears (**Figure 4.12**), simply enter the word or phrase you want to locate on the Web page and then click on your browser's Find (or Find Next) button.

Avoiding long print jobs

Imagine hitting your Print button and then discovering that the "Web page" you're printing is actually 28 pages long. And all you wanted was a couple of telephone and fax numbers that appear about two-thirds of the way through the document.

The secret to avoiding a problem like this is to activate your browser's Print Preview feature *before* hitting the Print button.

If you're using IE 5 (Windows or Mac) or Netscape 4 for Windows, you'll find the Print Preview link (**Figure 4.13**) on the File menu. (Unfortunately, at this writing Netscape 4 for Macintosh and Netscape 6 for Windows and Mac don't offer Print Preview.) Using Print Preview, find the page that contains the information you're after. (You'll probably have to "zoom in" to read the text and the page numbers that appear in the footer.) Then print just the page (or pages) you need.

Alternatively, with both IE and Netscape, you can highlight the text you're interested in and then copy and paste it to another application, like Word or Notepad, using the keyboard shortcuts [Ctrl][C] to copy and [Ctrl][V] to paste (⌘[C] and ⌘[V] on the Macintosh). Then print it from there.

✔ Tip

■ From time to time, you'll encounter a Web page that won't display properly in the Print Preview window. The header and footer may be there, for example, but the main text—the portion you're most interested in printing—will be blank. When that happens, try sending the page to yourself as an e-mail message using the Send (or Send Page) link on the File menu.

Opening a second Web browser

Sometimes the Web is painfully slow and a complicated search can seem to take forever to finish. When that happens, consider opening a *second* browser window so that you can go about your business and check back in a couple of minutes.

With IE, the command sequence is File and then New, Window (**Figure 4.14**). With Netscape, click on File and then New Navigator Window (New Navigator on the Mac).

Alternatively, with both IE and Netscape, you can use the keyboard shortcut [Ctrl][N] (⌘[N] on the Mac).

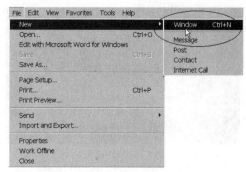

Figure 4.14 You can open a second Web browser window from the Internet Explorer File menu, as shown here. Netscape Navigator works much the same way.

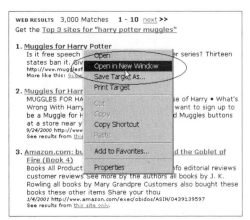

Figure 4.15 We've right-clicked on Muggles for Harry Potter to bring up the menu that includes an option for opening the link in a new browser window.

Viewing search results in a new window

How many times has this happened to you? You've initiated a search and produced a list of results that looks quite promising. You begin clicking on individual items, and the links on those pages, to see if they contain the information you're after. Eventually, you want to get back to your original results list. But it's buried so far down in the Back button's list that you can't easily find it. Or it may have even disappeared completely.

You can avoid this problem by keeping your search results on the screen and viewing individual results in a *new* window. Here's the technique: Instead of *clicking* on a link, do a *right-click* (Control-click on the Macintosh) and choose the menu option for opening it in a new window (**Figure 4.15**).

Dealing with broken links and "Page Not Found" messages

Some percentage of your searches are bound to lead you to Web pages that no longer exist. When that happens, try deleting everything after the last slash in the URL that appears in your browser's Address or Location box. Then press Enter. It may very well be that the Web site you're after still exists—it's just a particular file that's been eliminated or renamed.

PART 2

THE BIG SIX
SEARCH ENGINES

The Big Six
Search Engines

Once you've got a basic understanding of search engines and searching (either through direct experience or by reading Part 1), you'll be ready for these chapters on six of the very best search engines:

◆ **AltaVista**

◆ **Google**

◆ **HotBot**

◆ **Lycos**

◆ **Northern Light**

◆ **Yahoo!**

As you can see, the search engines are presented in alphabetical order. Feel free to skip around, perhaps starting with a search engine you've used before or heard the most about.

And remember, it's not necessary to master all six of these search engines. Use the information presented here to learn about the particular strengths of each one. Work through the step-by-step examples, and try some sample searches of your own with the book opened to the appropriate Quick Reference guide.

Once you've identified the search engine you like best, consider making it the default starting location for your Web browser, as suggested in Chapter 4. Add the others to your browser's Bookmarks or Favorites list so that you can get to them quickly when you need to consult a second (or third) search engine.

ALTAVISTA

altaVista:

Good to Know

- AltaVista is a favorite of professional searchers because of its large database, powerful search features, and search customization options.

- It's one of the few search engines to offer full Boolean and case-sensitive searching, along with a variety of field-search and language options to help you target your searches.

- Developed in 1995 at Digital Equipment Corporation in Palo Alto, California, AltaVista has been awarded more search-related patents than any other company in the world.

- AltaVista is majority-owned by CMGI, an Internet development and operating company. But Compaq (which had acquired the search engine with its 1998 purchase of Digital) holds a small stake as well.

AltaVista is one of the most powerful and comprehensive search engines available today. Launched in 1995 as a pioneering effort to index the full text of the World Wide Web, it has evolved over the years from a pure search engine to a portal service offering the usual assortment of news headlines, shopping, free e-mail, and advertising. But AltaVista's primary emphasis is still very much on *searching*.

If you've never used a search engine before, you'll be pleased to discover how quickly— and precisely—you can find information with AltaVista. All it takes is a little practice and the mastery of a few simple techniques that we'll cover in this chapter.

Experienced searchers will appreciate the fact that AltaVista offers full Boolean search capabilities, case-sensitive searching, and a range of field-search options that is second to none. AltaVista is also one of the few search sites to provide a customization feature that goes beyond mere cosmetics. With AltaVista, you can tailor the search form to limit your queries to pages written in a particular language. And you can specify the amount of detail presented in your search results, as well as the number of items presented on each page.

To take full advantage of AltaVista's power and sophistication, you'll need to spend some time familiarizing yourself with its various search forms. (The rules for entering a query differ depending on which form you're using.) Once you've learned your way around, you may well decide to join the legions of professional searchers who've made AltaVista their search engine of choice.

✔ Tips

- The AltaVista database is created by a spider program known as Scooter (**Figure 5.1**). Scooter constantly roams the World Wide Web, collecting some 10 million Web pages each day and delivering them to AltaVista, where special software indexes every word. Scooter's work is supplemented by information provided to AltaVista by Web site creators.

- If you'd like to know more about the AltaVista spider, database, and indexing methods, click on Submit a Site on the AltaVista home page. Then click on How AltaVista Works.

- Although the AltaVista spider software is apparently quite good at finding new Web pages, it falls short when it comes to weeding out dead ones. In the most recent "Dead Links Report" from Search Engine Showdown, AltaVista ranked worst among the major search engines.

  For current rankings and information on how the dead links survey is conducted, go to www.searchengineshowdown.com.

- As you explore the Web, you may come across sites that offer search capabilities "powered by AltaVista" (**Figure 5.2**). Many of the search skills and strategies presented in this chapter—particularly the ones summarized in the Quick Reference tables—are applicable at these sites as well.

Figure 5.1 The AltaVista spider, affectionately known as Scooter and represented by this smiling image, is actually a very sophisticated software program that constantly scours the Web for new and updated pages.

Figure 5.2 Web sites that display this logo have a built-in search capability provided by AltaVista, so you can apply much of what you learn in this chapter to those sites as well.

Contact Information

AltaVista Company
Palo Alto, California
650-320-7700 (voice)
650-320-7720 (fax)
www.altavista.com

ALTAVISTA

The AltaVista Home Page

AltaVista is constantly tinkering with its home page (www.altavista.com), so we can't guarantee that it will look exactly like the one shown in **Figure 5.3**. Features come and go, especially those not directly related to searching.

What we'll focus on here are the most important search-related features on the AltaVista home page—the ones we think you'll find most useful for day-to-day searching. As you'll soon discover, AltaVista offers a range of options for finding information on the Web. So whether you're a complete novice, a seasoned researcher, or somewhere in between, chances are you'll find that AltaVista has you covered.

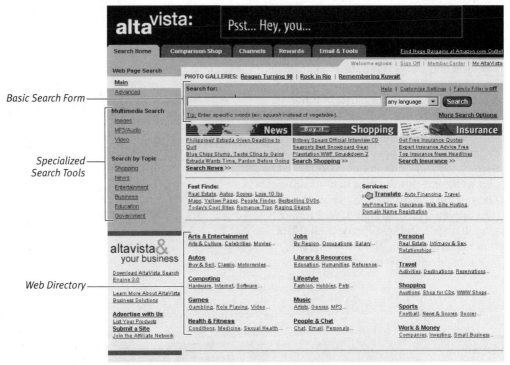

Figure 5.3 The AltaVista home page is crammed with features. From a searcher's perspective, the most important are the Basic Search form, the Web directory, and the specialized search tools accessible via links on the left side of the page.

Basic Search form

Many people find that AltaVista's Basic Search form (**Figure 5.4**) is the only one they ever need. It works just fine for most occasions, and even allows you to limit your searches to pages presented in a particular language. Just use the drop-down menu (**Figure 5.5**) to make your selection.

You can search for a phrase by enclosing the words in quotes, and use plus and minus signs to include (+) or exclude (-) words. You can also zero in on a specific part of a Web page by incorporating one of AltaVista's many field-search terms in your query.

We'll cover field searching and other aspects of using the Basic Search form in more detail later in this chapter.

Power Search

If you'd like a bit of guidance as you create your queries, click on More Search Options (**Figure 5.6**) near the Search button on the AltaVista home page. With the Power Search form (**Figure 5.7**), you can create sophisticated queries without the hassle of using special search terms.

Specifically, you can limit your searches by date, language, geography, and Web address. You can focus on three specific page elements—title, text, or links to URLs. And you can control the number of listings to be displayed on each page of your results (from 10 to 50), and specify that if AltaVista finds multiple pages at the same Web site, only a single result will be presented.

Figure 5.4 You will probably do most of your AltaVista searches using the Basic Search form.

Figure 5.5 Choose English from the drop-down Languages menu if you want to limit your Web search to English-language pages.

Figure 5.6 Clicking on this link on the AltaVista home page takes you to the Power Search form.

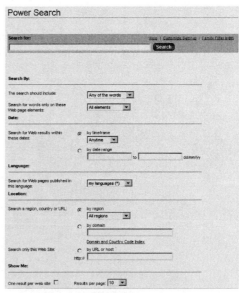

Figure 5.7 The Power Search form walks you through the process of building a complex query. Just make your selections from the drop-down menus and radio-button options.

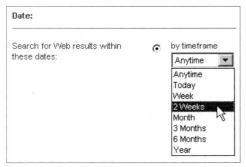

Figure 5.8 The Date section allows you to look for Web pages created or modified in the last two weeks, as shown here. You can also specify a range of dates.

Figure 5.9 This link on the AltaVista home page takes you to the Advanced Search form, favored by research professionals.

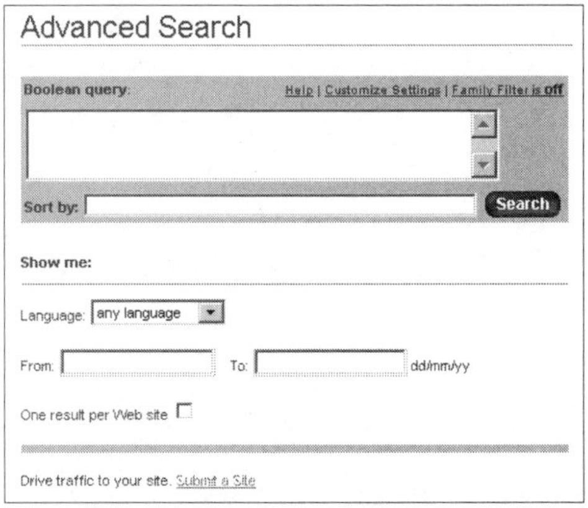

Figure 5.10 The Advanced Search form is the one to use if you prefer using Boolean expressions to search the Web. It also gives you more control over your search results than either Basic or Power Search.

Best of all, you're prompted through the entire process. All you have to do is make your selections by clicking on menu options and radio buttons (**Figure 5.8**).

✔ Tip

- If you like Power Search, try these specialty search options listed on the left side of the AltaVista home page. They apply the same menu/radio-button approach to finding specific types of information:

  Multimedia Search. For locating images, MP3/audio, and video files on the Web.

  Shopping. For comparison shopping at over 700 stores on the Web.

  News. For finding news articles that have appeared within the last two weeks.

  Entertainment. For locating entertainment news, audio and video clips, image files, radio broadcasts, and Web sites offering entertainment content.

  Business. For searching AltaVista's database of 1.8 million company fact sheets by name, ticker symbol, or domain name.

  Education. For limiting your search to Web sites with edu domain names.

  Government. For limiting your search to sites with gov domain names.

Advanced Search

For experienced searchers and others who prefer using Boolean operators in their queries, AltaVista's Advanced Search option (**Figure 5.9**) is the way to go.

On the Advanced Search form (**Figure 5.10**), you can create as complex a query as you like, using the full range of Boolean operators—AND, OR, AND NOT, NEAR, parentheses for enclosing nested expressions, and so forth. You can also limit your searches to Web pages written in a particular language and created or updated within a certain range of dates.

continues on next page

Finally, you can control the sort order for your results, giving more weight to certain words so that documents containing them appear higher on the list. And you can specify whether you want to see single vs. multiple results from each Web site.

For more on using this search form, see "Using Advanced Search" later in this chapter.

Web directory

When you're not exactly sure what you're looking for, or you simply want to get an idea of what the Web has to offer on a particular topic, try AltaVista's Web directory (**Figure 5.11**), provided by LookSmart.

To browse the directory, simply choose a main category and then "drill down" through the various subcategories.

To *search* rather than browse, click on a main category. (Any one will do.) Then type one or more keywords in the search form (**Figure 5.12**) and specify whether you want to search just that category or the entire directory. LookSmart automatically performs an AND search, looking for items that contain all the words in your query.

✔ Tip

- Phrase searching, plus and minus signs for including and excluding words, and Boolean operators are *not* allowed when searching the AltaVista/LookSmart directory. Consequently, when it comes to directory searches, Yahoo (www.yahoo.com) is a far better choice. For more on Yahoo, see Chapter 10.

Figure 5.11 AltaVista's Web directory is organized into 15 major categories and dozens of subcategories. If you don't see the topic you're looking for here, click on any link to access the directory's search form.

Figure 5.12 A search like this would find references to the words *song* and *lyrics* in the Music category of AltaVista's Web directory.

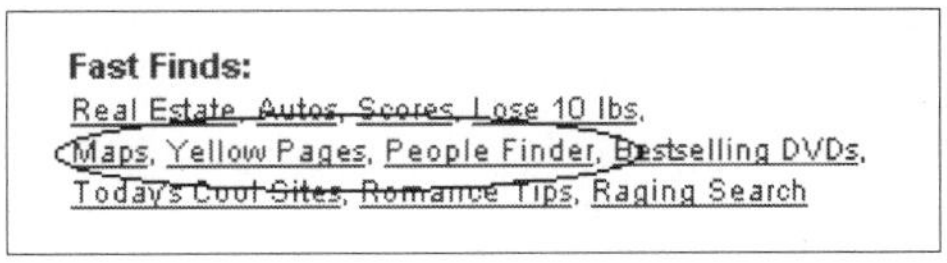

Fast Finds:
Real Estate, Autos, Scores, Lose 10 lbs,
Maps, Yellow Pages, People Finder, Bestselling DVDs,
Today's Cool Sites, Romance Tips, Raging Search

Figure 5.13 These specialty search tools come in handy for quick look-ups of maps and driving directions, business and residence addresses, and phone numbers.

from alta^{vista:}

Figure 5.14 Try Raging Search if you like AltaVista but prefer a "pure search engine" experience, without *any* portal features.

Other search-related tools

If you decide to make AltaVista your primary search site, you'll want to become familiar with its collection of specialty search tools, included in a section of the home page called Fast Finds (**Figure 5.13**). The ones you're likely to find most useful are Maps, Yellow Pages, and People Finder.

✔ Tips

- To save keystrokes, you can reach the AltaVista home page using the Web address www.av.com.

- For "pure AltaVista" searching without any of the usual portal features or advertisements, click on Raging Search on the AltaVista home page, or go directly to www.ragingsearch.com. Designed for hard-core search enthusiasts, Raging Search (**Figure 5.14**) uses the same database of Web pages as AltaVista and offers a full range of customization options.

- To make AltaVista your default home page, follow the instructions for "Customizing Your Web Browser" in Chapter 4.

- You can get back to the AltaVista home page at any time by clicking on Search Home or on the AltaVista logo at the top of most pages.

Searching with AltaVista

Now that you know your way around the AltaVista home page, let's do some searching. Despite its name, the Basic Search form is actually quite powerful. If you take full advantage of the tools that AltaVista makes available to you for use with Basic Search, you'll be amazed at how easily you can zero in on the information you're looking for on the Web.

In this section, we'll show you in step-by-step fashion how to enter search terms and special punctuation on the Basic Search form. For a summary of the material covered here, see the AltaVista Basic Search Quick Reference (**Table 5.1**).

Table 5.1

AltaVista Basic Search Quick Reference

FOR THIS TYPE OF SEARCH:	DO THIS:	EXAMPLE:
Plain-English Question	Simply type the question in the search form text box. Use as many words as necessary.	What is the date of the Battle of Trafalgar?
Phrase Search	Type the phrase as a sequence of words surrounded by **double quotes.**	`"Battle of Trafalgar"`
AND Search (multiple words and phrases, each of which *must* be present)	Use a **plus sign (+)** in front of each word or phrase that must appear in the results.	`+London + "art museum"`
OR Search (multiple words and phrases, any one of which may be present)	Type words or phrases separated by spaces, without any special notation.	`Stratford Shakespeare`
NOT Search (to exclude a word or phrase)	Use a **minus sign (–)** in front of a word or phrase you want to exclude from the results.	`+python −monty`
Case-Sensitive Search	Use lowercase to find any *combination* of uppercase and lowercase. Use capital letters (initial caps or a combination of uppercase and lowercase) to force an exact match of your search term. The first example would match *Bath* (but not *bath* or *BATH*). The second example would match *BATH* only.	`Bath` `BATH`
Date Search	Not available on the Basic Search form. Use Advanced Search or Power Search.	
Field Search	Type field-search keyword in lowercase, followed by a colon and your search word or phrase. (See **Table 5.2** for a complete list of field-search keywords.)	`title:"Victoria and Albert Museum"` `host:cambridge.edu` `domain:com`
Nested Search	Not available on the Basic Search form. Use Advanced Search or Power Search.	
Proximity Search	Not available on the Basic Search form. Use Advanced Search or Power Search.	
Wildcard Search	Use an **asterisk (*)** at the end of or within a word, along with at least three letters at the beginning of the search term.	`Brit*` `col*r`

Search for:

```
+London +"art museums"
```

Figure 5.15 To do an AND search on the Basic Search form, put a plus sign (+) in front of each term.

Search for:

```
+London +museum -"Victoria and Albert"
```

Figure 5.16 A minus sign (-) in front of a search term tells AltaVista to exclude Web pages containing that word or phrase.

Search for:

```
Trafalgar "Admiral Nelson"
```

Figure 5.17 To do an OR search, type the words (or phrases) separated by a space.

Search for:

```
+Brit* +monarchy
```

Figure 5.18 A search like this would locate references to both *British monarchy* and *monarchy in Great Britain*.

To enter a Basic Search query:

1. Go to www.altavista.com and type several unique keywords, a phrase in quotes, or a combination of words and phrases in the Basic Search form. Use a plus sign (+) in front of each word or phrase to tell AltaVista that they must *all* appear in your search results (**Figure 5.15**).

2. Use a minus sign (-) in front of any word or phrase you want to *exclude* from the search results. To find London museums *other than* the Victoria and Albert, use a search like the one shown in **Figure 5.16**.

3. To look for Web pages with references to *any* (but not necessarily *all*) of the terms in your query, type the words or phrases with a space between them. A search like the one in **Figure 5.17**, for example, would find all pages that have references to either *Trafalgar* or *Admiral Nelson*.

4. Use an asterisk (*) at the end of (or within) a word to do a wildcard search. Be sure to use at least three letters at the beginning of the search term or AltaVista will ignore the request. Using Brit* as a search term will find references to *Britain*, *British*, and *Britannia*, among others.

   For best results, combine a wildcard search term with at least one other unique keyword or phrase (**Figure 5.18**).

5. When you've finished entering your query, click on the Search button or press the [Enter] key to submit it.

continues on next page

SEARCHING WITH ALTAVISTA

✔ Tips

- You'll typically get much better results with AltaVista if you search for a phrase, or a combination of words and phrases, rather than a single word. If you're not sure what words and phrases to use, try entering your search as a question in plain English: What is the line of succession for the British monarchy?.

- AltaVista uses an automated process to detect commonly used phrases in your queries, even if you haven't enclosed the words in quotation marks. Consequently, you'll sometimes get the same results, with or without quotes (**Figure 5.19**).

  Still, it's a good idea to get into the habit of always enclosing phrases in quotation marks on the Basic Search form. After all, there's no way of knowing for sure exactly what AltaVista considers a "common phrase."

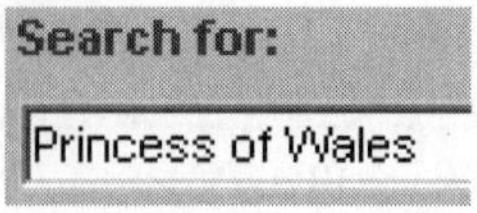

To make your search case-sensitive:

- ◆ Use initial caps or all caps as appropriate to search for a proper name or an acronym: Bath to search for the town of that name; BBC to find sites featuring the British Broadcasting Company.

✔ Tips

- Keep in mind that if you use any capital letters in your search request, AltaVista will perform a case-sensitive search. If, on the other hand, you enter your search terms in lowercase, you'll find all references to the term, regardless of case. Searching for bath, for example, will find references to bath, Bath, and BATH.

- When in doubt, enter your AltaVista search terms in lowercase. (If you're a two-finger typist who routinely turns on Caps Lock and pecks away, you're not likely to have much success with AltaVista.)

Search for:

Princess of Wales

Figure 5.19
Common phrases like this are included in AltaVista's phrase dictionary, so you'll get the same results with or without quotation marks.

- Case-sensitive searching comes in handy when you're looking for a company name that also happens to be a common word or phrase. Searching for next will return millions of hits. But a case-sensitive search for NeXT (or better yet "NeXT Inc") will help you zero right in on sites dealing with the company founded by Steve Jobs.

Figure 5.20
If a particular search returns a lot of foreign-language pages, you can eliminate them by using the languages menu.

Figure 5.21 Once you've customized the Language Options, AltaVista will automatically search for pages in your chosen language(s).

> 2. **Wolfgang Amadeus *Mozart***
> Wolfgang Amadeus **Mozart** (1756-1791) Bild: geboren: 27. Januar 1756 in Salzburg Bayern, heute Österreich) gestorben: 5. Dezember 1791 in Wien...
> URL: www.markus-hillenbrand.de/klassika/Kompo...zart/index.html
> Translate More pages from this site ▣ Related pages

Figure 5.22 For an instant translation to English, click on the Translate link in your search results.

> 1. **The *Mozart*Project**
> The life, times and music of Wolfgang Amadeus **Mozart**. Includes a complete Köchel listing, bibliography, **biography**, links to related sites and...
> URL: www.frontiernet.net/~sboerner/mozart/
> Directory Match: Wolfgang A Mozart Bios & Works
> Translate More pages from this site ▣ Related pages Facts about: Frontier Corp
>
> 2. ***Mozart*Discussion**
> Discussion of Wolfgang Amadeus **Mozart** on the web...
> URL: mozart.composers.net/wwwboard/index.html
> Translate More pages from this site ▣ Related pages
>
> 3. **The *Mozart*Project: Bibliography**
> HOME | **BIOGRAPHY** | COMPOSITIONS | SELECTED ESSAYS | BIBLIOGRAPHY **Mozart**'s Works and Writings. Anderson, Emily, ed. The...
> URL: trpe.reflektor.cz/mozart/books/index.html
> Translate More pages from this site ▣ Related pages
>
> 4. ***Mozart*, Wolfgang Amadeus: *Biography***
> Site @1996 Timothy A. Smith. Wolfgang Amadeus **Mozart** 1756-1791.
> Child prodigy **Mozart** made his first public appearance, at six years of age, in a...
> URL: jan.ucc.nau.edu/~tas3/wamozart.html
> Translate ▣ Related pages Facts about: Northern Arizona ...

Figure 5.23 Here's an example of how AltaVista presents search results for a query that includes the terms *Mozart* and *biography*.

To limit your search to a particular language:

1. Use the Basic Search form's drop-down menu (**Figure 5.20**) to make a language selection. Choosing English, for example, will ensure that only Web pages written in English will be included in your search results.

2. To permanently change the default setting to English (or whatever languages you prefer), click on Customize Settings and then on Language Options. Make your language selections and then click the Submit button.

3. The default language setting for your searches will now be my languages(*) (**Figure 5.21**).

✔ Tip

■ Another way of dealing with unfamiliar languages is to use AltaVista's translation tool, Babel Fish. If your results include a Web site in French, German, Italian, Portuguese, Russian, or Spanish, click on the Translate link (**Figure 5.22**) for an instant translation to English. It won't be perfect, but it could give you enough information to go on.

To view your search results:

1. Click on the Search button to the right of the search form text box and AltaVista will present your results, 10 to a page, with the best matches listed first (**Figure 5.23**). Your search terms will be highlighted in bold to make them easy to spot in the site descriptions. In Web page titles, which are bold to begin with, they'll be italicized.

continues on next page

2. Zero in on a typical entry (**Figure 5.24**) on the results page and you'll see that it includes the title of the document, a brief description provided by the person who created it (or, if a description has not been provided, the first couple of lines of text on the page), and the URL.

3. If your query matches multiple pages at a single Web site, AltaVista "clusters" the results and presents only one page from that Web site—a neat feature that allows you to get more variety in your results. To look at other pages from the site that match your query, click on the link labeled More pages from this site (**Figure 5.25**).

4. AltaVista also tells you exactly how many matches it found in its database (**Figure 5.26**). And if you scroll down to the bottom of the page, you'll find a word count for each of the keywords and phrases in your query (**Figure 5.27**), as well as the words (if any) that AltaVista ignored because they appear too frequently in its database.

This information can sometimes help you refine a search or identify problems. For example, if AltaVista found no instances of a particular term, it may be because you misspelled it.

5. If your search results look promising but you don't find exactly what you're looking for in the first couple of pages of results, you may want to modify your query and try again. For cases like this, AltaVista gives you the option of searching within the first set of results (**Figure 5.28**) instead of the entire database.

Figure 5.24 In addition to Web page title, description, and URL, this listing includes several links, including one for a match in the Web directory.

Figure 5.25 AltaVista presents a link like this whenever it finds your search terms on multiple pages at a single Web.

Figure 5.26 The first page of your search results will include information on the total number of Web pages found by AltaVista.

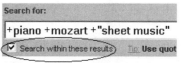

Figure 5.27 Near the bottom of your search results page, you'll find a word count for each of your search terms.

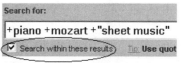

Figure 5.28 If you decide that your initial query was too broad, you might try adding another word or phrase and searching again *within* your original results.

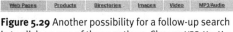

Figure 5.29 Another possibility for a follow-up search is to click on one of these options. Choose MP3/Audio, for example, to find sound files that match your search terms.

Figure 5.30 Your AltaVista results may include sections like these that can help clarify your search or locate sites that have been reviewed and approved for inclusion in the Web directory.

Figure 5.31 Don't get your hopes up when you find this section in your search results. It's often just an advertising gimmick.

6. With a single click, you can also direct your query to one of AltaVista's other search options (Products, Directories, Images, etc.) located above the search form on the search results page (**Figure 5.29**).

✔ Tips

- If your original search is quite general, your results may include a section labeled "Related Searches" to help you narrow the focus and home in on the information you're looking for. And if it matches a category in the AltaVista Web directory, you'll find them in a section labeled "See reviewed sites in" (**Figure 5.30**).

- You may also find a section of your search results labeled "AltaVista Recommends" (**Figure 5.31**). If so, don't be taken in by the fact that one of your search terms may be incorporated into the "recommendations." In most cases, following these links will simply lead you to generic promotional offerings by AltaVista advertisers.

- AltaVista allows you a great deal of control over the amount of detail included in your search results, as well as the number of items presented on each page. You can also turn bold highlighting of your search terms on or off. For more information, see "Customizing AltaVista" later in this chapter.

- For additional guidance in using the Basic Search form, click on the Help link above the Search button. AltaVista's help information is better than most—nicely organized and well written. You can even print out a "Cheat Sheet" with search examples and suggestions for getting better results from your AltaVista queries.

- Our only complaint about AltaVista's help information is that it doesn't always keep up with the changes being made at the site. From time to time, you'll encounter a reference to a feature that's no longer offered, which can be a bit disconcerting.

Improving Results with Field Search

It's not uncommon to enter a query on the AltaVista Basic Search form that returns hundreds, if not thousands, of Web pages— many of which have little or nothing to do with the information you're looking for.

When that happens, try adding one of AltaVista's *field-search* terms to your query. Field-search terms allow you to limit your search to specific parts (or *fields*) of Web pages.

You'll find a complete list of field-search terms that you can use on both the Basic and Advanced Search forms in the AltaVista Field Search Quick Reference (**Table 5.2**). The ones you are likely to find most useful are Title, Domain, Host, and Link.

✔ Tip

■ For point-and-click field searching, use AltaVista's Power Search form. It gives you the ability to incorporate some of the more popular field-search terms into your queries by making selections from drop-down menus and radio-button options.

Table 5.2

AltaVista Field Search Quick Reference

SEARCH TERM	DESCRIPTION	EXAMPLES
anchor:	Searches for Web pages that contain the specified hyperlink.	`anchor:"free product samples"`
applet:	Searches for Java applets. If you don't know the name of the applet, try combining an applet wildcard search with some other search term.	`applet:beeper` `+applet:* +Java`
domain:	Searches Web addresses for a specific domain (**com, edu, gov, net, org**, etc.) or two-letter Internet country code. (See Appendix B for a complete list.)	`domain:edu` `domain:uk`

host:	Searches just the *host name* portion of Web addresses.	`host:beatlefest.com`
		`host:oxford.edu`
		`host:BBC`

image:	Searches Web pages for the filenames of images matching your search term.	`image:ringo.gif` `image:*.gif`
like:	Searches for Web pages similar (or related in some way) to the specified URL.	`like:www.beatle.net`
link:	Searches for hypertext links (URLs) embedded in a Web page.	`link:www.songlyrics.com`
text:	Searches for text in the body of the Web page.	`text:"Strawberry Fields"`
title:	Limits search to the part of the Web page that the author labeled as the title.	`title:"John Lennon"`
url:	Searches for text in complete Web addresses (URLs).	`url:beatles.html`

Figure 5.32 A search for *John Lennon* in the *titles* of Web pages reduced the number of hits from several thousand to 153.

Search for:

+Beatles +domain:com

Figure 5.33 A search like this would help you locate Beatles-related sites in the U.S. that are commercial in nature.

To search Web page titles:

◆ Add a Title field search to your query. Let's say your initial search for "+"John Lennon" +lyrics results in too many hits. Try restricting your query to Web pages that include the singer/songwriter's name in the title: +title:"John Lennon" +lyrics (**Figure 5.32**). In most cases, you'll find that your search returns a much more manageable list of results.

To limit your search by Internet domain:

◆ Include a Domain field search in your query. For example, to focus on Web pages of commercial establishments, include +domain:com in your search request (**Figure 5.33**). You can also limit your search to Web pages for a *specific* domain name by including the entire name with the Domain search term. For example, using +domain:beatlefest.com in your query would limit your search to the Beatlefest Web site.

Here are the field-search terms for the most common Internet domains:

domain:com (commercial establishments)

domain:edu (educational institutions)

domain:gov (government agencies)

domain:mil (U.S. military)

domain:net (networks like AT&T and Sprint)

domain:org (non-profit organizations)

To limit your search by country:

◆ Do a Domain search for the country's two-letter country code. Adding +domain:uk to a Beatles search would limit the query to sites based in the United Kingdom (**Figure 5.34**).

✔ Tips

■ You can also use a Domain search to eliminate foreign-language sites from your search results. If you can't read French and want to avoid French-language pages, for example, you could add –domain:fr to your query. (Note the use of the minus sign.).

■ Remember, though, that AltaVista gives you the option of selecting your preferred language from a drop-down menu on the search form. You'll probably find that approach to be easier and more convenient than doing a Domain search.

■ See Appendix B for a complete list of Internet domains and country codes.

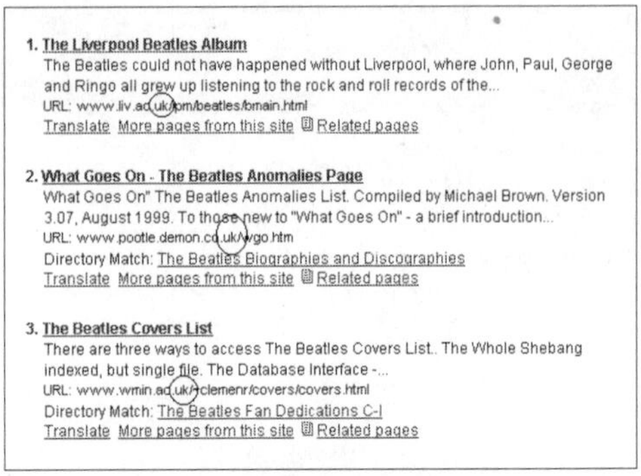

To limit your search by host name:

1. Use a Host field search to find all the Web pages "hosted" on a particular computer. A search for +host:harvard.edu, for example, would find Web pages hosted by a computer at Harvard University.

2. To exclude all such pages, put a minus sign (-) in front of the field-search term. A search like the one in **Figure 5.35**, for example, would help you locate sites that mention Harvard University while avoiding Harvard's own Web site.

To search for embedded links:

◆ Use a Link field in your query. The search term +link:www.songlyrics.com would help you identify Web pages that include embedded links to the Song Lyrics Web site.

Figure 5.34 If you include +domain:uk in your query, your search will be limited to Web sites in the United Kingdom, as shown here.

Figure 5.35 To exclude Web pages from a particular host system, use a Host field search preceded by a minus sign (-).

✔ Tip

■ Webmasters and Web site creators often use a Link search to find out who is sending traffic to their Web sites. It also provides a rough indication of a site's popularity—the more links, the more popular the site.

Using Advanced Search

Many AltaVista fans never venture beyond the search engine's main page. They master the Basic Search form and use it exclusively for most of their Internet searches. If they can't find what they're looking for with Basic Search, they just move on to another engine.

But power users and professional searchers will tell you that AltaVista's Advanced Search form (**Figure 5.36**) is worth taking the time to learn. In fact, some of what you've learned already about Basic Search applies to Advanced Search as well. The techniques for using wildcards, performing a case-sensitive search, and field searching are the same on both the Basic and Advanced Search forms.

continues on next page

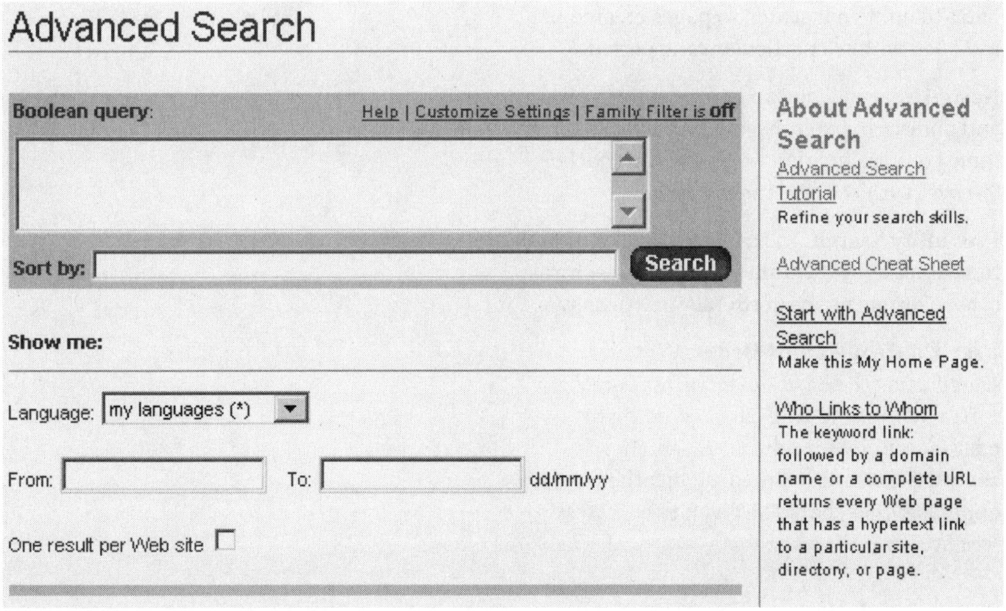

Advanced Search

Boolean query: Help | Customize Settings | Family Filter is **off**

Sort by: | Search |

Show me:

Language: my languages (*) ▾

From: | To: | dd/mm/yy

One result per Web site ☐

About Advanced Search
Advanced Search Tutorial
Refine your search skills.

Advanced Cheat Sheet

Start with Advanced Search
Make this My Home Page.

Who Links to Whom
The keyword link: followed by a domain name or a complete URL returns every Web page that has a hypertext link to a particular site, directory, or page.

Figure 5.36 AltaVista's Advanced Search form offers a number of search options not offered on the Basic Search form, including use of Boolean operators and date searching.

The rules for specifying phrases and for combining words and phrases are different, however.

Specifying Phrases. On the Advanced Search form, it is *not* necessary to enclose phrases in quotation marks. Whenever two or more words appear together without a Boolean operator between them, AltaVista interprets the words as a phrase.

Combining Words and Phrases. Instead of using plus and minus signs to require and exclude keywords and phrases, you must use the traditional Boolean operator AND (to require a term) and the somewhat less traditional AND NOT (to exclude a term). To search for several words or phrases, any of which *may* be present in your search results, you must link the terms with the Boolean operator OR.

Advanced Search also offers several very useful features not available with Basic Search:

Date Search. You can specify a range of dates to limit your search to pages created or modified within a particular time period.

Nested Search. You can group search words and phrases in parentheses in order to form more complex queries: (mystery AND (author OR novelist)) AND bestseller.

Proximity Search. You can use NEAR to find terms that appear within 10 words of each other: Catherine the Great NEAR biography.

User-Controlled Sort Order. When you search using the Basic Search form, AltaVista sorts and ranks your results according to relevance. But with Advanced Search, *you* control the sort order by specifying the words or phrases that should be given the greatest weight.

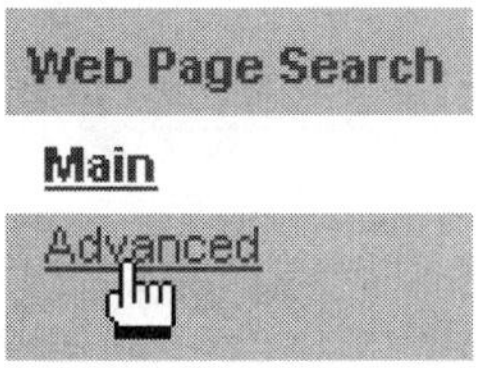

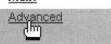

Web Page Search

Main

Figure 5.37 Use this link on the AltaVista home page to access the Advanced Search form.

Boolean query:

study abroad AND (Oxford OR Cambridge)

Figure 5.38 A Boolean query like this would find Web pages with references to the phrase *study abroad* (no quotes required) and either *Oxford* or *Cambridge*.

Sort by: Oxford Cambridge

Figure 5.39 Words typed in the "Sort by" box are given greater weight when AltaVista organizes your search results. Pages containing those words will be listed first.

From: 01/01/01   To: 31/12/01   dd/mm/yy

Figure 5.40 Specifying a range of dates like this would limit your search to Web pages created or modified during the 2001 calendar year.

One result per Web site

Figure 5.41 The check mark here tells AltaVista to "cluster" your results and show you only one page per Web site.

To search with Advanced Search:

1. Go to the AltaVista home page (www.altavista.com) and click on Advanced (**Figure 5.37**).

2. Type your search request in the area labeled "Boolean query" (**Figure 5.38**). Use AND, OR, and NEAR to combine words and phrases. To exclude a word, be sure to use AND NOT: Oxford AND NOT shoes. You can also use parentheses in your query to group words and phrases.

3. If there's any particular word or phrase that should be given greater weight in the presentation of search results, enter it in the "Sort by" area of the form (**Figure 5.39**). Boolean expressions are not allowed in this part of the search form.

4. To limit your search to documents created within a range of dates, enter that information in the form DD/MM/YY. Be sure to use a two-digit number for day, month, and year (**Figure 5.40**). And note that day (rather than month) comes first.

5. Use the drop-down menu if you want to limit your search by language, and click on the box labeled "One result per Web site" if you prefer not to see multiple pages from the same site (**Figure 5.41**).

6. Click on Search to enter your query. Your results will be presented in random order, unless you entered a word or phrase in the "Sort by" text box, as explained above. In all other respects, search results for Advanced Search are identical to what you get when you use the Basic Search form, described earlier in this chapter.

continues on next page

✔ Tips

- You can use uppercase or lowercase for Boolean operators on the Advanced Search form.

- Boolean operators are also allowed on the Power Search form, as long as you choose Boolean from the drop-down menu (**Figure 5.42**).

- To do a Boolean search for images, MP3/audio, or video files, you can use special versions of the Advanced Search form accessible by clicking on the appropriate multimedia search link (**Figure 5.43**) on the left side of the Advanced Search page.

- The AltaVista Advanced Search Quick Reference (**Table 5.3**) includes a summary of all the Advanced Search features and how to use them.

- For more tips and search examples, as well as a tutorial and "Cheat Sheet," click on Help on the Advanced Search form.

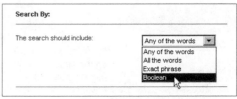

Figure 5.42 You can use Boolean operators on the Power Search form as long as you specify Boolean on the drop-down menu.

Figure 5.43 Use these links on the Advanced Search page to access special versions of the Advanced Search form tailored for finding image, MP3/audio, and video files.

Table 5.3

AltaVista Advanced Search Quick Reference

FOR THIS TYPE OF SEARCH:	DO THIS:	EXAMPLES:
Plain-English Question	Not recommended on Advanced Search form. Use Basic Search instead.	
Phrase Search	Just type the phrase in the search box (*without* quotation marks). AltaVista interprets as a phrase any words that appear together without a search operator between them.	`Tower of London`
AND Search (multiple words and phrases, each of which *must* be present)	Use AND between words or phrases to specify that both must be present in the results.	`Oxford AND Cambridge`
OR Search (multiple words and phrases, any one of which may be present)	Use OR between words or phrases to specify that you want to find references to either or both terms.	`Oxford OR Cambridge`
NOT Search (to exclude a word or phrase)	Use AND NOT in front of the word or phrase you want to exclude from the query.	`Oxford AND NOT Cambridge`
Case-Sensitive Search	Use lowercase to find any *combination* of uppercase and lowercase. Use capital letters (initial caps or a combination of uppercase and lowercase) to force an *exact match* of your search term, as shown in the example.	`Round Table`
Date Search	Type the range of dates you want to search in the From and To boxes, using the form DD/MM/YY. The example would search for dates between January 1, 2001, and December 3, 2001 (not March 12, 2001).	`From: 01/01/01` `To: 03/12/01`
Field Search	Type field-search keyword in lowercase, immediately followed by a colon and your search word or phrase. (See **Table 5.2** for a complete list of field-search keywords.)	`title:Castle Howard` `domain:com` `host:cambridge.edu`
Nested Search	Use **parentheses** to group search expressions into more complex queries. The example would find *Queen Mother* as well as *Queen Mum*.	`Queen (Mother OR Mum)`
Proximity Search	Use NEAR to find words or phrases that appear within 10 words of each other. The example would find *bed and breakfast* as well as *bed & breakfast* and *breakfast in bed*.	`bed NEAR breakfast`
Wildcard Search	Use an **asterisk (*)** at the end of or within a word with at least three letters at the beginning of the search term.	`bicycl*` `col*r`

USING ADVANCED SEARCH

Customizing AltaVista

If you use AltaVista a lot, you'll want to take advantage of its customization features. As we mentioned earlier in this chapter, AltaVista gives you more control than most search engines over how you search and how your results are displayed. You can also create your own personalized version of the AltaVista home page.

Here's a brief summary of the AltaVista customization features:

Results Options. This feature gives you complete control over the amount of detail displayed in your search results. It also allows you to specify the number of search results presented on each page, and whether your search terms should be presented in bold type so that they are easy to locate.

Language Options. You can change AltaVista's default language setting from any language to English, or whatever languages you can read and understand. Once you've identified your language preferences, AltaVista will automatically screen out Web pages written in other languages.

Family Filter. Allows you to set preferences for screening out objectionable material from your Web searches.

My AltaVista. Gives you the ability to pick and choose the "portal features" you find most useful, and decide how you want them arranged on the AltaVista home page.

To set Results Options:

1. Click on Customize Settings (**Figure 5.44**) on the AltaVista Basic Search form, or on the Advanced or Power Search form. That will take you to the Results Options page.

Figure 5.44 You'll find the Customize Settings link on all the major AltaVista search forms: Basic, Advanced, and Power Search.

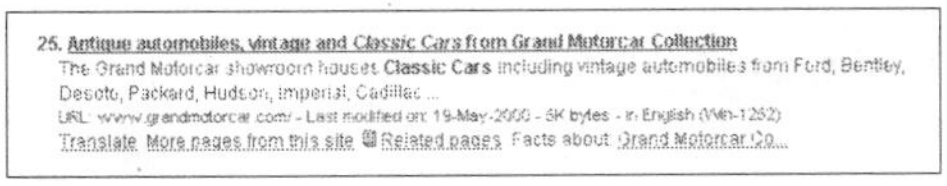

25. **Antique automobiles, vintage and Classic Cars from Grand Motorcar Collection**
The Grand Motorcar showroom houses **Classic Cars** including vintage automobiles from Ford, Bentley, Desoto, Packard, Hudson, Imperial, Cadillac...
URL: www.grandmotorcar.com - Last modified on: 19-May-2000 - 5K bytes - in English (Win-1252)
Translate. More pages from this site ■ Related pages. Facts about: Grand Motorcar Co...

Figure 5.45 Here's an example of what your AltaVista results will look like if you choose to display all available options.

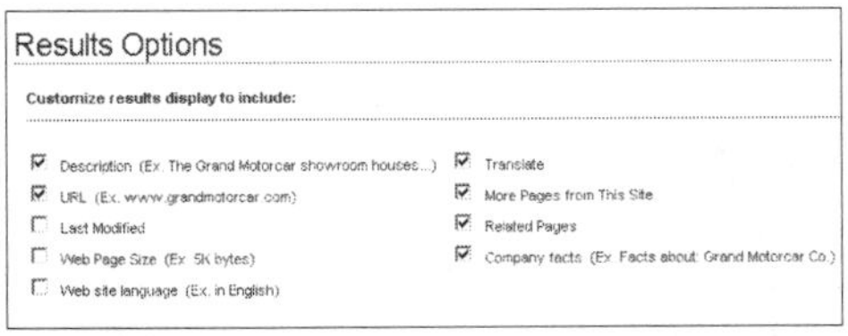

Results Options

Customize results display to include:

☑ Description (Ex: The Grand Motorcar showroom houses...)   ☑ Translate
☑ URL (Ex: www.grandmotorcar.com)   ☑ More Pages from This Site
☐ Last Modified   ☑ Related Pages
☐ Web Page Size (Ex: 5K bytes)   ☑ Company facts (Ex: Facts about: Grand Motorcar Co.)
☐ Web site language (Ex: in English)

Figure 5.46 If there's any particular item you would prefer not to see in your results, click on the box next to it to remove the check mark.

Figure 5.47 Increasing the number of results displayed on each page can be a time saver if you typically like to review 20 or more listings for your searches.

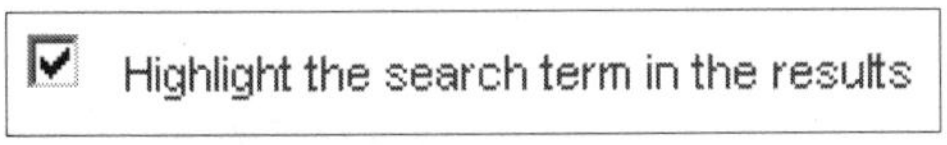

☑ Highlight the search term in the results

Figure 5.48 Remove this check mark to turn off highlighting of your search terms.

2. Scroll down the page and take a look at the example of how AltaVista displays search results (**Figure 5.45**). If there are any particular elements that you would like to remove, just click on the box next to the item to eliminate the check mark (**Figure 5.46**).

If you're not sure whether or not to exclude an item, leave it checked until you've had more experience with AltaVista. At a minimum, you'll certainly want to keep Description and URL. We also find that Last Modified and More Pages from This Site come in handy from time to time.

For an explanation of each item, scroll down the page and click on the Help link.

3. Once you've decided on the amount of detail to be included in your search results, use the drop-down menu (**Figure 5.47**) to choose the number of listings you want AltaVista to display on each page. The default setting is 10, but you can increase it to as many as 50.

The advantage to doing so is that when you're reviewing your search results, you can simply scroll down the page, instead of having to load a new page for every 10 results.

4. Next, decide whether you want your search terms presented in bold in your search results. If so, make sure that there is a check mark in the Highlight box (**Figure 5.48**).

5. When you are finished setting your Results Options, click on the Submit button and AltaVista will begin using them immediately. To change them at any time, just repeat the steps presented here.

To set Language Options:

1. Click on Customize Settings on the AltaVista Basic Search form and then on Language Options (**Figure 5.49**).

2. Make your language selections by clicking on the box next to any language (**Figure 5.50**). Most Web pages are presented in English, but if you want to ensure that your results include *only* English-language pages, click on the box for English. Once you've done that (and made the setting permanent as described below), you won't have to bother with the drop-down languages menu on the AltaVista Basic, Advanced, and Power Search forms.

3. If you've selected languages that use non-Roman alphabets (Chinese, Czech, Greek, Hebrew, Japanese, Korean, Polish, or Russian), be sure to complete the sections on encoding options.

4. Finally, click on the Submit button. From this point forward, the default setting on the AltaVista search form's drop-down languages menu will be my languages(*) (**Figure 5.51**).

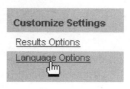

Figure 5.49 Click here to access the Language Options page.

Figure 5.50 The Language Options page allows you to limit your searches to English or more than two dozen other languages.

Figure 5.51 After setting Language Options, your searches will automatically default to your chosen language(s).

Figure 5.52 Click here to set up the Family Filter.

Figure 5.53 AltaVista gives you three filtering options, shown here.

Figure 5.54 Password protection is an optional feature with the Family Filter.

Figure 5.55 This link on the AltaVista search form tells you that the Family Filter is set to filter *all* Web content.

To set the Family Filter:

1. Click on Family Filter is off (**Figure 5.52**) on the AltaVista home page to access the Family Filter Setup Page.

2. Choose your filter preferences (**Figure 5.53**) by clicking the radio button to indicate whether you want to screen Multimedia Only (the default) or All Web content. To eliminate filtering completely, click on the radio button for None.

3. To activate password protection— optional, but probably a good idea if your objective is to prevent young family members from accessing inappropriate material—choose a password and enter it twice in the boxes provided (**Figure 5.54**).

4. Then click on the Done button to submit your Family Filter preferences.

5. If you have chosen to filter all Web content, when you return to the AltaVista search form, the Family Filter will be on (**Figure 5.55**). If you've chosen to filter multimedia content only, the filter will be activated only when you use one of the Multimedia search forms.

✔ Tips

- AltaVista's Family Filter works only for Web pages written in English.

- The Family Filter uses *cookie* technology to save your filter settings. If you have set your Web browser to reject cookies, you'll have to reset the Family Filter each time you visit AltaVista. (For more on this topic, including how to turn cookies back on, return to the Family Filter Setup Page and click on Frequently Asked Questions.)

CUSTOMIZING ALTAVISTA

To create your own AltaVista home page:

1. Click on My AltaVista (**Figure 5.56**) on the AltaVista home page.

2. Next click on Sign Up. You'll be asked to choose a member ID and password and to provide your name, address, and other information, most of which is optional.

3. Once you've completed the form, click on Next and you'll find yourself on the Customize My AltaVista page. Choose the features you want for each column of the AltaVista home page by clicking on the item and then on the Add button. Be sure to place AltaVista Search in one of the columns (**Figure 5.57**).

4. If you change your mind about a feature, just click on it again in the My Choices menu and then use the Remove button to delete it.

5. Once you've made all of your selections, click on the Done button.

6. Certain features can be further customized by clicking on the EDIT link (**Figure 5.58**) on your My AltaVista page.

7. You can, of course, return to the Customize My AltaVista page at any time to add or remove features.

8. To make My AltaVista your browser's default home page, click on Make this my start page and follow the instructions provided for Windows and Macintosh users.

✔ Tips

■ One disadvantage of the My AltaVista page is that it doesn't include links to Advanced Search, Power Search, Multimedia Search, and so forth. To use these search options, you first have to return to the AltaVista home page by clicking on Search Home or on the AltaVista logo at the top of the My AltaVista page.

Figure 5.56 Click on this link to create your own personalized version of the AltaVista home page.

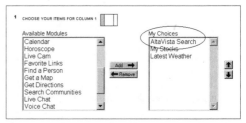

Figure 5.57 Three items have been selected for Column 1 of the My AltaVista page, including the AltaVista Basic Search form.

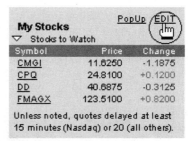

Figure 5.58 To further personalize a feature on your My AltaVista page, click on its EDIT link.

■ You can customize your My AltaVista page so that the Basic Search form is the only item that appears on it. But if using a stripped-down AltaVista without any of its "portal" features is what you're after, you might want to try Raging Search (www.ragingsearch.com) instead. It uses the same database of Web pages as AltaVista and gives you all the same great customization features.

GOOGLE

Google is the newest of the Big Six search engines, but it's giving established competitors like AltaVista (www.altavista.com) and even Yahoo (www.yahoo.com) a run for their money. The company made headlines in June 2000 with the announcement that its Googlebot spider had indexed more than a billion Web pages—the first (and at this writing still the only) search engine to reach that milestone.

More importantly, Google gets high marks for the *relevancy* of its search results. Using a patent-pending technology, Google not only searches for keywords and phrases, it also employs sophisticated *link analysis* and *data mining* techniques to determine how search results are ranked and presented.

The underlying theory is that the best Web sites on a particular topic will have been discovered by other Web users, who will then include links to those pages in their own Web sites. So the more popular a site—based on the number of other sites that link to it—the higher it appears in your search results.

Google doesn't give you nearly as much control over your queries as AltaVista, HotBot, and Northern Light. You can't use Boolean operators other than OR, for example, nor can you do case-sensitive or wildcard searches. Phrase searches are problematic: If the phrase you're searching for includes a common word like *about* or *with*, Google will ignore it.

Good to Know

◆ Created at Stanford in 1998, Google is one of the top-rated search sites, earning high praise for its simple interface, spot-on search results, and ad-free home page.

◆ Google's database is the largest of all the leading search engines, with more than 1.2 billion Web pages.

◆ Search results include matches from Google's gigantic database as well as the human-compiled Web directory created by the Open Directory Project.

◆ Google is currently the only search engine that indexes the full text of PDF files and includes them in search results.

◆ Boolean operators and other "power search" capabilities are fairly limited, but Google does such a good job of producing relevant results that it doesn't matter for most searches.

But frankly, these limitations aren't really a problem for most day-to-day search tasks. As long as you give Google two or three unique keywords to work with, there's a good chance you'll find what you're looking for within the first few listings in your search results.

✔ Tips

- Google was created in 1998 by Stanford doctoral students Larry Page and Sergey Brin, who dropped out of the computer science program, got venture-capital funding, and launched the service as a privately-held company in 1999.

  Sound familiar? That's probably because Yahoo was also created (four years earlier) by a pair of Stanford doctoral students.

- Both Yahoo and Netscape Search (search.netscape.com) have licensed the Google technology, so when you search at those sites, your results are coming (at least in part) from the Google database.

- Prepare to be amazed the first time you do a Google search. Because the work is spread out over a network of some 6,000 PCs, most searches take less than half a second.

- *Google* is a play on the word *googol* (**Figure 6.1**), coined in 1938 by an American mathematician's nine-year-old nephew. The boy had been asked by his uncle what word he would use for a truly gigantic number, represented by a one followed by 100 zeros.

  Google's founders chose the name to convey their commitment to organizing the immense body of information available on the Web. Today, a billion pages. Tomorrow, a googol!

- For more information about Google—press releases, corporate history, job openings, products from the company store—click All About Google on the search engine's home page.

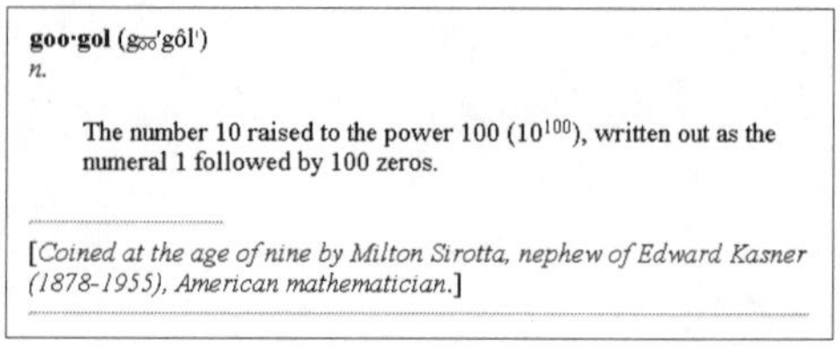

goo·gol (gōō'gôl')
n.

The number 10 raised to the power 100 (10^{100}), written out as the numeral 1 followed by 100 zeros.

[*Coined at the age of nine by Milton Sirotta, nephew of Edward Kasner (1878-1955), American mathematician.*]

Figure 6.1 The word *google* is based on a mathematical term coined in 1938 by a young boy named Milton Sirotta.

Contact Information

Google, Inc.
Mountain View, California
650-330-0100 (voice)
650-618-1499 (fax)
www.google.com

GOOGLE

The Google Home Page

If you prefer to do your Web searches in a clutter-free environment, you'll *love* the Google home page (**Figure 6.2**). Talk about a search engine that's focused on searching! No Web directory to browse. No portal features like news headlines, weather reports, and stock quotes to procrastinate with. No banner ads (with their annoying animated graphics) to distract you.

The Google home page is devoted *exclusively* to its search form. The Web directory and advanced features like field searching and language options are all relegated to underlying pages.

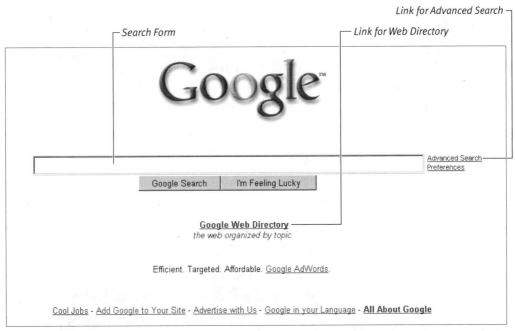

Figure 6.2 The Google home page is the least cluttered of all the leading search engines. The search form gets exclusive billing, and there are no banner ads.

Search form

The Google search form (**Figure 6.3**) consists of a box for entering queries along with your choice of two buttons to send them off for processing:

◆ Google Search. This is the one you'll use most of the time. It works just like you'd expect—processing your query and producing a list of results.

◆ I'm Feeling Lucky. This button automatically takes you to the first Web page in your search results, instead of displaying the list—an interesting idea, but not all that necessary. Google returns search results with such blinding speed (usually a half second or less) that skipping the results list doesn't save that much time.

Google defaults to doing an AND search, looking for *all* the words that you type in the search box, so plus signs (+) aren't necessary. The only Boolean operator that's recognized by Google is OR, which must be typed in full caps: genetics OR genome.

Advanced Search option

The Advanced Search link (**Figure 6.4**) on the Google home page takes you to a fill-in-the-blanks form that you can use for somewhat more sophisticated queries (**Figure 6.5**). You can limit your search to specific Web page fields (titles, URLs, domains, and links) or to pages written in a particular language.

The Advanced Search form also allows you to display more search results per page (up to 100) and gives you access to several topic-specific search tools: Apple Macintosh, BSD Unix, Linux, U.S. government, and universities.

Figure 6.3 Google gives you two choices for submitting a query: Google Search to display a list of results and I'm Feeling Lucky to go directly to the first item on the list.

Figure 6.4 Google's Advanced Search option gives you access to some additional features not available on the home page.

Figure 6.5 Using this form on the Advanced Search page, you can create more complex queries and exercise some control over how your results are presented.

Figure 6.6 Google doesn't display its Web directory on the home page. You have to click this link to display it.

Figure 6.7 Once you're on the Google Web Directory page, you can search the directory or "drill down" through its many categories and subcategories.

Figure 6.8
You can customize a handful of Google search options using the Preferences link.

Figure 6.9 To get back to the Google home page from anywhere within the site, click the company logo.

Google Web Directory option

The Google Web Directory link (**Figure 6.6**) takes you to a hierarchical guide to the Web, organized into 16 major topic categories and dozens of subcategories (**Figure 6.7**). Like a number of leading search engines, Google gets its Web directory from the Open Directory Project (dmoz.org), a volunteer effort to identify and catalog the best Web sites, based on the judgments of human beings rather than automated spider programs.

When you enter a query using the Google search form, your results automatically include matching categories and sites from the Web directory. But on occasion, you may want to browse the directory or do a search of its contents, instead of searching the entire Web. That's what the Google Web Directory link is for.

✔ Tips

- The Preferences link (**Figure 6.8**) on the Google home page gives you access to several useful customization options. You can set language preferences, increase the number of results per page from 10 to 100, specify that your results be displayed in a new browser window, and turn on content filtering. For more on Google preferences, see "Customizing Google" later in this chapter.

- To make Google your default home page, follow the instructions for "Customizing Your Web Browser" in Chapter 4.

- You can get back to the Google home page at any time by clicking the Google logo (**Figure 6.9**) at the top of every page within the site.

THE GOOGLE HOME PAGE

Searching with Google

Doing a search from the Google home page is pretty straightforward. There are no drop-down menus or radio buttons to consider. Just type several unique words or phrases in the search box and click Google Search to submit your query. Chances are, you'll get pretty good results most of the time.

If you decide to make Google your primary search engine, however, there are a few basic things you should know about entering and combining keywords that can help you search with more precision. To refine your queries even further, you can include field-search terms to zero in on Web page titles, URLs, domain names, and links.

To enter a query:

1. Go to the Google home page (www.google.com) and type several descriptive words, or a phrase in quotes, in the search box (**Figure 6.10**).

   By default, Google does an AND search, looking for *all* the words, so there's no need to put plus signs (+) in front of required words. In fact, if you do use plus signs, Google typically ignores them.

   The only time you need to use a plus sign is when you are searching for a very common word (or *stopword*), like *about* or *for* or *with* (**Figure 6.11**). In that case, the plus sign signals Google that the word should *not* be treated as a stopword: +about guides, for example, to search for information on the company that creates the About guides to the Internet (www.about.com).

2. To tell Google that you want to do an OR search, type your search words separated by OR in full caps: hilary OR hillary, for example, to look for either spelling of the name (**Figure 6.12**). You *must* use full caps for OR so that Google knows to treat it as a Boolean operator.

Figure 6.10 When you type multiple words in the search box, Google assumes you want to find *all* the words. There's no need to link them with AND or put plus signs (+) in front of them.

Figure 6.11 Plus signs are only required for very common words, which Google typically ignores. A search like this tells Google not to ignore the word *about*.

Figure 6.12 Use the Boolean operator OR in full caps to tell Google that you want to look for one word *or* the other.

Your search - **"first lady"** OR **"laura bush"** - did not match any documents.

Figure 6.13 You'll get an error message like this if you use quotation marks in an OR search. The same query without quotes (first lady OR laura bush) works fine.

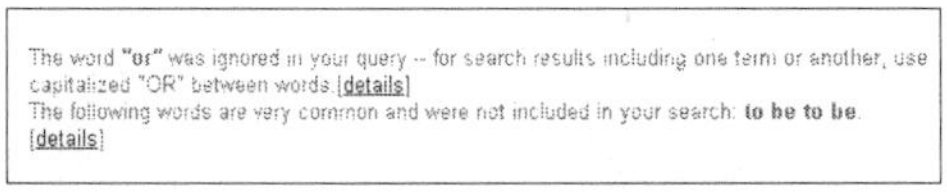

The word **"or"** was ignored in your query -- for search results including one term or another, use capitalized "OR" between words [details]
The following words are very common and were not included in your search: to be to be. [details]

Figure 6.14 A Google search for the famous line "to be or not to be" from Hamlet turns up empty, even when the words are enclosed in double quotes.

To look for phrases with OR, type them *without* quotes: first lady OR laura bush. Otherwise you'll get a "no results found" message (**Figure 6.13**).

3. If you want to exclude a certain word or phrase from your search results, use a minus sign (-) directly in front of it: Portobello –mushrooms, for example, if you're looking for a restaurant named Portobello rather than the fungus.

✔ Tips

- Except for the OR operator, Google isn't sensitive to case. You can type search words and phrases in uppercase, lowercase, or a combination and you'll get the same results.

- With most of the leading search engines, you can search for a phrase—even one that's composed almost entirely of stopwords—by enclosing the phrase in double quotes. Not so with Google. Try searching for **"to be or not to be"** and you'll be advised that *to*, *be*, and *or* have all been ignored because they are so common (**Figure 6.14**).

  When that happens, you can redo your Google search, putting plus signs in front of the words that were ignored the first time around. (Don't put plus signs in front of all the words, though, or you'll be back to square one.)

  Alternatively, try another search engine. Lycos (www.lycos.com) is an especially good choice, because it will *not* ignore common words that are part of a phrase enclosed in double quotes.

To view your search results:

1. Click Google Search (or hit Enter) to display your results, 10 to a page, with your search terms highlighted in bold and presented with a few words of surrounding text from the Web page. Google "clusters" results and presents only two Web pages from any given site—one indented below the other—in order to give you more variety in your search results (**Figure 6.15**).
2. To "uncluster" the results and view additional pages from a particular Web site, click the More results from link (**Figure 6.16**).
3. In some cases, Google also gives you the option of clicking a Cached link (**Figure 6.17**) to display a copy of the Web page at the time it was indexed by the Google spider. If you have a problem linking to the current version of the Web page (because the site is down, for example), try retrieving the cached version.
4. Your search results may include items that begin with a [PDF] label (**Figure 6.18**). Google is in the process of indexing the full text of Adobe PDF (Portable Document Format) files that are available on the Web. If you have the Adobe Acrobat Reader installed, you can download and view these items by clicking the link next to the [PDF] label. If not, click Text version to view the document as a text file.

Human Genome Project
Human Genome Project Information
Human Genome Project Publications
Division of Extramural Research (DER): HGP
National Human Genome Research Institute (NHGRI)

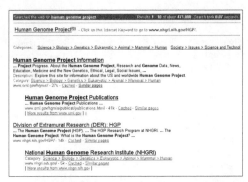

Figure 6.15 Google puts your search terms in bold to make them easy to spot and presents only two Web pages from any given site, one indented below the other.

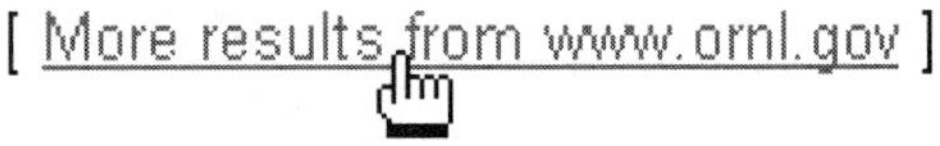
[More results from www.ornl.gov]

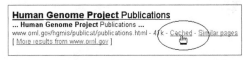

Figure 6.16 To "uncluster" your results and view more Web pages from a given site, click the More results from link.

Human Genome Project Publications
... Human Genome Project Publications ...
www.ornl.gov/hgmis/publicat/publications.html - 41k - Cached - Similar pages
[More results from www.ornl.gov]

Figure 6.17 If you have trouble connecting to a Web site listed in your search results, click Cached to display a copy of the page as it looked when last visited by the Google spider.

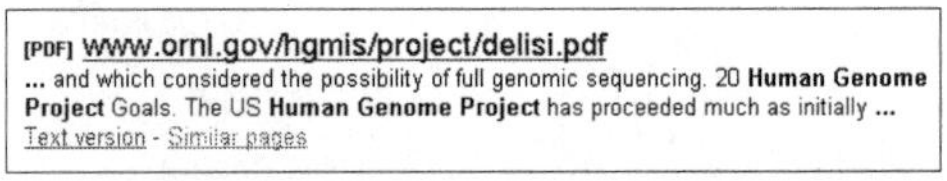
[PDF] www.ornl.gov/hgmis/project/delisi.pdf
... and which considered the possibility of full genomic sequencing. 20 Human Genome Project Goals. The US Human Genome Project has proceeded much as initially ...
Text version - Similar pages

Figure 6.18 You have two options with PDF files: click the link following the [PDF] label to view the file with the Adobe Acrobat Reader, or click Text version to view it as a text file.

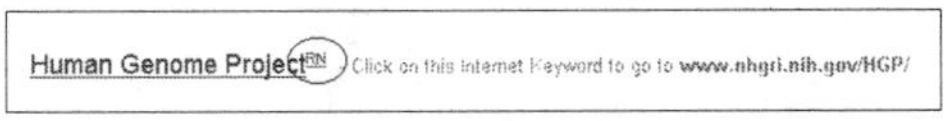

Figure 6.19 RealNames (ʀɴ) keywords like Human Genome Project shown here can be typed in the Internet Explorer Address box in place of a complicated Web address.

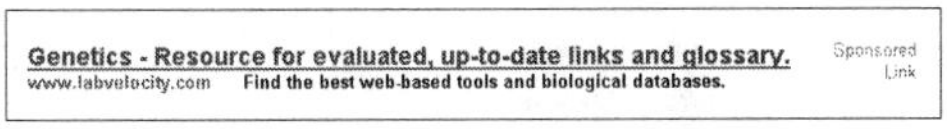

Figure 6.20 Google doesn't allow banner ads, but your search results may include a Sponsored Link in a shaded area like this (or in a small box on the right side of the screen).

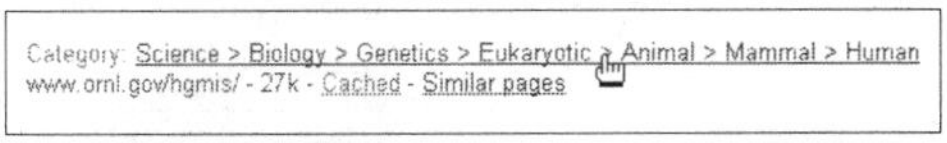

Figure 6.21 Category links, labeled as such and easily recognizable by the greater-than (>) symbols separating the various subtopics, can help you find Web pages with related content.

Figure 6.22 In addition to finding out how many search results were located (and how quickly), you can use the statistics bar to get a definition for any search word or phrase that's underlined.

✔ Tips

- The ʀɴ designation next to an item on the search results page (**Figure 6.19**) means that the word you have searched for is a brand, product, service, or company name that has been registered as an Internet keyword with RealNames (www.realnames.com). Companies pay $100 a year or more for the right to "own" a particular RealNames keyword, which can be entered directly into the Internet Explorer Address box in place of the URL. (Microsoft owns a 20 percent stake in RealNames.)

  You'll typically find RealNames results (if any) at the top of the Google results list, along with Sponsored Links—discrete text advertisements related to your search request (**Figure 6.20**).

- Each item on the Google search results page includes a Similar pages link that's intended to help you find other sites that might be of interest. Sometimes it works, sometimes it doesn't.

  A more consistently effective way to find related sites is to click the Category link (**Figure 6.21**), if there is one. That will take you to the appropriate spot in the Google Web directory, where you will find "related sites" that have been chosen by human beings, not an automated "scout" program.

- The statistics bar (**Figure 6.22**) at the top of the search results page displays your query and tells you how many results were found and how long the search took. If one of your search terms is underlined, you can click on it for an instant definition.

To refine a Google query:

1. Try adding another unique word to the search box at the top of the search results page (**Figure 6.23**) and submitting your query again. Since Google looks for *all* the words in your query, this has the effect of searching *within* your original results (also known as *set searching*). It's faster than scrolling to the bottom of the page and using the `Search within results` option.

2. As you may recall from our discussion of keywords in Chapter 2, one of the best ways to narrow the focus of a search is to zero in on Web page *titles*. With Google, you can use `allintitle:` followed directly (no space after the colon) by a phrase in quotes or multiple words that you'd like to find in Web page titles:
`allintitle:human genome project history`
(**Figure 6.24**).

To do an OR search of words in titles, use `intitle:` followed directly by two or more words separated by spaces:
`intitle:genome DNA mapping`.

✔ Tips

- You can also use URL, domain, and link field-search terms in your Google queries. For examples, see the Google Quick Reference (**Table 6.1**).

- For even easier field searching, click `Advanced Search` and use the fill-in-the-blanks form and drop-down menus to focus on Web page titles, URLs, domain names, and links.

- Google's search tips and help information are splendid—written in plain English and covering just about any question you might have about how to construct a query and interpret the results. You'll find a `Search Tips` link on every search results page or by clicking `All About Google`.

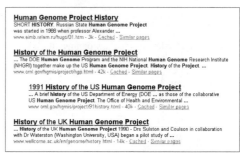

Figure 6.23 You can refine a Google search by simply adding another word to your query and running the search again.

Human Genome Project History
SHORT **HISTORY**. Russian State **Human Genome Project** was started in 1988 when professor Alexander ...
www.eimb.relam.ru/hugo/01.htm - 3k - Cached - Similar pages

History of the Human Genome Project
... The DOE **Human Genome** Program and the NIH National **Human Genome** Research Institute (NHGRI) together make up the US **Human Genome Project**. **History** of the **Project**. ...
www.ornl.gov/hgmis/project/hgp.html - 42k - Cached - Similar pages

1991 **History** of the US **Human Genome Project**
... A brief **history** of the US Department of Energy (DOE ... as those of the collaborative US **Human Genome Project**. The Office of Health and Environmental ...
www.ornl.gov/hgmis/project/91history.html - 40k - Cached - Similar pages

History of the UK Human Genome Project
... **History** of the UK **Human Genome Project** 1990 - Drs Sulston and Coulson in collaboration with Dr Waterston (Washington University, USA) began a pilot study of ...
www.wellcome.ac.uk/en/genome/history.html - 14k - Cached - Similar pages

Figure 6.24 To produce these results, we searched for `allintitle:human genome project history`. Note that all of our search terms appear in bold in the Web page titles.

Table 6.1

Google Quick Reference		
FOR THIS TYPE OF SEARCH:	DO THIS:	EXAMPLES:
Plain-English Question	Simply type a phrase or question that expresses the idea or concept, using as many words as necessary.	Who invented the steam engine?
Phrase Search	Type the phrase surrounded by **double quotes**. (Common words will be ignored, even with quotes.)	"industrial revolution"
AND Search (multiple words and phrases, each of which must be present)	Type the words (or phrases in quotes) separated by a space, without any special punctuation.	Edison "light bulb"
	Use a **plus sign (+)** only if one of the words in your query is a very common word (or *stopword*). The second example would help you find guides at the popular About.com Web site dealing with history.	+about guides history
OR Search (multiple words and phrases, any one of which may be present)	Type words or phrases (no quotes allowed) separated by **OR** (full caps required).	phonograph OR speaking machine
NOT Search (to exclude a word or phrase)	Use a **minus sign (–)** directly in front of the word or phrase you want to exclude.	Lincoln –"town car"
Case-Sensitive Search	Not available.	
Date Search	Not available.	
Field Search	Type the field-search term followed by a colon and the search word or phrase. Note that there is no space after the colon. (For fill-in-the-blanks field searching, use Advanced Search.)	
	Titles. Use `allintitle:` or `intitle:` with one or more search words. The first example would look for *both* words in page titles, the second *either* word.	allintitle:inventions inventors intitle:inventions inventors
	URLs. Use `allinurl:` or `inurl:` with one or more words you want to find in the URL. The first example would look for *both* words, the second *either* word.	allinurl:pdf 1099 inurl:patents trademarks
	Domains. Use `site:` followed by a domain name or type (com, edu, gov, etc.), along with the search word or phrase you want to find at that site or domain type.	site:nationalgeographic.com inventions site:gov patents
	The first example would find pages at the National Geographic Web site that include the word *inventions*. The second would find government (gov) Web sites that include the word *patents*.	
	Links. Use `link:` with a specific Web address to find all pages that link to that address. The example would find pages that link to the U.S. Patent and Trademark Office (www.uspto.gov).	link:www.uspto.gov
	Note: You *cannot* combine a `link:` search term with another search word or phrase.	
Nested Search	Not available.	
Proximity Search	Not available.	
Wildcard Search	Not available.	

Using Advanced Search

Many diehard Google fans never avail themselves of the offerings on the Advanced Search page (**Figure 6.25**). In most cases, that's because searching from the Google home page produces such consistently good results. Why bother mastering advanced techniques when typing a few unique words and phrases gets the job done so effectively?

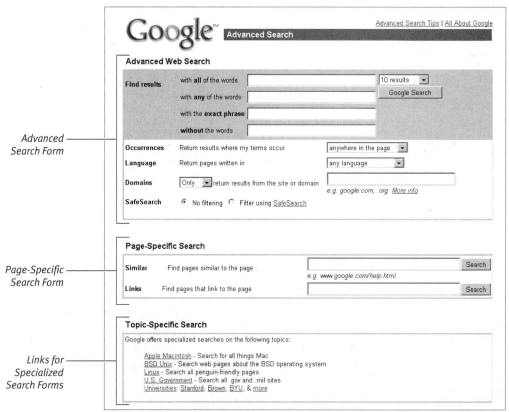

Advanced Search Form

Page-Specific Search Form

Links for Specialized Search Forms

Figure 6.25 Google's Advanced Search page lets you create more complicated queries using fill-in-the-blanks forms and drop-down menus.

Figure 6.26 Creating an "advanced" search couldn't be easier. You're prompted for each of the available options.

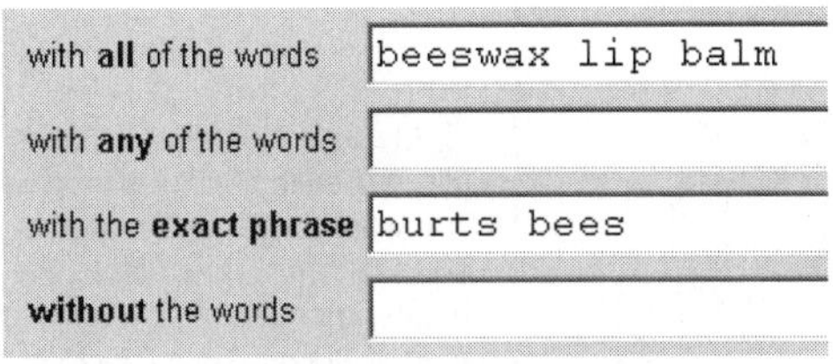

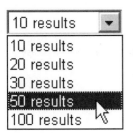

Figure 6.27 You can type words in one or more of these four search boxes to tell Google you want to do an AND, OR, phrase, or NOT search.

Figure 6.28 If you like being able to scroll quickly through 20 or more search results, you can boost the number presented on each page to a maximum of 100.

Well, the fact is, *Advanced Search* is actually a bit of a misnomer for this page. *Power-Assisted Search* comes closer to describing what you'll find here. For certain types of queries, you can save keystrokes and avoid having to remember (and correctly type) special search terms and punctuation. Just fill in the blanks and choose options from the appropriate drop-down menus and away you go!

The Advanced Search page also lets you control certain aspects of how your search results are presented, with options for increasing the number of results per page, choosing your preferred language, and filtering out content that you may find offensive.

To enter an Advanced Search query:

1. Click Advanced Search on the Google home page and use the fill-in-the-blanks form at the top of the page (**Figure 6.26**) to construct your query. Start by entering your search words or phrases in the appropriate search boxes, depending on whether you want to look for *any* of the words, *all* the words, the *exact phrase*, pages *without* a certain word, or a combination (**Figure 6.27**).

   There's no need to use any punctuation, as long as you enter your search terms in the right boxes. To look for a phrase, for example, type it in the "exact phrase" box without quotation marks. To do a NOT search, type *just* the word you want to exclude (no minus sign) in the box labeled "without the words."

   Searches are *not* case sensitive, so you'll get the same results using uppercase, lowercase, or a mix of the two.

2. If you prefer to see more than the standard 10 results per page (so that you can scroll through them more quickly), use the drop-down menu (**Figure 6.28**) to boost the number as high as 100.

continues on next page

3. To limit your search to Web page titles or URLs, make a selection from the Occurrences menu (**Figure 6.29**). This has the same effect as using one of Google's field-search terms (allintitle:, intitle:, allinurl:, inurl:) in your query.

4. If you'd like to restrict your search to Web pages written in English or some other language, use the Language menu (**Figure 6.30**). Google's default setting is any language.

5. Use the Domains option to limit your search to a specific domain name or type (com, edu, gov, org, net, etc.). This is similar to using Google's site: field-search term.

For example, type npr.org in the Domains search box to tell Google to look for your search words only at the NPR Web site (**Figure 6.31**). Or type org if you want to focus on all sites that are classified as non-profit organizations.

To specifically avoid the NPR site, change the "return results from" drop-down menu in the Domains section from Only to Don't.

6. When you're ready to submit your query, click Google Search. (Hitting Enter doesn't work here.)

✔ Tips

■ Google presents search results the same way, whether you do your search from the Google home page or the Advanced Search page. For details, see "Searching with Google" earlier in this chapter.

■ You can permanently change your settings for language, number of search results per page, and content filtering using Google's Preferences feature. For details, see "Customizing Google" later in this chapter.

Figure 6.29 The Occurrences menu lets you focus your search on Web page titles or URLs.

Figure 6.30 Most Web pages are written in English, but if you want to make sure that you see only English-language pages, change the Language menu from any language to English.

Figure 6.31 The Domains section makes it easy to limit your search to a specific Web site, in this case npr.org.

USING ADVANCED SEARCH

Figure 6.32 Instead of looking for Web pages that are similar to www.burtsbees.com, we've specified that we want to locate all the pages that link to it.

To search for similar pages or links:

1. Scroll down to the Page-Specific Search area of the Advanced Search page and enter a Web address in either the Similar or Links box (**Figure 6.32**).

2. Type a Web address in the Similar box to find other Web pages with content that is similar or related, based on information collected and analyzed by Google's automated "scout" program. Then click Search to submit your query.

3. Alternatively, type a Web address in the Links box and click Search to find pages that link to that site. (This produces the same results as using a link: field-search term in a Google query.)

✔ Tips

- Of the two Page-Specific Search options, you'll probably find Links to be the most useful. Webmasters and Web site creators often do link searches to get a handle on a site's popularity—the more links, the more popular the site.

- Link searches can also be quite effective in tracking down similar or related Web sites. If you're a fan of Burt's Bees, for example, a link search for www.burtsbees.com could help you locate other Web sites that offer beeswax products.

To do specialized searches:

1. Scroll down to the Topic-Specific Search area (**Figure 6.33**) of the Advanced Search page and click one of the links for Google's specialized search tools. Options include: Apple Macintosh, BSD Unix, Linux, U.S. Government, and Universities.

2. Choose Apple Macintosh, for example, and you'll be presented with a special Google search form (**Figure 6.34**) that you can use to search for "all things Mac"—without including the words *apple* or *macintosh* in your queries.

✔ Tip

■ Just for fun, we tried searching for pie using the Apple Macintosh search form, expecting that we might get a "no results found" message. Instead, the first two pages of search results were dominated by Web pages offering apple pie recipes! Clearly, these specialized tools are works in progress.

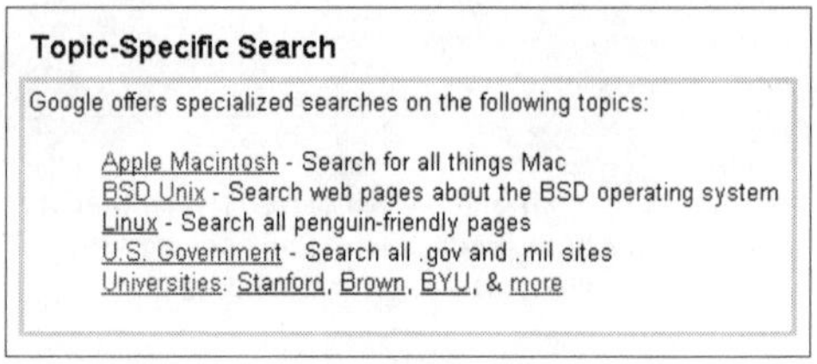

Topic-Specific Search

Google offers specialized searches on the following topics:

Apple Macintosh - Search for all things Mac
BSD Unix - Search web pages about the BSD operating system
Linux - Search all penguin-friendly pages
U.S. Government - Search all .gov and .mil sites
Universities: Stanford, Brown, BYU, & more

Figure 6.33 Each of these links leads to a special Google search page.

Search for Apple/Macintosh-related sites using Google:

web search tools

[Google Search]   [I'm Feeling Lucky]

Figure 6.34 Search for web search tools on the Apple Macintosh search form shown here and Google will know that you don't want to see PC/Windows tools.

Figure 6.35 The Preferences page lets you change Google's default language settings and control certain aspects of how your results are displayed.

Figure 6.36 Google "speaks" more than a dozen languages, which you can choose from the Interface Language menu.

Figure 6.37 With the Interface Language menu set to French, Google's I'm Feeling Lucky button is now J'ai de la chance!

Figure 6.38 The Search Language area of the Preferences page lets you limit your Google searches to Web pages written in one or more languages.

Customizing Google

Google doesn't currently offer much in the way of customization features. You can't change the content and layout of the home page, for example, nor can you save Google searches to be run again periodically.

What you *can* do is control the language that Google uses to communicate with you as you do your searches. You can also make a couple of adjustments in the way your results are presented, and turn on Google's SafeSearch content filter if you wish.

The customization process only takes a minute—there's no sign-up requirement or membership form to fill out and only a few options to consider. It's certainly worth doing if you decide to make Google your primary search engine.

To customize Google:

1. Go to the Google home page (www.google.com) and click Preferences to access the page that allows you to customize your search settings (**Figure 6.35**).

2. The first two settings have to do with language preferences. If English isn't your native tongue, you can use the Interface Language menu (**Figure 6.36**) to change Google's tips and messages to another language (**Figure 6.37**).

   Then, if you want make sure that your Google results never include Web pages written in languages you don't understand, use the Search Language area (**Figure 6.38**) to limit your results to specific languages. (You can click as many boxes as you wish.)

3. The next two settings give you a small measure of control over how your search results are presented (**Figure 6.39**).

continues on next page

Many Web searchers prefer to boost the Number of Results setting from the default of 10 results per page to as many as 50 or 100. (It makes it easier and faster to scroll through a large number of results, or to search them with your browser's Find feature.)

The Results Window option lets you specify that whenever you click an item on your Google search results page, a new browser window will be opened to display it. Like the number of results per page, this is a personal preference that may or may not be important to you.

4. The last option on the Preferences page lets you turn SafeSearch content filtering on and off (**Figure 6.40**). With SafeSearch turned on, most Web pages containing pornography and explicit sexual content are blocked from your search results.

5. When you're finished customizing Google, click Save Preferences (**Figure 6.41**).

✔ Tips

- Your Google Preferences settings apply to searches from both the Google home page and the Advanced Search page.

- If you decide to make Google your primary search engine, you may want to customize your Web browser so that it takes you to Google automatically whenever you go online, and whenever you hit your browser's Home button. You can tell your browser to use either the Google home page or the Advanced Search page as its default home-page location, using these addresses:

  http://www.google.com
  (Google home page)

  http://www.google.com/advanced_search
  (Advanced Search page)

  If you're not sure how to set your Web browser's home-page location, see "Customizing Your Web Browser" in Chapter 4.

Figure 6.39 These settings let you increase the number of items displayed on each page of your Google results, and specify that you want to open search results in a new browser window.

Figure 6.40 You can automatically filter out most sexually explicit material by turning on Google's SafeSearch content filter.

Figure 6.41 Be sure to save your settings before leaving the Preferences page.

HOTBOT

Good to Know

◆ HotBot rivals AltaVista in the breadth and sophistication of its search offerings, including search customization features.

◆ Powered by Inktomi, one of the largest and most frequently updated search engine databases, HotBot is a top choice of professional searchers.

◆ Because of its easy-to-use interface, with drop-down menus and radio buttons that allow you to create complex and precisely targeted queries, it's also extremely popular with less-experienced searchers.

◆ Launched in 1996 by Wired Digital, HotBot was acquired in 1998 by the company that owns and operates the Lycos search engine.

HotBot was launched in 1996 as a joint venture between Wired Digital (creators of *Wired* magazine) and Inktomi, a company that makes high-end computer workstations. The *Wired* connection helps explain the site's bilious lime-green color scheme. (If you've ever read—or *tried* to read—the magazine, you know what we mean.) Inktomi's role was to create the search engine software for HotBot—most notably *Slurp*, the spider responsible for crawling the Web and assembling documents into a searchable database.

Now owned by Terra Lycos (which also operates the Lycos search engine), HotBot is very popular with technically savvy Web searchers, who appreciate the ease and speed with which it allows you to search the Web. But it doesn't get nearly as much traffic (or press attention) as rival search sites AltaVista, Google, and Yahoo. That's a shame, because for all of its speed and sophistication, HotBot is also an excellent search engine for inexperienced searchers.

The HotBot search form accepts special punctuation marks and Boolean operators for those who want to use them in their queries. But the form also offers drop-down menus and radio-button selections that allow you to essentially point and click your way through even the most complex searches.

Within about a second, you'll have your results, sorted according to how well they match your search criteria. If you don't find exactly what you're looking for, you can easily refine your query by adding more terms or limiting the search by date, location, or media type. You can also do *set searching*, limiting a follow-on search to just those Web pages that were returned the first time around.

For those occasions when you want to browse or search the Web by topic, the HotBot home page includes a subject guide provided by the Open Directory Project. It's certainly worth getting to know, especially if you plan to do most of your searching with HotBot.

Just keep in mind that HotBot's main focus is its lightning-fast search capability. For sheer speed, comprehensiveness, and ease of use, HotBot is a real winner.

✔ Tips

- The name *Inktomi* (pronounced "**INK**-teh-me") comes from a Lakota Indian legend about a resourceful spider known for its ability to defeat its enemies through wit and cunning.

- Inktomi and its Web-crawling associate Slurp are obviously doing something right. As you may recall from our discussion of search engines in Chapter 1, Inktomi's GEN3 database of Web pages is among the largest of all the major search engines.

- HotBot, AOL Search, and MSN Search (as well as a number of other search engines) are all "powered by Inktomi" (**Figure 7.1**). But at this writing, HotBot is one of the few to offer Inktomi's GEN3 database. Both AOL Search and MSN Search use a version of the Inktomi database that's roughly one-quarter the size of GEN3.

- To read more about the technology behind Slurp, visit the Inktomi Web site (www.inktomi.com) and click on About Inktomi.

Figure 7.1 Inktomi helped launch HotBot some years ago and now provides the search engine software and database for a number of sites on the Net.

Contact Information

Wired Digital, Inc.
A Division of Terra Lycos
San Francisco, California
415-276-8400 (voice)
415-276-8499 (fax)
www.hotbot.com

The HotBot Home Page

Unlike many of its rivals, the HotBot home page (**Figure 7.2**), with its distinctive lime-green and navy-blue color scheme, is designed primarily for searching. Advertising banners and promotional offers are kept to a minimum, and traditional "portal features" like news headlines, stock quotes, and shopping services are relegated to underlying pages.

Furthermore, if you find that the default search settings on the home page don't meet all of your day-to-day requirements, you can customize the page in a variety of ways, adding the features you need and removing those that you rarely use.

Let's take a look at the HotBot home page and its most important search-related features.

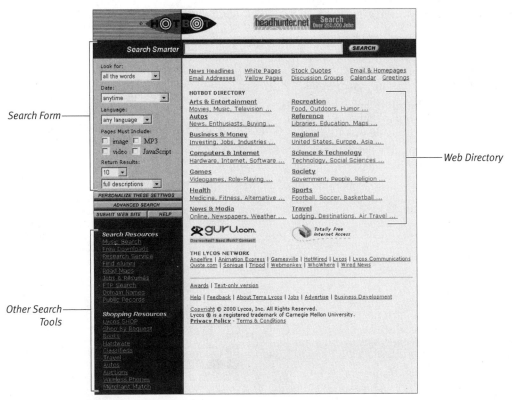

Search Form —

Other Search — Tools

Web Directory

Figure 7.2 The HotBot home page.

Search form

Using the HotBot search form (**Figure 7.3**) couldn't be easier—whether you're an accomplished search professional or a first-timer. For the professionals, the form allows the use of plus and minus signs to include (+) or exclude (-) words and phrases, as well as the Boolean operators AND, OR, and NOT. For less experienced searchers, simply typing several unique keywords (or even a question in plain English) will typically produce excellent results.

Tools for refining a search

Novice and professional searchers alike will appreciate the tools HotBot offers on its home page for refining a search (**Figure 7.4**). Using drop-down menus, you can specify whether you want to search for all the words, the default setting (similar to a Boolean AND search), or one of the other options (**Figure 7.5**).

You can also limit your search by date and language (**Figure 7.6**). And you can specify that certain types of files appear on the page (**Figure 7.7**). Finally, you can make adjustments in how your search results are presented, increasing the number of items per page from 10 to as many as 100 and specifying the amount of detail to be included (**Figure 7.8**).

Figure 7.3 Typing a few unique keywords in the HotBot search form is the first step in performing a search.

Figure 7.4 This part of the search form makes it easy to refine your query. Just use the drop-down menus to tell HotBot what and how you want to search.

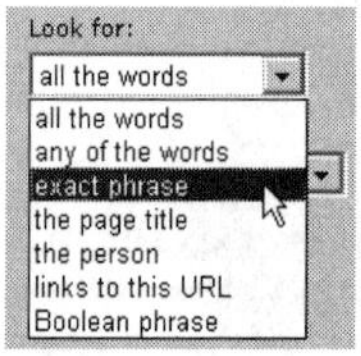

Figure 7.5 The Look For menu's default setting tells HotBot to do an all the words search. But if you've typed a phrase in the search box, you'll get better results with exact phrase.

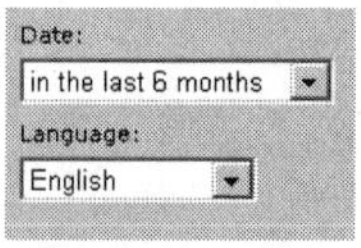

Figure 7.6 Here, we've set the Date and Language options to focus on recently updated Web pages that are presented in English.

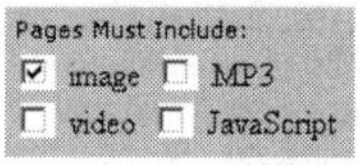

Figure 7.7 Searching for special file types is relatively easy with HotBot, since you can specify right on the search form that your results must include a certain type of file.

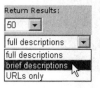

Figure 7.8 HotBot lets you decide how your results are presented—the number per page (increased here from 10 to 50) and the amount of detail for each listing.

Figure 7.9 Clicking on this button takes you to the Advanced Search page, which offers even more options for refining your HotBot queries.

Figure 7.10 HotBot leads the pack when it comes to search customization options. To see for yourself, click on this button.

> **HOTBOT DIRECTORY**
>
> **Arts & Entertainment**
> Movies, Music, Television ...
>
> **Autos**
> News, Enthusiasts, Buying ...
>
> **Business & Money**
> Investing, Jobs, Industries ...
>
> **Computers & Internet**
> Hardware, Internet, Software ...
>
> **Games**
> Videogames, Role-Playing ...
>
> **Health**
> Medicine, Fitness, Alternative ...
>
> **News & Media**
> Online, Newspapers, Weather ...
>
> **Recreation**
> Food, Outdoors, Humor ...
>
> **Reference**
> Libraries, Education, Maps ...
>
> **Regional**
> United States, Europe, Asia ...
>
> **Science & Technology**
> Technology, Social Sciences...
>
> **Society**
> Government, People, Religion...
>
> **Sports**
> Football, Soccer, Basketball ...
>
> **Travel**
> Lodging, Destinations, Air Travel ...

Figure 7.11 The Web directory on the HotBot home page is created and maintained by thousands of volunteer editors under the auspices of the Open Directory Project.

- Once you've found the right topic in the HotBot directory, your next hurdle is to figure out what the rules are for entering a search. Here again, HotBot falls short, offering no guidance whatsoever.

  It took a visit to the Open Directory help page (dmoz.org/searchguide.html) to clarify that you can use plus and minus signs, phrases in quotes, and the Boolean operators AND, OR, and ANDNOT (no space) in your directory queries.

✔ Tips

- For even more search options, click on Advanced Search (**Figure 7.9**).

- If you find yourself frequently changing HotBot's default settings, or going to the Advanced Search page to use the features offered there, you should definitely consider using the Personalize These Settings option (**Figure 7.10**). It allows you to change the defaults and add (or remove) features on the search form. For details, see "Customizing HotBot" later in this chapter.

Web directory

HotBot's Web directory (**Figure 7.11**) provides an alternative method for finding information on the Internet. Instead of searching a vast database of Web pages for the information you're after, you can browse or search a much smaller collection of sites, organized into 14 subject categories and dozens of subcategories.

The content and organization of the directory are the work of the Open Directory Project (dmoz.org), a volunteer effort to catalog the Web. As you might guess, the directory is modeled after Yahoo (www.yahoo.com) and offers many of the same features and functions.

✔ Tips

- One big drawback to HotBot's Web directory is that there's no way to *search* (rather than *browse*) the entire directory. Your only choice is to pick a topic and then search that specific topic and its related subtopics. (Yahoo and the Open Directory Project's own Web site don't have this limitation.)

Other search-related tools

You'll find three sets of links on the HotBot home page for specialized search tools. The one right below the search form (**Figure 7.12**) gives you one-click access to searches for News Headlines, Email Addresses, White Pages, Yellow Pages, and Stock Quotes. There's also a link for Discussion Groups that you can use to search Usenet newsgroups.

A second set of links under the heading "Search Resources" (**Figure 7.13**) takes you to a variety of search services, some of them free, some not. Click on Road Maps, for example, and you'll find yourself at the MapQuest Web site (www.mapquest.com), where you can do a free search for maps and driving directions. Click on Research Service, on the other hand, and you'll be taken to Electric Library (www.elibrary.com), a subscription-only service that offers a 30-day free trial but then charges $60 per year (or $10 per month) for unlimited searching.

Finally, under "Shopping Resources" (**Figure 7.14**), you'll find links to various searchable shopping services offered by Lycos (one of HotBot's sister companies) and its advertising partners—AutoTrader for new and used car information, Barnes & Noble for books, Trip.com for travel, and so forth.

News Headlines   White Pages   Stock Quotes
Email Addresses Yellow Pages Discussion Groups

Figure 7.12 These links right below the HotBot search form give you quick access to current news articles, phone numbers, addresses, stock quotes, and newsgroups.

Figure 7.13 HotBot's Search Resources menu gives you one-click access to some the Net's best special-purpose search tools.

Figure 7.14 These links take you to shopping sites run by Lycos and other online merchants who have paid to "own" a particular link.

Figure 7.15 The HotBot Help information is nicely organized and provides answers to frequently asked questions.

✔ Tips

- HotBot's Discussion Groups link gives you limited access to Deja (formerly Deja News), a search service that specializes in Usenet newsgroups, among other things. To take full advantage of Deja's newsgroup-search capabilities (covered in Chapter 15), use the Deja Web site (www.deja.com).

- The exact lineup in the Search Resources and Shopping Resources menus may change from time to time as search engine partners come and go. But you can count on the fact that this part of the HotBot home page will always offer some excellent tools to complement your HotBot Web searches.

- For instructions on making HotBot your default home page (**Figure 7.15**), click on Help and then on Getting Started. Or follow the instructions for "Customizing Your Web Browser" in Chapter 4.

- You can return to the HotBot home page at any time by clicking on the HotBot logo at the top of the page.

Searching with HotBot

Having covered the basic elements of the HotBot home page, let's do some actual searching and see how HotBot presents the results.

To enter a HotBot query:

1. Go to the HotBot home page (www.hotbot.com) and type several unique keywords, a phrase in quotes, or a combination of words and phrases in the search form (**Figure 7.16**). You can use plus and minus signs to require (+) and exclude (-) search terms, although plus signs aren't really necessary if you leave the Look For menu set to all the words.

2. By default, HotBot performs an AND search, looking for Web pages that contain all the words in your query. To change that, use the Look For menu (**Figure 7.17**) to select one of the other options:

   ◆ any of the words
   Similar to a Boolean OR search.

   ◆ exact phrase
   No need to enclose the phrase in quotation marks if you use this option. You'll typically get the same results with or without quotes.

   ◆ the page title
   To look for your search terms in the *titles* of Web pages.

   ◆ the person
   To tell HotBot to look for *near matches* to your query. Typing Lee Iacocca and selecting the person, for example, will find references to that exact name as well as *Iacocca, Lee* and *Lee A. Iacocca.*

   ◆ links to this URL
   To find Web pages that include hyperlinks to a specific URL—a technique often used by Web site creators to get a measure of their sites' popularity. To work properly, your search must include the Web site's *complete* URL.

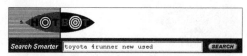

Figure 7.16 Type this query and by default HotBot will look for *all the words*, even though you haven't used plus signs or Boolean ANDs.

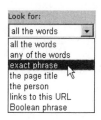

Figure 7.17 You can easily change the default search setting to one of several other options on the Look For menu.

Figure 7.18 HotBot can handle Boolean expressions like this. Just be sure to select `Boolean phrase` on the Look For menu.

Figure 7.19 You can make a HotBot search case sensitive by using the exact combination of uppercase and lowercase letters that you want to find in a particular word.

For example, to find Web pages that link to MapQuest, you would need to type `http://www.mapquest.com` in the HotBot search form.

◆ `Boolean phrase`
To tell HotBot that you've typed a Boolean expression in the search form (**Figure 7.18**). You can use AND, OR, NOT, phrases in quotes, and parentheses in constructing a Boolean query. The Boolean operators can be typed in either uppercase or lowercase.

To make your search case-sensitive:

1. The first thing you need to know is that when you type a search word in lowercase, HotBot assumes that you want to search for *all* combinations of lowercase and uppercase. Type `jeep` in the search form, for example, and HotBot will look for *Jeep* and *JEEP* as well as *jeep.*

2. To limit your search to an exact combination of uppercase and lowercase letters (for example, to find the company names *HotWired* or *NeXT*), type the words using the specific combination of uppercase and lowercase letters that you want to find (**Figure 7.19**).

✔ Tips

■ Case-sensitive searching comes in handy when you're looking for the name of a person or place, which will almost always be presented with initial caps. Company names, on the other hand, can trip you up, since they often use unexpected combinations of uppercase and lowercase (as in the examples above). If you're not sure how a company name is likely to be presented on a Web page, try searching first with all lowercase.

■ Remember that if you use even a *single* uppercase letter in a search term, HotBot will assume that you want to do a case-sensitive search.

To do a wildcard search:

1. Use an asterisk (*) or a question mark (?) along with at least two adjacent characters in your search term.

2. An asterisk matches *zero or more characters* anywhere in a word or string of characters (beginning, middle, or end). For example, a search for realt* would match both *realty* and *realtor*.

3. A question mark matches a *single* character anywhere in a word or string of words. The search term alumn? would find both *alumna* and *alumni* but not *alumnus* or *alumnae*.

✔ Tip

■ HotBot's wildcard capability is temperamental. Sometimes it works; sometimes it returns a "no results found" message. As a fallback, you can, of course, simply do an *any of the words* (Boolean OR) search for the word variations you had hoped to find with the wildcard character.

To view your search results:

1. Once you've entered your query, click on Search to submit it. Your results will be presented 10 to a page, along with the total number of matches found (**Figure 7.20**). As you may recall, these results come from the Inktomi database.

2. Each listing will include what HotBot calls "full descriptions"—Web page title, one to four lines of text, date created or modified, and URL (**Figure 7.21**).

3. HotBot "clusters" results, meaning that if your query matches multiple pages at a single Web site, only one page from that site will be listed. To see all the matching pages from a particular site, click on the link telling HotBot to show you the results for this site only (**Figure 7.22**).

Figure 7.20 Here's an example of HotBot search results. Note that the first line tells you the total number of matches in the Inktomi database.

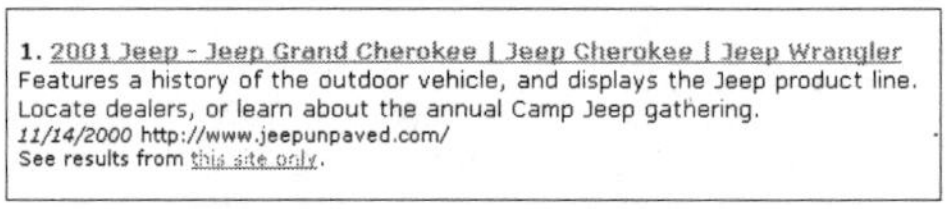

Figure 7.21 The "full description" of a Web site in HotBot's search results includes page title, a few lines of text, date, and URL.

Figure 7.22 HotBot shows you only one matching page per Web site, but you display the rest by clicking on this link.

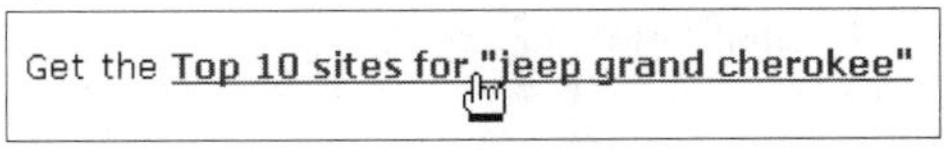
Get the Top 10 sites for "jeep grand cherokee"

Figure 7.23 To view the most popular sites for your query, click on this link. The information comes from a service called Direct Hit.

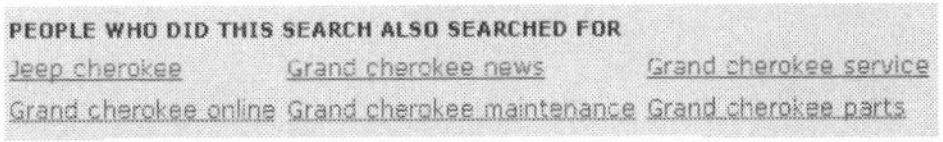
PEOPLE WHO DID THIS SEARCH ALSO SEARCHED FOR
Jeep cherokee
Grand cherokee news
Grand cherokee service
Grand cherokee online
Grand cherokee maintenance
Grand cherokee parts

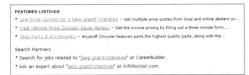

Figure 7.24 HotBot sometimes offers suggestions of other search terms that might help you refine your search.

FEATURED LISTINGS
Low Price Quotes on a New Grand Cherokee - Get multiple price quotes from local and online dealers on...
Free Vehicle Price Quotes! Save Money! - Get the invoice pricing by filling out a three minute form...
Jeep Parts & Accessories - Wyckoff Chrysler features parts the highest quality parts, along with the...
Search Partners
Search for jobs related to "jeep grand cherokee" at CareerBuilder.
Ask an expert about "jeep grand cherokee" at InfoRocket.com.

Figure 7.25 Advertisers pay for the privilege of being featured like this on the HotBot search results page.

Results for
jeep grand cherokee
SEARCH
Search within these results
PEOPLE WHO DID THIS SEARCH ALSO SEARCHED FOR
NEW SEARCH
REVISE OPTIONS
ADVANCED SEARCH

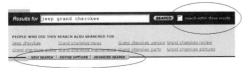

Figure 7.26 HotBot offers several options for doing a follow-on search. Your best bet is often to search again *within* your original results.

4. The first page of results will often include a section labeled "Top 10 Matches" or a link you can click on to view the "Top 10 sites" for your query (**Figure 7.23**). These results come from a service called Direct Hit, a "popularity engine" that ranks Web sites based on how often they are clicked on by users of Direct Hit's own Web site (`www.directhit.com`).

5. Your results may also include suggestions for refining your search (**Figure 7.24**) and "featured listings" from HotBot and Lycos advertising partners (**Figure 7.25**).

6. If you don't see exactly what you're looking for in the first couple of pages of your HotBot search results, you have several options (**Figure 7.26**):

   Search within these results. Entering a modified query and clicking on the box next to this option allows you to do a *set search*—that is, to search again *within* your original results.

   New Search. Clicking on this tab takes you back to the HotBot home page, where you can enter an entirely new query.

   Revise Options. Clicking here takes you back to the home page, where you'll find your original query ready and waiting to be modified.

   Advanced Search. Clicking on this tab takes you to the Advanced Search page and automatically enters your original query in the search form.

7. If you're still not satisfied, you can automatically send your query to the Lycos search engine for a "second opinion."

continues on next page

✔ Tips

- For best results with HotBot, use at least two or three search terms and be as specific as possible.

- To limit your results to Web pages written in English, use the search form's Language menu.

- If you prefer to see more results per page, use the Return Results area of the search form to increase the number (up to 100). You can also control the amount of detail presented for each listing by choosing `brief descriptions` (to eliminate the date and URL) or `URLs only`.

- To permanently change your Return Results settings, click on `Personalize These Settings`. The Personalize page also allows you to turn off Web page "clustering," which it refers to as "disabling the 'Best Page Only' filter" (**Figure 7.27**).

- For additional search tips and techniques, click on `Help` on the HotBot home page. You'll also find a summary of HotBot search features and syntax in the HotBot Quick Reference (**Table 7.1**).

Figure 7.27 You can turn off Web page "clustering" by disabling this option on the Personalize page.

Table 7.1

HotBot Quick Reference	
FOR THIS TYPE OF SEARCH:	DO THIS:
Plain-English Question	Simply type the question in the search form and select all the words from the search form's Look For menu.
Phrase Search	Type the phrase with or without quotes and select exact phrase on the Look For menu. To look for multiple phrases, or a phrase and a single word, put the phrase in quotes and select all the words from the Look For menu.
AND Search (multiple words and phrases, each of which *must* be present)	Type words and/or phrases and select all the words from the Look For menu. You can use a **plus sign (+)** in front of each word or phrase, but it's not really necessary with an all the words search. You can also combine words and phrases with **AND** and select Boolean phrase from the menu.
OR Search (multiple words and phrases, any one of which may be present)	Type words or phrases separated by spaces and select any of the words from the menu. Alternatively, combine words and phrases with **OR** and choose Boolean phrase from the menu.
NOT Search (to exclude a word or phrase)	Use a **minus sign (-)** in front of a word or phrase you want to exclude from the results. Or use **NOT** in front of the word or phrase and specify Boolean phrase.
Case-Sensitive Search	Use lowercase to find *any combination* of uppercase and lowercase. Use capital letters (initial caps or a combination of uppercase and lowercase) to force an *exact match* of your search term.
Date Search	Use the Date menu on the HotBot home page to select a timeframe (one week to two years). Alternatively, you can use the Date meta words after:, before:, or within: in your query. For examples, see the HotBot Meta Words Quick Reference (**Table 7.2**). For point-and-click date searching, use Advanced Search.
Field Search (Web page titles)	Use the Look For menu on the HotBot home page to specify that you want to search the page title. Or you can use the HotBot meta word title: in your query. (See **Table 7.2** for examples.)
Field Search (geography, domain, or domain type)	Use the HotBot meta word domain:. For example, use domain:jp to look for sites in Japan. Use domain:com to look for commercial sites in North America. For more examples, see **Table 7.2**. Alternatively, you can click on Advanced Search and use the Location/Domain section to focus your search on a particular geographic region, country, domain, or domain type (com, edu, gov, etc.).
Field Search (multimedia)	Use the Pages Must Include section on the HotBot home page to look for image, video, MP3, or JavaScript files. For an expanded list of multimedia options, click on Advanced Search. Alternatively, you can use feature: meta words in your queries on the HotBot home page to find plug-ins, embedded scripts, Java applets, audio and video files, etc. (See **Table 7.2** for a complete list.)
Nested Search	Combine search terms with parentheses and select Boolean phrase from the Look For menu.
Proximity Search	Not available.
Wildcard Search	Use an **asterisk (*)** with at least two adjacent characters to search for zero or more characters anywhere in a word or string of characters (beginning, middle, or end). Use a **question mark (?)** with at least two adjacent characters to search for a single character. For example, car* would match *cars*, *cart*, *carrot*, and *cardiovascular*. But car? would only match *cars*, *cart*, and other four-letter words.

Improving Results with Field Search

As you may recall from our discussion of the HotBot home page, you can easily limit your queries to certain specific Web page elements (or *fields*) using the search form's drop-down menus and radio buttons (**Figure 7.28**):

Figure 7.28 We've changed the search form's default settings to zero in on specific Web page elements— title, date, and file type.

- ◆ To focus on *titles* of Web page, use the page title option on the Look For menu.

- ◆ To look for Web pages created or modified within a certain *timeframe*, use the Date menu.

- ◆ To find *image*, *video*, *MP3*, and *JavaScript* files, click on the appropriate radio button in the Pages Must Include section.

But these options are but a fraction of HotBot's field-search capabilities. To take full advantage of the entire range of options, you need to know about *Advanced Search* and HotBot *meta words*. Of the two, Advanced Search offers by far the easier method for doing field searches, so let's start with it.

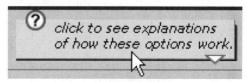

Figure 7.29 If this is your first visit to the Advanced Search page, be sure to click here to display brief explanations of all the options.

To do field searching with Advanced Search:

1. Click on Advanced Search on the HotBot home page. When the Advanced Search page appears, click on the special button (**Figure 7.29**) located directly below the search form to display explanations of all the options.

2. Type your query in the search form and make your selection on the Look For menu, just as you would on the HotBot home page.

3. The Date section (**Figure 7.30**) expands on the date-searching capabilities of the main search form. In addition to looking for Web pages created or modified within a certain timeframe, you can fill in a precise date and specify Before or After.

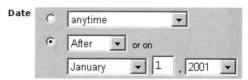

Figure 7.30 The Date section lets you focus on very recent (or very old) Web pages.

IMPROVING RESULTS WITH FIELD SEARCH

Figure 7.31 The Pages Must Include section helps locate sites offering special types of files. You can click on as many items as you wish, and specify one or more file extensions as well.

Figure 7.32 We used the link to HotBot's domain and country code Index to find the code for Spain (es).

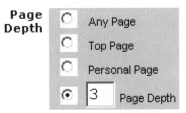

Figure 7.33 How deep into a Web site do you want HotBot to search? You can use Page Depth to specify the number of pages.

```
title:"Jeep Grand Cherokee"        SEARCH
```

Figure 7.34 A search like this would limit your query to Web pages that include the phrase *Jeep Grand Cherokee* in the title.

Figure 7.35 Here we combined two field-search terms to locate education (edu) Web sites that link to the Internet Movie Database (imdb.com).

4. The Pages Must Include section (**Figure 7.31**) gives you additional options for locating multimedia files, Java applets, and other special file types. You can also look for a specific file extension (GIF, JPEG, TIFF, etc.) You can even click on multiple entries if you like.

5. The Location/Domain section (**Figure 7.32**) lets you focus your search on a particular continent, country, domain name, or type of domain (com, edu, gov, etc.).

To target a particular country, you'll need the country's two-letter Internet code (cl for Chile, es for Spain, etc.). For a list, click on Domain and country code index or see Appendix B.

6. Finally, the Page Depth section (**Figure 7.33**) gives you control over how deep into the Web site your search will go. If you want to search only top-level pages (typically a Web site's home page), choose Top Page. Otherwise, specify a number and click on the Page Depth radio button.

To do field searching with meta words:

1. You can incorporate one or more of HotBot's field-search terms, called *meta words*, right into your queries.

For example, instead of using the Look For menu's the page title option to search for the phrase *Jeep Grand Cherokee* in the titles of Web pages, you can type title: "Jeep Grand Cherokee" in the HotBot search form (**Figure 7.34**).

2. Similarly, you can use the domain: field-search term to look for specific domain names or types of domains, and linkdomain: to find Web pages that link to specific sites. You might even combine these two field-search terms to look for, say, education (edu) domains that link to a particular Web site (**Figure 7.35**).

continues on next page

IMPROVING RESULTS WITH FIELD SEARCH

3. You can search for a veritable laundry list of special Web page elements and multi-media files (audio and video files, scripts, Java applets, etc.) using the `feature:` meta word. To look for images of Jeeps (**Figure 7.36**), try a HotBot search for `feature:image Jeep`.

4. The Date meta words `after:`, `before:`, and `within:` are designed to allow more precise searching than the Date menu on the main search form. You could, for example, use both `after:` and `before:` in a Boolean expression to search for Web pages created or modified within a specific time period.

HotBot cautions, however, that the Date meta words work correctly only if used as part of a Boolean expression. You cannot use them with plus (+) and minus (-) signs.

So `jeep AND within:3/months` should produce good results.

But `+jeep +within:3/months` will result in an error message.

Figure 7.36 Use the HotBot meta word `feature:image` along with another unique keyword (in this case `Jeep`) to locate sites that include graphics like this.

✔ Tips

- For the most part, HotBot's meta words duplicate the search capabilities provided on the main search form and the Advanced Search page. Unless you're a power searcher, you'll probably find it easier to use the point-and-click approach rather than incorporating meta words into Boolean expressions.

- The Date meta words (`after:`, `before:`, and `within:`) are great in theory, but they don't always work as promised. We've had trouble with them from time to time, and the HotBot technical support group has been unable to explain or duplicate the problem.

- For a summary of meta words, along with search examples, see the HotBot Meta Words Quick Reference (**Table 7.2**).

- For more advice on using HotBot meta words, including a current list of the ones that are available, click on `Help` on the HotBot home page and then on `Advanced Search`.

Table 7.2

HotBot Meta Words Quick Reference*	
META WORD FORMAT	**WHAT IT DOES**
`title:`*word*or *phrase*	Searches Web page titles for the word or phrase you specify. For example, `title:Edmund's` or `title:"car guides"`.
`domain:`*name*	Restricts search to the domain name selected. Domains can be specified up to three levels: `domain:com`, `domain:ford.com`, `domain:www.ford.com`.
`linkdomain:`*name*	Restricts search to pages containing links to the domain you specify. For example, `linkdomain:edmunds.com` finds pages that point to the Edmund's Car Guides Web site.
`outgoingurlext:`*extension*	Restricts search to pages containing embedded files with a particular extension. For example, `outgoingurlext:ra` finds pages containing RealAudio (RA) files.
`depth:`*number*	Limits how deep within a Web site your search goes. To go three pages deep, use `depth:3`.
`feature:acrobat`	Detects Acrobat files.
`feature:applet`	Detects embedded Java applets.
`feature:activex`	Detects ActiveX controls or layouts.
`feature:audio`	Detects audio formats.
`feature:embed`	Detects plug-ins.
`feature:flash`	Detects Flash plug-in HTML.
`feature:form`	Detects forms in HTML documents.
`feature:frame`	Detects frames in HTML documents.
`feature:image`	Detects image files (GIF, JPEG, etc.).
`feature:script`	Detects embedded scripts.
`feature:shockwave`	Detects Shockwave files.
`feature:table`	Detects tables in HTML documents.
`feature:video`	Detects video formats.
`feature:vrml`	Detects VRML files.
`scriptlanguage:javascript`	Allows you to search for pages containing JavaScript. (Note that lowercase is required for `javascript`.)
`scriptlanguage:vbscript`	Allows you to search for pages containing VBScript. (Note that lowercase is required for `vbscript`.)
`after:`*dd/mm/yy*	Use in a Boolean expression to restrict search to pages created or modified *after* the specified date: `Explorer AND after:31/12/00`. (Note that date format is day/month/year.)
`before:`*dd/mm/yy*	Use in a Boolean expression to restrict search to pages created or modified *before* the specified date: `Corvette AND before:30/6/99`. (Note that date format is day/month/year.)
`within:`*number/unit*	Use in a Boolean expression to search for pages created or modified within a specified time period. Units can be expressed in days, months, or years: `(Jeep Cherokee OR "Grand Cherokee") AND within:3/months`.

*Note: The words shown in italics *are variables. You'll find examples of the terms you can use for each of these variables in the column labeled "What It Does."*

IMPROVING RESULTS WITH FIELD SEARCH

Customizing HotBot

The overall content and layout of the HotBot home page are essentially a take-it-or-leave-it affair. You can't eliminate the Web directory, for example, or move it to a different location on the page, as you can with, say, AltaVista and Yahoo. Nor can you change the color scheme or add features for tracking your stocks or monitoring the weather, as you can with most search engines that double as "portal" pages.

What you *can* do, however, is tailor the search form to your particular style of searching. You can pick and choose from a long list of search options, select the settings you use most often, and arrange to have your chosen settings appear automatically whenever you do a HotBot search.

If you decide to make HotBot your primary (or backup) search engine, you'll definitely want to take advantage of its search-form customization features. It's easy to do and will save you time in the long run.

To customize HotBot's search form:

1. Go to the HotBot home page (www.hotbot.com) and click on Personalize These Settings to access the Personalize HotBot page (**Figure 7.37**). For helpful tips on what each setting does, click on the explanations link.

2. Search options that currently appear on the HotBot home page will have a check mark next to them. To add or remove an option, click on the box to make the check mark appear or disappear.

3. Use the drop-down menu next to each option to change its default setting (**Figure 7.38**). If you typically change the Look For menu to Boolean phrase, for example, make that the default. Similarly, if you want to avoid pages written in foreign languages, change the Language menu to English.

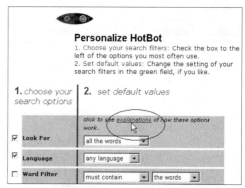

Figure 7.37 The Personalize HotBot page walks you through the process of customizing the search form.

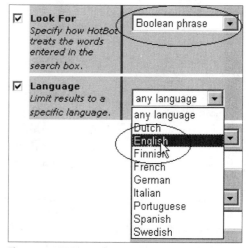

Figure 7.38 We've made Boolean phrase and English the default settings for the Look For and Language menus respectively.

CUSTOMIZING HOTBOT

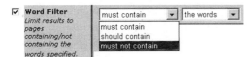

Figure 7.39 Putting a Word Filter section on the search form gives you another method for requiring or excluding search terms.

Figure 7.40 Here's our customized version of the settings on the HotBot search form.

4. Adding a Word Filter option (**Figure 7.39**) to the search form lets you specify words or phrases that *must*, *should*, or *must not* appear in your search results.

5. Once you've made all the changes, click on Okay to get back to the HotBot home page, where you'll find your customized search settings all ready for your next search (**Figure 7.40**).

6. To change your default settings at any time, just return to the Personalize HotBot page, make your new selections, and click on Okay. To get back to HotBot's original settings, click on reset defaults.

✔ Tips

- The Personalize HotBot page gives you the option of turning on a feature called *word stemming*. With this feature enabled, HotBot automatically searches for variations of certain terms. Type thought, for example, and HotBot will look for that word as well as *think* and *thinking*.

  It's an interesting notion. But since there's no way of knowing for sure what word variations HotBot can handle automatically, we prefer to make our own decisions about the search terms to be included in our queries.

- HotBot's customization feature uses *cookie* technology to remember your settings. If you've disabled cookies in your Web browser, your settings can't be saved.

  For step-by-step instructions on enabling cookies using Internet Explorer or Netscape, go to the HotBot home page and click on Help and then on Advanced Search.

continues on next page

■ What about saving a complex search, along with your search settings, so that you can run it again from time to time? HotBot doesn't currently offer a Saved Searches feature, but here's a technique that works:

Type your query in the search form on the HotBot home page, select your settings, and click on Advanced Search. Then add the resulting page to your Bookmarks or Favorites list and choose a descriptive name, like HotBot Search: Glossbrenner Book Reviews. (By default, it will be called HotBot: SuperSearch.) To run the search, just select it from your Bookmarks or Favorites list and click on the Search button.

Lycos

Good to Know

◆ Developed in 1994 at Carnegie Mellon University, Lycos is now owned by Terra Lycos, a Spanish company that also owns HotBot and a number of other popular Web sites.

◆ The highly acclaimed Lycos spider is still used for building certain specialty databases, but the site is now powered by the FAST search engine.

◆ The Lycos Web directory comes from the Open Directory Project.

◆ Lycos ignores all Boolean operators, so you can't search with much precision. But it's a good choice for doing multimedia searches, and for finding phrases that include common stopwords.

One of the oldest Internet search engines, Lycos was developed in 1994 by artificial-intelligence expert Michael "Fuzzy" Mauldin at Carnegie Mellon University. The name comes from the Latin for *wolf spider*, a creature Mauldin has long admired for its tenacity at searching for and finding its prey.

Now a commercial enterprise, Lycos is owned by Terra Lycos, a Spanish conglomerate whose mission is "to be the most visited online destination in the world." In pursuit of that goal, Terra Lycos also owns and operates rival search engine HotBot (www.hotbot.com) and a number of other popular Web sites, including MatchMaker (www.matchmaker.com), Quote.com (www.quote.com), and WhoWhere? (www.whowhere.com).

Under the new ownership, the highly acclaimed Lycos spider has been relieved of many of its former duties. Most Lycos search results now come from FAST, a relatively new but increasingly formidable contender among the leading search technologies. (The FAST database currently ranks second—behind Google (www.google.com)—in the ongoing competition for the largest collection of Web pages.)

Lycos

The job of creating and maintaining the Lycos Web directory has been farmed out as well. It's currently provided by the Open Directory Project (`dmoz.org`).

One thing that hasn't changed at Lycos is the emphasis on making multimedia searches as easy as possible. You can use a special search form to locate images, audio files, and video files by simply clicking the appropriate radio button. With a properly equipped Web browser, you can even view or listen to the files as they are being downloaded to your computer. A separate MP3 search option gives you access to the FAST database of more than one million music files in the popular MP3 format.

The major drawback to searching with Lycos is that you're limited to fairly basic queries. You can search for phrases in quotes and use plus and minus signs to require (+) or exclude (-) words and phrases. But try using Boolean operators (AND, OR, NOT, NEAR, ADJ, etc.) in your queries—as the help information says you can do using the Advanced Search form—and you'll find that Lycos treats them like any other search term, looking for every occurrence of *AND*, for example, and presenting it in bold in your search results.

Contact Information

Lycos, Inc.
A Division of Terra Lycos
Waltham, Massachusetts
781-370-2700
www.lycos.com

Figure 8.1 FAST, the search engine that powers Lycos, maintains a fairly low profile. The company uses its home page (www.alltheweb.com) to demonstrate its search technology.

✔ Tips

- If you're interested in Internet history, pay a visit to Michael Mauldin's Lazy Toad Ranch Web site (www.lazytd.com) and click on Fuzzy and then professional web page. Once there, you can read the original patent for the Lycos spider and listen to several RealAudio interviews with Mauldin.

- FAST (short for FAst Search and Transfer) was launched in 1999 by a Norwegian company. You can search FAST directly— without the Lycos interface—by going to the company's demonstration Web site at www.alltheweb.com (**Figure 8.1**). The site doesn't get much publicity because, instead of competing head-on with the leading search engines, FAST concentrates on selling its search technology to other companies.

- For more information about the company behind Lycos—recent press releases, the management team, how to invest in the company—click on About Terra Lycos at the bottom of the Lycos home page.

The Lycos Home Page

Before doing any real searching, let's take a look at how the Lycos home page (**Figure 8.2**) is organized. The key features to zero in on are the Basic Search form, the Advanced Search option, the Web directory, and links for accessing other search-related tools.

Figure 8.2 The Lycos home page includes the Basic Search form and links for a variety of other search-related tools. To display the Web directory, you have to click the Websites link.

Figure 8.3 This is the Basic Search form. It defaults to an AND search, so a query like the one shown here would find pages that include both *oyster* and *mushrooms*.

Figure 8.4 Use this link for Advanced Search, which gives you access to a number of options not available with the Basic Search form on the Lycos home page.

Figure 8.5 This drop-down menu on the Advanced Search form lets you specify whether you want to do an AND, OR, or phrase search.

Figure 8.6 Select one of these options on the Advanced Search form to limit your search by content, do field searches, find pages written in a specific language, or locate embedded links.

✔ Tip

■ The Lycos help information includes a wonderful section on using Boolean operators (AND, OR, NOT, NEAR, ADJ, etc.) on the Advanced Search form. Trouble is, none of them work. Search for Bush NEAR Cheney, for example, and Lycos will return Web pages that contain the words *Bush*, *near*, and *Cheney*, all of which will be presented in bold in the search results.

Basic Search form

The search form on the Lycos home page—which we'll refer to as the Basic Search form to distinguish it from the one on the Advanced Search page—consists of a search box and a Go Get It! button for submitting your query (**Figure 8.3**). No drop-down menus or special options of any kind. This is basic searching with a capital *B*!

Just type several words (or a phrase in quotes) and click Go Get It!. Lycos performs an AND search by default, looking for *all* the words and phrases that you type in the search box. So it's not even necessary to use plus signs.

Advanced Search option

For more control over your Lycos searches, click on the link for Advanced Search (**Figure 8.4**) to the right of the Go Get It! button. With Advanced Search, also known as Lycos Pro, you can use a drop-down menu to specify that you want to do an AND, OR, or phrase search (**Figure 8.5**).

You can also limit your search in a variety of ways by selecting radio buttons or filling in the blanks for one of four search options (**Figure 8.6**):

Content. To look for information in one of 15 broad categories from Autos to Weather. Three of the 15 categories are devoted to finding multimedia and MP3 music files.

Page Field. To focus your search on Web page titles, or to limit your query to a specific Web address or domain name.

Language. To search for Web pages in languages other than English.

Link Referrals. To find all the Web pages that link to a specific site.

Web directory

Like its sister company HotBot, Lycos gets its Web directory from the Open Directory Project (dmoz.org), a volunteer effort to catalog the Web using an approach similar to Yahoo (www.yahoo.com). But instead of letting you browse and search the Web directory from its home page, Lycos makes you work a bit:

◆ **To Browse the Directory**. Click on Websites (**Figure 8.7**) on the Lycos home page. You can then "drill down" through the Web directory's 15 topic categories (**Figure 8.8**) and dozens of subcategories.

◆ **To Search the Directory**. Click on Advanced Search on the Lycos home page, type a word or phrase in the search box, and use the drop-down menu to specify whether you want to do an AND, OR, or phrase search. Then select the Open Directory radio button and click Go Get It! to display your results (**Figure 8.9**).

✔ Tips

■ The section of the Lycos home page called Topics on Lycos (shown in Figure 8.2) looks like a traditional Web directory. But it's actually a set of pointers to other Lycos services. Click Finance, for example, and you'll be taken to Quote.com (www.quote.com), a Lycos subsidiary that offers stock quotes and investment information. Careers leads to a special Lycos page devoted to job-search and resume-posting services and information.

■ You can create your own "personalized" version of the Lycos home page that includes the Web directory. To learn how, see "Customizing Lycos" later in this chapter.

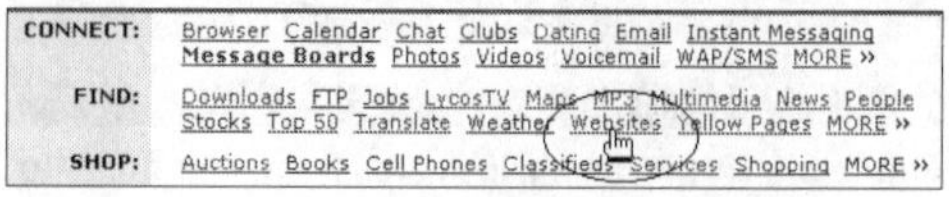

Figure 8.7 Instead of featuring its Web directory on the home page, Lycos makes you click the Websites link to display it.

Figure 8.8 The Lycos Web directory, organized into the 15 major categories shown here, is provided by the Open Directory Project.

Figure 8.9 A Web directory search for mushrooms turned up Web sites in a number of categories and subcategories, designated with greater-than (>) symbols.

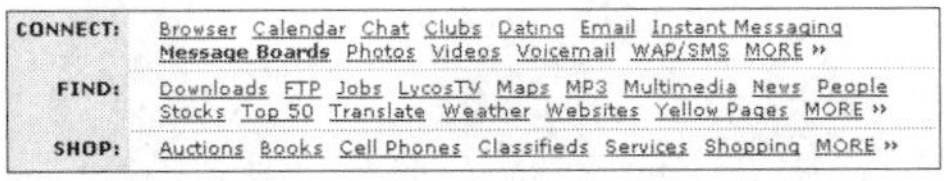

Figure 8.10 Links for other Lycos search tools are organized into three categories: Connect, Find, and Shop. Additional tools are available by clicking MORE.

Figure 8.11 The Site Map's Find menu presents most of the home page's Connect, Find, and Shop tools into a single list, organized alphabetically.

Figure 8.12 Use these links at the bottom of the Lycos home page to access country-specific versions of the search engine.

Other search-related tools

Like all good general-purpose search engines, Lycos offers a number of other search tools for handling some of the most common day-to-day questions and concerns. What's the weather forecast for this weekend? Where is the nearest one-hour photo lab and what's the best route to take to drive there? Is tonight's episode of *The West Wing* a new show or a repeat?

You'll find links for many of these special-purpose tools—Maps, Weather, Yellow Pages, and more (**Figure 8.10**)—right below the Basic Search form. For a complete list, organized alphabetically (**Figure 8.11**), click on one of the MORE links. They all lead to the same place—a page that features the Lycos Site Map.

✔ Tips

■ The Site Map serves as a master directory for the Lycos site. You can access the Site Map at any time by clicking the Site Map link at the top the page.

■ Lycos offers several country-specific editions of its search service, accessible from a set of links at the bottom of the home page (**Figure 8.12**). If you live in one of these countries, or simply want to practice searching in a language other than English, give the non-U.S. versions of Lycos a try.

continues on next page

- If you're a parent with young children, be sure to check out Lycos Zone (**Figure 8.13**), a special version of the search service designed for kids. You can go directly to the Web site (www.lycoszone.com) or click on Kids in the Topics on Lycos section of the home page.

  You might also want to use the SearchGuard feature to filter the text and images that are presented at the main Lycos Web site. To set up filters, click Parental Controls on the Basic or Advanced Search form.

- To make Lycos your default home page, follow the instructions for "Customizing Your Web Browser" in Chapter 4.

- You can get back to the Lycos home page from anywhere in the site by clicking on the Lycos Home link at the top of the page.

Figure 8.13 Lycos Zone offers search tools, homework helpers, online stories, reading lists, and games for pre-school and school-age children.

Figure 8.14 Type a search like this in the Basic Search form and Lycos will assume that you want to find pages that include references to all three terms. You don't have to use plus signs or AND.

Searching with Lycos

Having learned your way around the Lycos home page, the next step is to do some searches using the Basic Search form. Your options here are fairly limited, but with the right choice of keywords and phrases, you may very well find what you're looking for.

If not, you can always try the Advanced Search form, which gives you more options for targeting your query. Or you can submit your search to HotBot (Lycos's sister company) for a "second opinion."

To enter a Basic Search query:

1. Go to the Lycos home page (www.lycos.com) and type two or three search terms, a phrase in quotes, or a plain-English question in the search box (**Figure 8.14**).

2. You can put a plus sign (+) directly in front of a word or phrase to require that it be included in your search results: +"mad cow" +symptoms. Lycos automatically performs an AND search, however, looking for *all the words* you specify. Consequently, you don't have to use plus signs in front of required search terms. You'll get the same results with or without them.

3. To do an OR search, looking for *any of the words* you type in the search box, enclose the words in parentheses: ("mad cow" BSE), for example, to find Web pages that include references to either *mad cow* or *BSE* (the acronym for the disease's official medical name). This technique isn't documented by Lycos, but it works!

4. Use a minus sign (-) directly in front of a word or phrase to exclude it from your results: "mad cow" -humor, for example, to avoid turning up a lot of joke pages in your search.

continues on next page

✔ Tips

■ As with most search engines, it's a good idea to use two or three search terms and to be as specific as possible. To find information on identifying mushrooms that are safe to eat, for example, don't just type mushrooms in the search box. Instead, try mushrooms edible poisonous.

If you don't find what you're looking for in the first couple of pages, refine your query with Advanced Search, or try another search engine.

■ Lycos searches are *not* case-sensitive. You'll get the same results whether you use uppercase, lowercase, or a combination.

■ Unlike some search engines that ignore common words (often referred to as *stopwords*) in phrases, Lycos will look for *every* word you include in a phrase search. We take advantage of that capability for tracking reviews of one of our recent books, *About the Author*.

A Lycos search for "About the Author" Glossbrenner produces excellent results. The same search on Google returns a message advising us that "*about* is a very common word and was not included in your search."

Figure 8.15 Lycos search results are organized into as many as four sections. The section name (in this case *Popular*), appears in a shaded box, followed by the results for that section.

[POPULAR | **WEB SITES** | **NEWS ARTICLES** | **SHOPPING**]

Figure 8.16 You can jump to any section on the search results page by clicking on its link.

To view your search results:

1. Click Go Get It! to submit your query. Your results (**Figure 8.15**) will be organized into as many as four sections: Popular, Web Sites, News Articles, and Shopping.

2. You can scroll down the page or jump directly to any section by clicking on its link (**Figure 8.16**):

   Popular results (usually no more than three or four Web sites) come from one of two sources. Lycos editors may have selected them as the most relevant sites for a particular search. Or the Direct Hit "popularity engine" may have identified them as being the top choices, based on user activity at Direct Hit's own Web site (www.directhit.com). Your Lycos search results may or may not include this section.

   Web Sites results include topic categories and Web sites found in the Open Directory Project's Web directory, as well as Web sites from the FAST search engine and the Lycos spider. The topic categories (if any) will be presented first, followed by a numbered list of Web sites. To view additional sites, 10 to a page, click on More Web Sites.

   News Articles results come from several leading news wires and include stories related to your search that have appeared within the past week. Your results may or may not include this section.

   Shopping results (if any) come from Lycos Shop (shop.lycos.com), an online shopping service sponsored by Lycos to help buyers and sellers find each other.

continues on next page

SEARCHING WITH LYCOS

3. Scan the Web page title and description
(**Figure 8.17**) for results that appear on
the first couple of pages. If the description is presented in a foreign language,
click Translate to convert it to English,
compliments of Systran Software
(www.systransoft.com). Don't expect
perfection, but it may be worth a shot if
you're looking for some obscure piece of
information that's not available elsewhere.

4. Lycos gives you the option of doing a
follow-on search, focusing on the results
of your original query. (This is often
referred to as *set searching*.) To do that,
type a word or phrase in the search box.
You can leave or delete what's already
there—you'll get the same results either
way. Then click the Search these results
box (**Figure 8.18**) and submit your query
with Go Get It!.

5. If your follow-on search isn't successful,
you can automatically submit your query
to HotBot by clicking the Second opinion?
link at the bottom of the search results
page (**Figure 8.19**).

✔ Tips

- As you may recall from our discussion
of field searches in Chapter 2, one excellent way to refine a search is to look for
words in the *titles* of Web pages.

 If you get too many irrelevant hits with a
search for mad cow symptoms, for example,
you could do a follow-on search of just
those results by typing title:"mad cow"
in the search box. Then click Search
these results and Go Get It! for a more
precisely focused set of results.

 Additional field-search options are available on the Lycos Advanced Search form,
covered in the next section of this chapter.

Figure 8.17 Individual entries on the search results
page include Web page title (underlined), brief
description, Web address, and a Translate link that
you can use if the information in presented in a
language you don't understand.

Figure 8.18 As a follow-up to our search for mad cow
symptoms, we've specified that we want to search our
original results for pages that include the word .

Figure 8.19 Lycos makes it easy to get a "second
opinion" from HotBot, which, as you may recall, is
owned by the same company.

- Unfortunately, Lycos doesn't give you any
control over how your search results are
displayed. You can't change the number
of results per page, for example, or modify
the order in which they are listed.

- For a summary of Lycos search terms and
syntax, see the Lycos Quick Reference
(**Table 8.1**). To access the Lycos help
information, click the Help link at the
bottom of the Lycos home page.

Table 8.1

Lycos Basic Search Quick Reference*		
FOR THIS TYPE OF SEARCH:	DO THIS:	EXAMPLES:
Plain-English Question	Simply type a phrase or question that expresses the idea or concept, using as many words as necessary.	Are oyster mushrooms poisonous?
Phrase Search	Enclose the phrase in **double quotes**.	`"edible mushrooms"`
AND Search (multiple words and phrases, each of which *must* be present)	Type words or phrases separated by a space, without any special punctuation. By default, Lycos searches for *all* the words in your query, so even though **plus signs (+)** are allowed, you'll get the same results without them. The two examples shown here would return identical results: Web pages that contain both the phrase *oyster mushrooms* and the word *recipes*.	`"oyster mushrooms" recipes` `+"oyster mushrooms" +recipes`
OR Search (multiple words and phrases, any one of which may be present)	Enclose the words or phrases in **parentheses**. The example would find Web pages that include references to either *edible mushrooms* or *mycology*.	`("edible mushrooms" mycology)`
NOT Search (to exclude a word or phrase)	Use a **minus sign (-)** in front of a word or phrase you want to exclude from your results.	`mushrooms -recipes`
Case-Sensitive Search	Not available.	
Date Search	Not available.	
Field Search	To search titles of Web page documents, use `title:` directly in front of a word or phrase. (Note that there's no space between the colon and the search term.) For URL and Host/Domain, and Link Referral field searches, use Advanced Search.	`title:mushrooms` `title:"mushroom gardening"`
Nested Search	Not available.	
Proximity Search	Not available.	
Wildcard Search	Not available.	

* Note: This table applies to searches using the form on the Lycos home page. For Advanced Search, see **Table 8.2**.

SEARCHING WITH LYCOS

Using Advanced Search

The first thing you need to know about the Lycos Advanced Search form (**Figure 8.20**) is that it's really not all that advanced.

Power searchers who are familiar with earlier versions of Advanced Search (also known as Lycos Pro) will be disappointed to discover that Boolean operators no longer work. The Lycos help information goes into great detail about using AND, OR, NOT, NEAR, and other Boolean operators in Advanced Search queries. But somewhere along the way, Lycos has lost the ability to recognize these terms as having special meanings, and it treats them like any other search term in your query.

So why use Advanced Search? There are several features that you may find yourself needing from time to time that are not offered on the Lycos Basic Search form:

◆ Focusing your search on specific *types* of information—multimedia files, for example, or recent news articles, or personal home pages.

◆ Looking for words in Web page *URLs* (short for Uniform Resource Locators, the technical term for Web addresses) or just the *domain name* portion of the Web address. (You can also search Web page *titles* using a fill-in-the-blank approach instead of the `title:` field-search term that's required on the Basic Search form.)

◆ Limiting your search to a specific *language*.

◆ Finding Web pages that *link* to a particular site.

You may also prefer the method used on the Advanced Search form for specifying AND, OR, and phrase searches using a drop-down menu (**Figure 8.21**).

Figure 8.20 The Advanced Search form, while not really all that advanced, provides several features not available when you search from the Lycos home page.

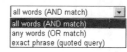

Figure 8.21
The Advanced Search form defaults to an AND search, but you can specify an OR or phrase search using this drop-down menu.

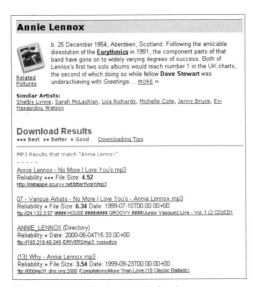

Annie Lennox

b. 25 December 1954, Aberdeen, Scotland. Following the amicable dissolution of the **Eurythmics** in 1991, the component parts of that band have gone on to widely varying degrees of success. Both of Lennox's first two solo albums would reach number 1 in the UK charts, the second of which doing so while fellow **Dave Stewart** was underachieving with *Greetings* ... MORE »

Related Pictures

Similar Artists:
Shelby Lynne, Sarah McLachlan, Lisa Richards, Michelle Cote, Jenny Bruce, Evi Hasapidou Watson

Download Results
••• Best •• Better • Good   Downloading Tips

MP3 Results that match "Annie Lennox"
- - - - -
Annie Lennox - No More I Love You's.mp3
Reliability: ••• File Size: **4.52**
Http://datapipe.scurvy.net/btterflygrrl/mp3

07 - Various Artists - No More I Love You's - Annie Lennox.mp3
Reliability: • File Size: **6.34** Date: 1999-07-10T00:00:00+00
ftp://24.132.3.57 /#### HOUSE ####/#### GROOVY ####/Junior Vasquez Live - Vol. 1 (2 CD)/CD1

ANNIE_LENNOX (Directory)
Reliability: • Date: 2000-06-04T15:33:00+00
ftp://193.219.49.249 /DRIVERS/mp3_rusiuotos

(13) Why - Annie Lennox.mp3
Reliability: • File Size: **3.54** Date: 1999-09-23T00:00:00+00
ftp://000mp31.dhs.org:2000 /Compilations/More Than Love (18 Classic Ballads)

Figure 8.22 MP3 files by a particular singer are a snap to find using the Music by Artist radio button in the Content section of the Advanced Search form.

Figure 8.23 The Content section's Multimedia radio button lets you search a vast database of audio and video files as well as images, like this one of Vermeer's famous painting, "The Milkmaid."

Multimedia Search

SEARCH: ● All ○ Pictures ○ Audio ○ Video
FOR: [   ] Search!
Controls are OFF   Search Help

Figure 8.24 Using this special Multimedia search form, you can specify one of three types of files—Pictures, Audio, or Video—instead of looking for all three at once.

To search for specific types of information:

1. Enter your query in the Advanced Search form and make a selection from the Content section to focus on one of 15 broad categories of information, instead of searching the entire Web.

   Options include Autos, Books, Downloads, Dictionary, FTP Search, Home Pages, Multimedia, Music by Artist, Music by Songs, News, Open Directory, Recipes, Stock, and Weather.

2. To find MP3 files of Annie Lennox songs (**Figure 8.22**), for example, type "Annie Lennox" in the search form and click the Music by Artist radio button before submitting your query with Go Get It!.

3. To locate images of Vermeer's painting of "The Milkmaid," type Vermeer Milkmaid in the search box, click the Multimedia radio button, and then click Go Get It! to find several examples like the one in **Figure 8.23**.

✔ Tips

- If you click a category's link (instead of its radio button), you'll be taken to a special search page customized for that category.

  Click Multimedia, for example, to access the Lycos search form for finding images, audio files, and video files (**Figure 8.24**).

  Click Open Directory to display the Lycos Web directory (provided by the Open Directory Project).

- Lycos ignores case on both the Basic and Advanced Search forms, so you can use any combination of uppercase and lower-case and you'll get the same results.

USING ADVANCED SEARCH

To look for words in Web page titles, URLs, or domain names:

◆ Click Page Field and use the form presented there (**Figure 8.25**) to narrow your focus by typing a search word in the Title, URL, or Host/Domain search boxes. Let's step through for an example for each of these options:

◆ **Title**. If you're looking for information about a particular California wine called Sequoia Grove, type "Sequoia Grove" in the primary search box on the Advanced Search form and type California wines in the Title search box. Then click Go Get It!.

By limiting your search to Web sites that include the phrase *California wines* in their titles, you're much more likely to find sites that *feature* (as opposed to simply *mentioning*) wines produced in California.

◆ **URL**. To limit your search for Sequoia Grove to the Wine.com Web site, type "Sequoia Grove" in the primary search box and wine.com in the URL search box, Click Go Get It! to submit your query.

◆ **Host/Domain**. To find education sites dealing with French wines, type "French wines" in the primary search box and edu in the Host/Domain box. Submit your query by clicking Go Get It!. (For a list of other Internet domains, see Appendix B).

✔ Tips

■ For best results, avoid using quotation marks and other punctuation in the Title, URL, and Host/Domain search boxes.

■ You're not required to enter a search term in the primary search box when you do a Page Field search. You could, for example, leave the primary search box empty and type French wines in the Title box to find all Web sites that have the words *French wines* in their titles.

Figure 8.25 The Page Field options let you focus your search on Web page titles, URLs, and domain names.

Figure 8.26 You can limit your results to pages written in a specific language—English or two dozen other choices—by clicking the appropriate radio button on this list.

Figure 8.27 With Link Referrals, you can track down Web sites similar to one you like, or get a measure of a specific site's popularity, as indicated by the number of other sites that link to it.

To limit a search by language:

◆ Click Language to display the list of languages that are available on Lycos (**Figure 8.26**). Then simply type your query in the search box and click the radio button for the language of your choice.

For example, type "Chianti" in the search form, select the Italian radio button, and click Go Get It!. Your search results will be limited to Web pages presented in Italian.

To find Web pages that link to a specific site:

◆ Click Link Referrals and type the URL for the site you'd like to find out about in the Your URL box (**Figure 8.27**).

If you're a fan of *The Wall Street Journal's* Wine site, for example, and want to find Web sites that link to it—in hopes of discovering some new sites that might be of interest to you as well—type wine.wsj.com in the URL box and click Go Get It!.

✔ Tips

■ If your search results include a lot of links from *within* the Web site that you entered in the Your URL box, type the *same* URL in the Exclude this Host box and run the search again.

■ Webmasters and Web site creators often use link referrals as a rough measure of a site's popularity. Try it with your own Web site if you have one.

USING ADVANCED SEARCH

Table 8.2

Lycos Advanced Search Quick Reference		
FOR THIS TYPE OF SEARCH:	**DO THIS:**	**EXAMPLES:**
Plain-English Question	Simply type a phrase or question that expresses the idea or concept, using as many words as necessary. Leave the drop-down menu set to all words (AND match).	What are the best French table wines?
Phrase Search	Type the phrase without any special punctuation and choose exact phrase (quoted query) from the drop-down menu.	French table wines
	Alternatively, you can type the phrase in **double quotes** and leave the drop-down menu set to all words (AND match).	"French table wines"
AND Search (multiple words and phrases, each of which *must* be present)	Type the words (or phrases in quotes) in the search form and leave the drop-down menu set to all words (AND match).	California "Cabernet Sauvignon"
OR Search (multiple words and phrases, any one of which may be present)	Type the words (or phrases in quotes) in the search form and choose any words (OR match) from the drop-down menu.	"sparkling wine" Champagne
NOT Search (to exclude a word or phrase)	Use a **minus sign (-)** in front of a word or phrase you want to exclude from the results.	Chardonnay -California
Case-Sensitive Search	Not available.	
Date Search	Not available.	
Field Search	Click Page Field and use the fill-in-the-blanks form to search Web page Title, URL, and Host/Domain fields. (For best results, avoid using quotation marks and other punctuation when using the Page Field option.)	
	Click Link Referrals and use the fill-in-the-blanks form to look for links to a specific Web page.	
	For examples, see "Using Advanced Search" on pages 130–133.	
Nested Search	Not available.	
Proximity Search	Not available.	
Wildcard Search	Not available.	

Figure 8.28 To make Lycos your Web browser's default home page, type http://www.lycos.com in Internet Explorer's home page Address box as shown here (or Netscape's home-page Location box).

Customizing Lycos

If you decide to make Lycos your primary search engine, you may want to think about customizing it to reflect the way you search and the types of information that are of particular interest.

There are two options for you to consider:

◆ **Basic or Advanced Search as Browser Home Page**. If the search form on the Lycos home page works for you most of the time, fine. But if instead you find yourself doing most of your searches using the Advanced Search form, you can make it your Web browser's default home-page location.

◆ **Standard or Personalized Lycos**. If you decide to stay with the Basic Search form on the Lycos home page, you have another decision to make: Do you want to stick with the default settings for content and layout or "personalize the page"?

To make Lycos your home page:

1. Decide which of the two search forms you want to use on a regular basis—Basic or Advanced.

2. Access your Web browser's home-page setup feature and type the complete Web address for the page containing the search form you prefer into the home page Address or Location box (**Figure 8.28**):

http://www.lycos.com (if you prefer to do most of your searches using the Basic Search form).

http://lycospro.lycos.com (if you prefer the Advanced Search form).

✔ Tip

■ If you're not sure how to access your Web browser's home-page setup feature, see the section in Chapter 4 called "Customizing Your Web Browser."

To personalize the Lycos home page:

1. Click Sign up (**Figure 8.29**) in the Personalize Lycos section of the Lycos home page to display the membership form for new users

2. Complete the form and then click the Sign Me Up! button at the bottom of the page to submit it. (Pay careful attention to the Special Offers section to avoid inadvertently signing yourself up for lots of junk mail.)

3. Once your membership has been accepted (it only takes a few seconds), you can use the My Page Setup feature (**Figure 8.30**) to pick and choose the information you want to have on your page.

   For example, to display the Lycos Web directory on your home page, click the My Page Setup Add link. Then click the Lycos Directories radio button in the Resources & Search section of the Add/Remove Boxes page (**Figure 8.31**).

4. Once you've chosen the sections you want on your page, some of them—like stock reports, TV listings, weather forecasts, and so forth—can be further tailored using Edit links (**Figure 8.32**).

Personalize Lycos
My Lycos: Sign up | Log in

Figure 8.29 You'll find this link for personalizing Lycos on the left side of the Lycos home page.

My Page Setup

Boxes:
Add | Remove | Move
Change Box Size

Page:
Change Colors
Add a Page

Figure 8.30 My Page Setup lets you add and remove Lycos features, move and resize them on the page, and choose your own color scheme.

Resources & Search
☐ People Finder
☐ Road Maps
☐ Yellow Pages
☑ Lycos Directories

Figure 8.31 You can display the Lycos Web directory on your personalized Lycos page by clicking Add in My Page Setup and then selecting the Lycos Directories radio button.

Figure 8.32 Some features that you add to your personalized Lycos page can be customized to your liking using an Edit link.

Track this Search

Figure 8.33 You can have Lycos "track a search" and send you e-mail notices when it finds new information. But you have to set up a special e-mail account to take advantage of the service.

✔ Tips

- You can easily switch back and forth between the standard Lycos home page and your personalized page, using the links for Lycos Home (to get back to standard Lycos from your personalized page) and My Lycos (to get to your personal page from the Lycos home page).

- Lycos offers a Track this Search option (**Figure 8.33**) for queries made using the Basic Search form. Unfortunately, no details are provided, other than a vaguely worded statement that you'll be notified by e-mail of "changes to your search." Worse still, you have to set up a special Lycos e-mail account in order to receive the notices.

    If you need a feature like this, try Northern Light (www.northernlight.com) instead. Their Search Alert Service is well documented, easy to set up, and works with your regular e-mail account. (See Chapter 9 for more on Northern Light.)

CUSTOMIZING LYCOS

NORTHERN LIGHT

Northern Light

Good to Know

- Launched in 1997, Northern Light handles plain-English queries and complex Boolean expressions equally well.

- What sets it apart from its rivals is that it lets you *simultaneously* search both the Web and a database of some 25 million full-text documents from 7,100 other sources—making it an especially good choice for researching news stories and business information.

- Northern Light also has a unique approach to organizing search results into "folders" of related information, so that you can find what you're looking for more quickly.

- Its Search Alert Service, providing e-mail notification of updates to saved searches, is the best of all the leading search engines.

Housed in an old mill building in Cambridge, Massachusetts, Northern Light was launched in 1997 by a small team of librarians, information industry professionals, and software engineers. For almost two years they had labored to create a service that would address the shortcomings of conventional search engines—most notably the difficulty of finding quality information and the total lack of organization. "The Web is the ultimate expression of the problem of too much data and not enough information," says company CEO David Seuss.

When Northern Light came on the scene—joining well-established rivals like AltaVista, Excite, HotBot, Lycos, and Yahoo—the search community embraced it immediately, recognizing that it was indeed a search engine with a difference. Billed as a "research engine," Northern Light made headlines not only for the size of its database, but also because of two unique features that address the problems of information quality and organization.

continues on next page

◆ **Special Collection**. The best information on a particular topic may or may not exist on the Web, so Northern Light lets you simultaneously search both Web pages and its Special Collection database of full-text journals, books, magazines, newswires, and reference sources. The database includes more than 25 million documents dating back to 1995, from over 7,100 sources.

You can search and view summaries of articles for free and then buy the full text for a small fee (typically $1 to $4) charged to a major credit card. Northern Light is so confident you'll be satisfied, they offer a money-back guarantee.

◆ **Custom Search Folders**. To address the organization problem, Northern Light offers a unique approach to presenting your search results—sorting them into "folders" that it creates on the fly based on subject, source, type of document, and sometimes language.

Search for chocolat, for example, and your results might be organized into folders labeled *Movies* (because of the award-winning Miramax film), *Food & Beverages Industry*, *Recipes*, and *Documents in French*, among others.

Custom Search Folders are Northern Light's way of asking, "Is this what you mean?" and helping you move quickly to the right set of information.

Northern Light is designed to handle both plain-English queries and complex Boolean expressions equally well, making it a good choice for searchers of all experience levels.

And once you've developed a particularly effective query on a subject that you want to stay on top of, you can take advantage of the free Search Alert Service. All it takes is a single click, and you'll be notified by e-mail whenever Northern Light finds new information on the Web or in the Special Collection database.

Contact Information

Northern Light Technology, Inc.
Cambridge, Massachusetts
617-621-5100 (voice)
617-621-3459 (fax)
cs@northernlight.com
www.northernlight.com

NORTHERN LIGHT

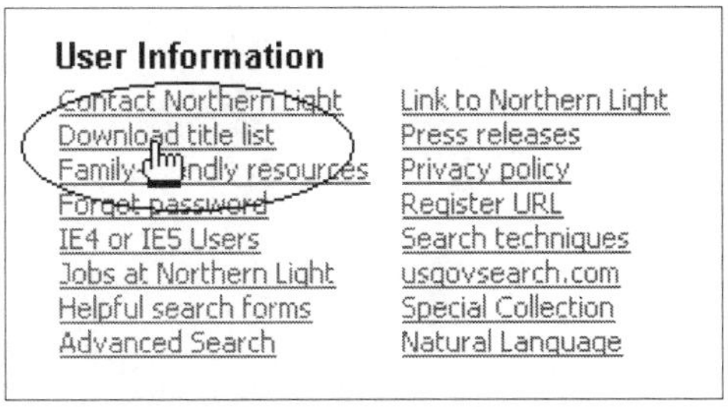

User Information

Contact Northern Light   Link to Northern Light
Download title list   Press releases
Family-friendly resources Privacy policy
Forget password   Register URL
IE4 or IE5 Users   Search techniques
Jobs at Northern Light   usgovsearch.com
Helpful search forms   Special Collection
Advanced Search   Natural Language

Figure 9.1 You can download a list of all the publications represented in the Special Collection database by clicking this link.

Figure 9.2 A painting of the clipper ship *Northern Light* hangs in the lobby at the company's headquarters.

Help
Accounts
About
Alerts
Portfolio

Figure 9.3 To learn more about Northern Light's history, management team, and awards, click the About link.

✔ Tips

■ Knowing that serious searchers will want to know exactly what sources are represented in the Special Collection, Northern Light makes the complete list available. Just click Download title list in the User Information area of the home page (**Figure 9.1**).

■ The company's name and logo were inspired by the clipper ship *Northern Light* (**Figure 9.2**), built in Boston in 1851. Based on a radical new design, the ship became known for its speed and ground-breaking technology.

■ For more information on Northern Light—company history, industry awards, customer comments, and so forth—click About (**Figure 9.3**) on the home page.

The Northern Light Home Page

In keeping with its research orientation, the Northern Light home page (**Figure 9.4**) includes both a basic search form, called Simple Search, as well as links for Power Search and several specialized search options. The only portal-type services you'll find on the home page are the day's news headlines and a small space devoted to the Dow Jones Industrial Average.

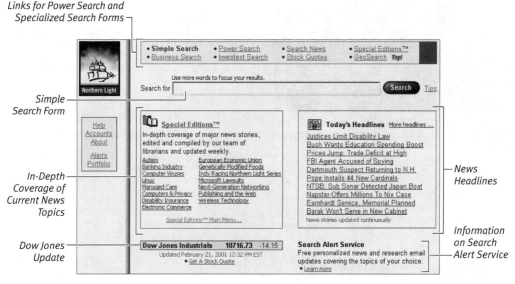

Figure 9.4 The Northern Light home page.

Figure 9.5 A plain-English question like this works fine with Northern Light.

Figure 9.6 This set of links on the Northern Light home page gives you access to Power Search and several other specialized search forms.

Figure 9.7 The Power Search form makes it easy to create a complex query by simply filling in the blanks and choosing radio buttons and menu options.

Simple Search form

The Simple Search form (**Figure 9.5**) lets you simultaneously search both the Web and Northern Light's Special Collection database of documents from non-Web sources. You can enter a query as a plain-English question: What companies are included in the dow jones industrial average?. Or you can type a complex Boolean expression: (DJIA OR "dow jones industrial average) AND companies AND list. Either way, you'll typically get excellent results.

Northern Light automatically searches for *all* the words in your query, so it's not necessary to use plus signs (+) or AND to require that a word or phrase appear in your search results.

Power Search option

Clicking Power Search in the set of links (**Figure 9.6**) at the top of the Northern Light home page takes you to a form that helps you search with more precision by focusing on specific subjects, sources (Special Collection or World Wide Web), document types, and dates (**Figure 9.7**).

You can also do a variety of field searches (title, URL, publication name, domain type), look for documents written in a particular language, and sort your results by date—all using a fill-in-the-blanks form.

Other search options

In addition to Power Search, the links at the top of the Northern Light home page give you access to several more narrowly focused search forms:

◆ Search News lets you search a two-week archive of articles and press releases from dozens of newswires, including AP Online, UPI, and PR Newswire (**Figure 9.8**). You can limit your results by timeframe and topic and sort results by relevance or date.

◆ Business Search gives you access to a form designed for serious business researchers (**Figure 9.9**). Special features include the ability to limit your search to a specific company, industry, market research firm, or business publication.

◆ Investext Search allows you to search or browse thousands of investment research reports written by analysts at brokerage houses, investment banks, and research firms throughout the world. Searches and report summaries are free. Full-text reports range in price from ten dollars to several hundred dollars

◆ Stock Quotes takes you to a form that lets you search for stock symbols, stock quotes, company news and financial information, and SEC filings.

◆ GeoSearch is a relatively new search offering that helps you locate Web sites offering products and services in a particular geographic area. You can search within a specified distance (up to 100 miles) from a street address, city, or Zip code.

Figure 9.8 The Search News form is optimized for finding press releases and news articles that have appeared in the last two weeks.

Figure 9.9 The Business Search form is your best bet for locating information on a specific company.

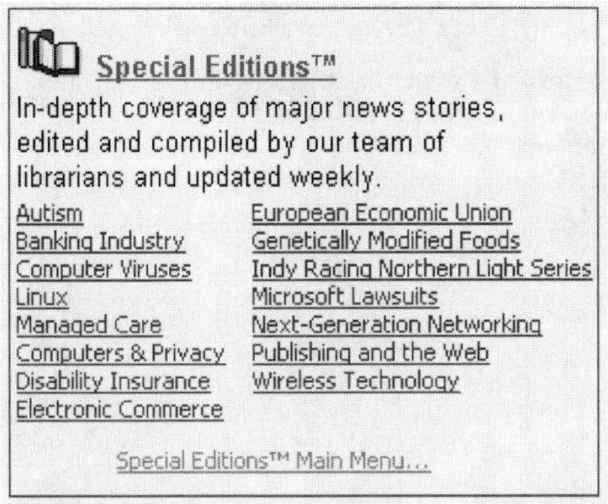

Special Editions™

In-depth coverage of major news stories, edited and compiled by our team of librarians and updated weekly.

Autism   European Economic Union
Banking Industry   Genetically Modified Foods
Computer Viruses   Indy Racing Northern Light Series
Linux   Microsoft Lawsuits
Managed Care   Next-Generation Networking
Computers & Privacy   Publishing and the Web
Disability Insurance   Wireless Technology
Electronic Commerce

Special Editions™ Main Menu...

Figure 9.10 Northern Light librarians and information specialists update this area of the home page each week to reflect major news stories.

✔ Tips

- An area of the Northern Light home page called Special Editions (**Figure 9.10**) features several current news stories, with information compiled and edited by staff librarians and information specialists. For the complete list of stories, click Special Editions Main Menu.

- You'll find explanations of each of the Northern Light search forms and tips for using them on the Search Help page. To get there, click Help on the Northern Light home page and then click Search Help. Or click Tips next to the Search button on any search form.

- To make Northern Light your browser's default home page, see "Customizing Your Web Browser" in Chapter 4.

- To return to the Northern Light home page, click Simple Search or the company logo that appears at the top of most pages within the site.

THE NORTHERN LIGHT HOME PAGE

Searching with Northern Light

You'll probably do most of your Northern Light searches using the Simple Search form on the home page, so that's what we'll focus on here.

Once you've learned to enter a Simple Search query and work with the results, using Northern Light's other search forms will be a snap. The same basic rules apply throughout the site, and searches that require complicated Boolean expressions and field-search terms on the Simple Search form can be accomplished by filling in the blanks with Power Search and the specialized Business and Investext forms.

To enter a Simple Search query:

1. Go to the Northern Light home page (www.northernlight.com) and type a question, several descriptive words, a phrase in quotes, or a Boolean expression in the search box (**Figure 9.11**).

   Northern Light automatically searches for *all* the words, so you don't have to use the Boolean operator AND or put plus signs (+) in front of required words.

2. To tell Northern Light to look for *any* of the words, use the Boolean operator OR: wireless OR "mobile commerce".

3. If you want to specifically exclude a certain word or phrase from your results, put a minus sign (-) directly in front of it: wireless -paging. Or use the Boolean operator NOT: wireless NOT paging.

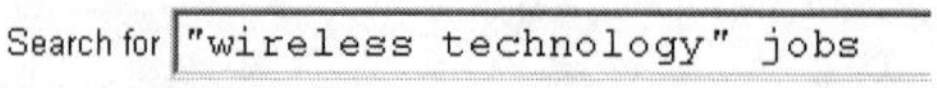

Search for `"wireless technology" jobs`

Figure 9.11 A search like this tells Northern Light to look for both the phrase *wireless technology* and the word *jobs*.

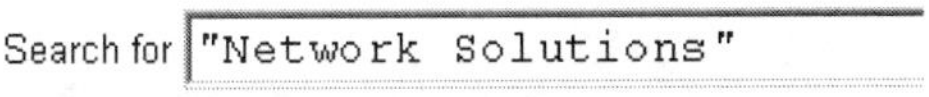

Search for | "Network Solutions"

Figure 9.12 To find the company called Network Solutions, it's a good idea to type the name with initial caps.

✔ Tips

- The Boolean operators AND, OR, and NOT can be typed in uppercase or lowercase.

- Strictly speaking, Northern Light searches are *not* case sensitive. You'll get the same *set* of results whether you use uppercase, lowercase, or a mix of the two. However, if you're looking for a proper name, it's a good idea to type it exactly as you'd expect it to appear in a document (**Figure 9.12**). When you use initial caps (or any mix of uppercase and lowercase), *exact* case matches will appear higher in the results list, making them easier to find.

- Northern Light automatically looks for both the singular and plural forms of your search terms. Type technology, for example, and it looks for *technology* and *technologies*.

- For other types of word variations, you can use an asterisk (*) as a wildcard to look for multiple characters within or at the end of a word. For example, technolog* would find *technology*, *technologies*, *technological*, and *technologist*. Just be sure to use at least four other characters preceding the asterisk. To look for a *single* character, use a percent sign (%) as the wildcard: adapt%r to find references to *adapter* and *adaptor*.

- Unlike some search engines, Northern Light will *not* ignore common words (*stopwords*) in phrases, so a search for a phrase like "to be or not to be" is never a problem.

To view your search results:

1. Click Search (or hit Enter) to display your results, 10 to a page, with your search terms highlighted in bold and presented along with a few words of surrounding text or a brief description of the Web page or document. The total number of items found is also displayed, along with your original query (**Figure 9.13**).

   For Web sites (**Figure 9.14**), Northern Light gives you an indication of the type of information you'll find there (articles and general information, company background, directories and lists, and so forth), the date the site was last updated, and the type of site (commercial, non-profit, government, etc.).

   For Special Collection documents (**Figure 9.15**), you're provided with the document type (article, press release, industry overview, etc.), publication date, and source.

2. To view a specific item on the list, click its title. For Special Collection documents, you'll be shown an abstract and given an opportunity to purchase the document for a small fee (**Figure 9.16**).

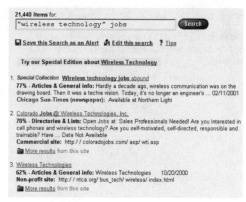

Figure 9.13 Your search results will typically include both Web pages and documents from the Special Collection database.

Figure 9.14 Here's an example of how Web site information is presented on the Northern Light results page.

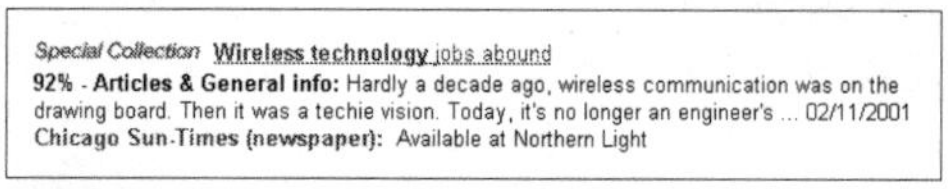

Figure 9.15 Items from the Special Collection database are clearly identified as such, and include the publication name and date.

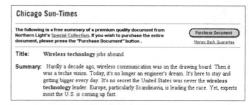

Figure 9.16 Article summaries like the one shown here are free, but you have a to pay a small fee to purchase the full text.

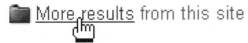

Figure 9.17 Click this link to "uncluster" search results and view additional pages from a particular Web site or Special Collection document.

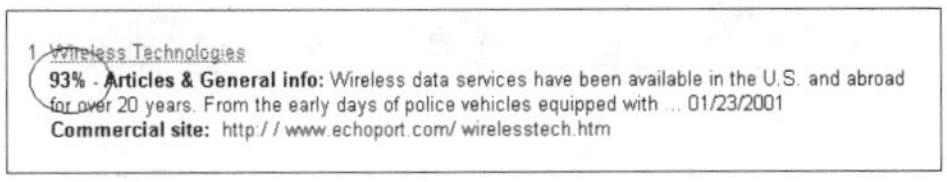

Figure 9.18 The percentage figure that appears with each item on the search results page gives you an indication of how well the item matches your query.

Figure 9.19
Northern Light organized the results from our search for "wireless technology" jobs into the Custom Search Folders shown here.

Figure 9.20 The Careers & Occupations folder was further broken down into these subfolders.

3. Northern Light "clusters" results and presents only one page from any given Web site or document. To view additional pages, go back to the search results page and click the item's More results link (**Figure 9.17**).

✔ Tips

■ Your Northern Light search results are displayed in order based on how well they match your search terms. Each item's *relevance rating*, expressed as a percentage, is included in your results (**Figure 9.18**).

■ You can override the relevance ratings and sort your results by date (from newest to oldest) by adding sort:date to your query and submitting it again.

To refine a Northern Light query:

1. The easiest (and often most effective) technique is to simply add another unique search word or phrase to the search box at the top of the page and submit your query again. Northern Light looks for *all* the words in your query, so this has the effect of searching *within* your original results (also known as *set searching*).

2. Another excellent way to refine a Northern Light search is to take advantage of the Custom Search Folders feature. Review the list of folders for your query (**Figure 9.19**) and identify the one that comes closest to the type of information you're looking for. Click on it to display a further breakdown of your results within that folder (**Figure 9.20**).

continues on next page

✔ Tips

■ Northern Light only produces Custom Search Folders for queries that result in a large number of hits.

■ Keep in mind that Custom Search Folders are created by Northern Light software. They are a neat innovation and work quite well for many types of searches. But they are no match for human-compiled directories and subject guides.

■ Since Northern Light doesn't offer its own Web directory, try one of these sites when you want to explore the Web by topic, with guidance from human beings:

About, The Human Internet Guide
www.about.com

Argus Clearinghouse
www.clearinghouse.net

Open Directory Project
dmoz.org

Yahoo
www.yahoo.com

To save a query and get e-mail alerts:

1. Click Save this Search as an Alert (**Figure 9.21**) on the results page for the search you want to save.

2. On the Search Alert Service page (**Figure 9.22**), enter a descriptive name for your Alert. (The name will be displayed in the subject line of e-mail messages that are sent to you.). You also have the option of limiting the Alert to documents dated in the last 90 days, and creating an additional Alert for news articles.

3. When you're finished, click the Save Alert button. From that point forward, whenever Northern Light discovers new information relating to your query, you'll be notified by e-mail.

🖫 Save this Search as an Alert

Figure 9.21 Once you've developed a query that produces good results, you can save it by clicking this link on the search results page.

Figure 9.22 Be sure to give your Alert a descriptive name, since that's what will appear in the subject line of e-mail messages notifying you of new information relating to your query.

✔ Tips

■ Northern Light's Search Alert Service is the best we've encountered among the leading Web search engines.

■ For a summary of the search rules presented in this section, see the Northern Light Quick Reference (**Table 9.1**).

■ For assistance with all aspects of Northern Light, click Help on the home page. You'll find that, in line with its emphasis on searching, the company has anticipated virtually any question you might have about the service.

Table 9.1

Northern Light Quick Reference

FOR THIS TYPE OF SEARCH:	DO THIS:	EXAMPLES:
Plain-English Question	Simply type a phrase or question that expresses the idea or concept, using as many words as necessary.	Where can I find information about study abroad programs in France?
Phrase Search	Type phrase surrounded by **double quotes**.	"youth hostel"
AND Search (multiple words and phrases, each of which must be present)	Type words (or phrases in quotes) separated by a space. You can also use **plus signs (+)** or **AND** operator if you're accustomed to doing so. All three examples would produce the same results.	Princeton "financial aid" +Princeton +"financial aid" Princeton AND "financial aid"
OR Search (multiple words and phrases, any one of which may be present)	Type words or phrases separated by **OR** (in uppercase or lowercase).	scholarship OR "student loan" OR grant
NOT Search (to exclude a word or phrase)	Use a **minus sign (-)** directly in front of the word or phrase you want to exclude. Alternatively, you can use **NOT** (uppercase or lowercase).	booksellers -Amazon.com booksellers NOT Amazon.com
Case-Sensitive Search	Strictly speaking, not available. Northern Light returns the same set of results regardless of case. But if you use mixed case, hits that make an *exact* case match will appear higher on the results list.	"Scholastic Aptitude Test"
Date Search	Not available with Simple Search form. Use Power Search or Business Search.	
Field Search	Type field-search term followed by a colon and the search word or phrase. *For Web pages and Special Collection documents:* title: (to look for words in Web page or document titles) url: (to look for words in Web page URLs) link: (to find Web pages or documents that include links to a specific site) text: (used with another field-search term to look for words in the *text* of Web pages or documents) *For Special Collection documents only:* company: (to find documents by company name) ticker: (to find documents by ticker symbol) pub: (to find documents in specific publication) recid: (to find document based on ID number from Northern Light article summary page) Note: For fill-in-the-blanks field searching, use Power, Business, or Investext search forms.	title:"Favorite Poem Project" url:booktv link:abouttheauthor.com url:npr.org text:"Car Talk" company:ebay ticker:MSO pub:business week recid:AA20010207020001236
Nested Search	Use **parentheses** to group Boolean expressions into more complex queries.	SAT AND ("sample test" OR "prep course")
Proximity Search	Not available.	
Wildcard Search	Use an **asterisk (*)** to search for *multiple* characters at the end of (or within) a word, or a **percent sign (%)** to look for a *single* character. Wildcard must be preceded by at least four other characters.	GRE test prep* gene%logy

Improving Results with Field Search

As you may recall from our discussion of keywords in Chapter 2, one of the best ways to narrow the focus of a search with any search engine is to zero in on specific *fields*. Searching the *titles* of Web pages and documents, for example, can reduce your results list considerably and help you find items that *feature* (instead of simply *mentioning*) your search terms.

With Northern Light's Simple Search form, you can use the field-search terms listed here to find Web pages and Special Collection documents. In each case, type your search word or phrase *immediately* following the colon, without leaving a space.

- `title:` To look for words or phrases in the titles of Web page or documents (**Figure 9.23**).

- `url:` To look for words in URLs.

- `link:` To find Web pages or documents that link to a specific site.

- `text:` Used in combination with another field-search term to find a word or phrase in the body of a Web page or document.

Several other Northern Light field-search terms apply only to Special Collection documents:

- `company:` To locate Special Collection documents by company name.

- `ticker:` To locate documents by a company's stock ticker symbol (**Figure 9.24**).

- `pub:` To find documents from a specific publication.

- `recid:` To find a document based on its ID number from the Northern Light article summary page.

Figure 9.23 By using `title:ISP` to look for *ISP* in the titles of Web pages and documents, we zeroed right in on a site offering "The Definitive ISP Buyer's Guide."

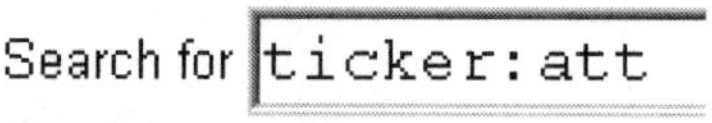

Search for `ticker:att`

Figure 9.24 You can use a `ticker:` field-search term to find Special Collection documents by a company's stock ticker symbol, in this case AT&T's.

Figure 9.25 In this example, we used `pub:` and `text:` field-search terms together to look for *Wall Street Journal* articles that mention the term *ISP* in the body of the article.

Figure 9.26 Both Power Search and Business Search let you limit your search to Web sites *or* Special Collection documents—a capability not offered on the Simple Search form.

SELECT DATE RANGE
Fill in one date field or both to narrow your results by date.
Start date: `01/01/01` End date: `03/31/01` *mm/dd/yyyy*

Figure 9.27 You can also do a date search on the Power and Business Search forms.

✔ Tips

■ If you want to search both the *body* of a Web page or Special Collection document as well as another field, you *must* include a `text:` field-search term in your query (**Figure 9.25**).

■ For more field-search examples, see the Northern Light Quick Reference (**Table 9.1**).

■ For even easier field searching, use Northern Light's Power, Business, and Investext search forms. All three offer a fill-in-the-blanks approach to field searches.

■ In addition to field searching, the Power Search and Business Search forms let you choose which Northern Light database you want to search—Web or Special Collection (Figure 9.26). You can also specify a date range for your query (**Figure 9.27**).

Customizing Northern Light

You can't change anything about the content and layout of the Northern Light home page—at least not at this writing. Nor can you set preferences for the way your search results are presented.

But if Northern Light becomes your search engine of choice, you may want to consider customizing your Web browser so that it takes you automatically to one of the Northern Light search forms whenever you go online or click your browser's Home button.

You might also want to set up a Northern Light account. It only takes a minute or two, and once you've gone through the process, whenever you want to purchase a document from the Special Collection, all you have to do is enter your username and password and the purchase will be charged to your credit card.

To make Northern Light your home page:

1. Decide which of the two search forms you want to use on a regular basis— Simple Search or Power Search.

2. Access your Web browser's home-page setup feature and type the complete Web address for the page containing the search form you prefer into the home page Address or Location box (**Figure 9.28**):

   http://www.northernlight.com
   (if you expect to do most of your searches using the Simple Search form).

   http://www.northernlight.com/power.html
   (if you prefer the Power Search form).

✔ Tip

■ If you're not sure how to access your Web browser's home-page setup feature, see "Customizing Your Web Browser" in Chapter 4.

Figure 9.28 To make Northern Light your Web browser's home page location, type the complete Web address in the Internet Explorer Address box (or the Netscape Location box).

Figure 9.29 Use the Accounts link on the Northern Light home page to set up a member account.

Figure 9.30 Once you've completed the Member Account form shown here, you'll be able to buy Special Collection documents, charging the fee to Visa, Mastercard, or American Express.

To set up a Northern Light account:

1. Go to the Northern Light home page (www.northernlight.com) and click Accounts (**Figure 9.29**).

2. On the Accounts page, click Create New Account to display the Member Account Set Up Page (**Figure 9.30**).

3. Complete the form. Then click OK to indicate your acceptance of the "terms of service" and to submit the form to Northern Light.

✔ Tip

■ Many of the documents in Northern Light's Special Collection database are available free of charge elsewhere on the Web. You'll find some of them in searchable archives maintained by the publications in which they originally appeared. You might also track them down at Web sites like FindArticles (www.findarticles.com) and NewsDirectory (www.newsdirectory.com). But you can't beat the convenience of having them searchable and available for viewing and printing at a single site. And with Northern Light's price of just $1 to $4 per document, it may not be worth your time to try to locate the free versions.

CUSTOMIZING NORTHERN LIGHT

YAHOO!

Technically speaking, Yahoo is not a search engine at all. It's actually a searchable subject directory. And its database—estimated at some two million Web sites—is a mere fraction of the size of its competitors. So how has Yahoo managed to become the Web's most popular search service? What is it that makes finding information with Yahoo so easy?

The answer lies in the fact that Yahoo is more of a hands-on operation than most other search sites. Instead of relying on automated search robots or spider programs to build its database, Yahoo maintains a staff of some 150 editors. Their job is to review information submitted by Web site creators and other Internet users and decide, first, whether a particular site merits inclusion in the Yahoo directory, and if so, under which category.

This is a time-consuming process, of course, so Yahoo supplements its human-compiled directory with listings from Google (www.google.com), one of the Web's largest spider-created databases. (See Chapter 6 for more on Google.)

The beauty of Yahoo is that when you enter a query, your search is run simultaneously against both the Yahoo directory *and* the Google database of more than a billion Web pages. If the search terms you've entered are found among Yahoo's own listings, those

Good to Know

- Yahoo is the Web's most popular search site.

- Created at Stanford University in 1994, it was the first major attempt at organizing and classifying the information available on the Internet.

- When you do a Yahoo search, you are actually searching both the Yahoo directory and the Google database of more than a billion Web pages.

- Yahoo is a good place to start when you need general information on a topic, or when you are not quite sure what you're looking for but have a sense that you'll recognize it when you see it.

matches will be presented first, followed by Web pages found in Google. If nothing is found in the Yahoo database, you'll at least have the Google results.

So why not just use Google to begin with?

You might very well prefer to start with Google when you're looking for something quite specific. But for those occasions when you want to explore what the Web has to offer on some very broad topic, or when you're not quite sure what you're after, a Yahoo search is often your best bet.

✔ Tips

- Yahoo was developed in 1994 at Stanford University by David Filo and Jerry Yang, graduate students in electrical engineering. At the time, they were simply interested in keeping track of their personal favorite sites on the Internet. But before too long, word got out and they began getting hundreds of messages a day alerting them to wonderful sites that should be added to the Yahoo directory.

  Eventually the workload started interfering with their studies, so the pair dropped out of school, raised a million dollars in venture capital, and turned their dorm-room project into one of the Internet's most popular (and successful) businesses.

- Today, most search engines include a human-compiled directory on their home pages—often the Open Directory (www.dmoz.org) or LookSmart (www.looksmart.com). But Yahoo develops its own subject directory and continues to set the standard. Its classification system is so detailed that the *San Jose Mercury News* has called Yahoo "the closest in spirit to the work of Linnaeus, the 18th-century botanist whose classification system organized the natural world."

Contact Information

Yahoo!, Inc.
Santa Clara, California
408-731-3300 (voice)
408-731-3301 (fax)
www.yahoo.com

YAHOO!

The Yahoo Home Page

One of the things you'll come to appreciate about Yahoo is that once you've learned your way around the home page (**Figure 10.1**), chances are that you won't have to relearn where things are anytime soon. Unlike most of the other major search sites, Yahoo settled on the overall organization and "look and feel" for its home page early on, and they're not constantly fiddling with it.

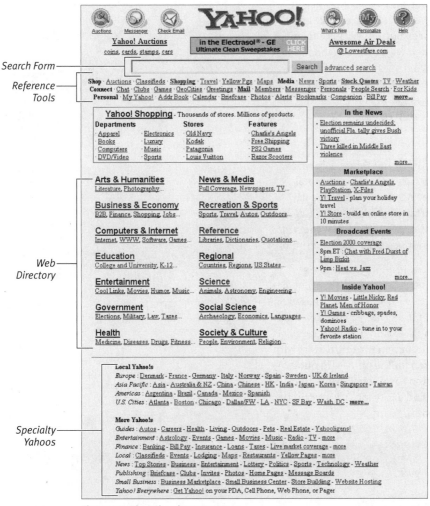

Figure 10.1 The Yahoo home page.

The Yahoo home page is designed not just for searching but as a "portal" page as well—offering news headlines, e-mail services, stock quotes, and so forth. From a searcher's perspective, the most important features to zero in on are the search form and the Web directory.

Here's a quick look at how to use those features, as well as a couple of other search-related tools.

Figure 10.2 The Yahoo search form.

Search form

To search Yahoo, type a word or phrase in the Yahoo search form (**Figure 10.2**) and click on the Search button. Within seconds, you'll be presented with a list of Yahoo topic categories and Web sites that match your request. If no matches are found, Yahoo will display Web pages found in the gigantic Google database of Web pages.

✔ Tips

■ Keep in mind that the Yahoo database is a *directory* rather than a traditional search engine database. Consequently, Yahoo doesn't index the full text of Web pages. Its database includes just the site's topic category, title, and a brief description.

■ To increase the likelihood of finding matches in the Yahoo (rather than Google) database, start with search terms based on the general subject that you're interested in. For example, to find manufacturers of antique reproduction furniture, start with a Yahoo search for the phrase (in quotes) "reproduction furniture". More than likely, you'll find a category with a number of possible sites.

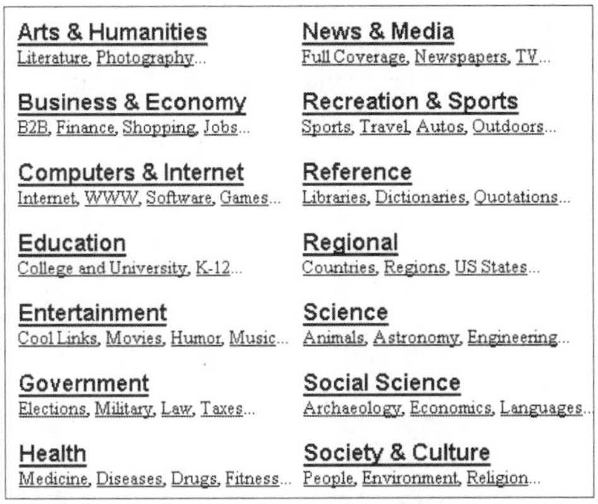
Arts & Humanities
Literature, Photography...
News & Media
Full Coverage, Newspapers, TV...
Business & Economy
B2B, Finance, Shopping, Jobs...
Recreation & Sports
Sports, Travel, Autos, Outdoors...
Computers & Internet
Internet, WWW, Software, Games...
Reference
Libraries, Dictionaries, Quotations...
Education
College and University, K-12...
Regional
Countries, Regions, US States...
Entertainment
Cool Links, Movies, Humor, Music...
Science
Animals, Astronomy, Engineering...
Government
Elections, Military, Law, Taxes...
Social Science
Archaeology, Economics, Languages...
Health
Medicine, Diseases, Drugs, Fitness...
Society & Culture
People, Environment, Religion...

Figure 10.3 Yahoo's Web directory categorizes sites into the 14 broad subject areas shown here.

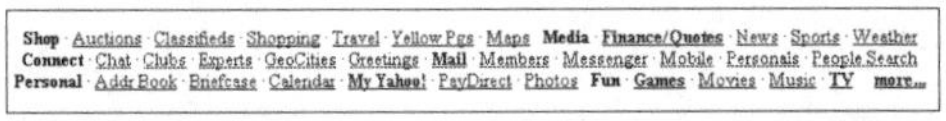
Shop · Auctions · Classifieds · Shopping · Travel · Yellow Pgs · Maps Media · Finance/Quotes · News · Sports · Weather
Connect · Chat · Clubs · Experts · GeoCities · Greetings · Mail · Members · Messenger · Mobile · Personals · People Search
Personal · Addr Book · Briefcase · Calendar · My Yahoo! · PayDirect · Photos Fun · Games · Movies · Music · TV more...

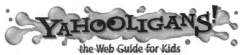

Figure 10.4 These reference tools on the Yahoo home page can help you find the answers to many common search questions.

YAHOOLIGANS!
the Web Guide for Kids

Figure 10.5 Yahooligans Web Guide for Kids is one of many specialized versions of the Yahoo search service, all accessible from links on the home page.

Web directory

When you simply want to explore what the Web has to offer on a rather broad topic, use the Web directory (**Figure 10.3**). Click on one of the 14 major topic categories and then work your way through the subcategories, moving from general to more specific information.

When you find a category that looks promising, you have the option of continuing to "drill down" further into the directory. Or you can do another keyword search of just that particular category.

Other search-related tools

If you decide to use Yahoo on a regular basis, there are two other search-related features on the home page that you'll want to explore and become familiar with:

- **Reference Tools**. Sometimes the fastest way to find a particular type of information is to use a specialized tool. Yahoo offers a collection of them (**Figure 10.4**) right below the search form. You'll find a shopping directory, business yellow pages, people-finding tools, maps and driving directions, classifieds and personals, daily news headlines, stock quotes, local weather and TV listings, sports scores, and more.
- **Specialty Yahoos**. The Yahoo home page also offers links for country-specific versions of its search service, regional directories for U.S. cities, and special Yahoo guides on subjects like autos, careers, personal finance, and real estate. There's also a link for Yahooligans, a version of the Yahoo search service designed just for kids (**Figure 10.5**).

continues on next page

✔ Tips

- You can tailor Yahoo to your personal interests and information needs by clicking on the Personalize link (**Figure 10.6**) at the top of the Yahoo home page. For more on this feature, see the section on "Customizing Yahoo" later in this chapter.

- To make Yahoo your default home page, follow the instructions for "Customizing Your Web Browser" in Chapter 4.

- To get back to the Yahoo home page at any time, click on the Yahoo logo that appears at the top of most pages, or look for the Yahoo! or Home link.

Figure 10.6 Click on the Personalize link in the Yahoo navigation bar to create your own customized version of the Yahoo home page.

```
+"music boxes" +collectible     [ Search ]
```

Figure 10.7 To do an AND search, put a plus sign (+) in front of each word or phrase.

Yahoo! Category Matches (1 - 1 of 1)

Business and Economy > Shopping and Services > Antiques and Collectibles > Mechanical Musical Instruments
  • Music Boxes

Yahoo! Site Matches (1 - 19 of 34)

Regional > U.S. States > Arizona > Cities > Phoenix > Business and Shopping > Shopping and Services > Antiques and Collectibles
  • Sorrento Music Boxes - offers Italian inlaid **music boxes**, jewelry boxes, and musical Capodimonte carousels.

Business and Economy > Shopping and Services > Antiques and Collectibles > Mechanical Musical Instruments
  • Mechantiques - dealer in antique mechanical musical instruments. Including disc or cylinder type **music boxes**, musical clocks, nickelodeons and more. Buy, sell, trade.
  • Mechanical Musical Memories - **music boxes**, phonographs, nickelodeons, player pianos, and band organs.

Business and Economy > Shopping and Services > Antiques and Collectibles > Books > Booksellers > Recreation and Sports > Antiques and Collectibles
  • Arlington Book Co. - specializes in books on barometers, clocks, fountain pens, furniture, jewelry, **music boxes**, tools, trademarks, watches, wristwatches, and related subjects.

Figure 10.8 Here's an example of how Yahoo presents search results. Category Matches come first, followed by Site Matches.

Web Page Matches (1 - 20 of about 802)

  • Collectible Music Boxes
    Collectible Music Boxes (Page 1 of 1). Item #. Description. Price. cmb-1 Picture. The box is in good ...
    http://www.tias.com/stores/lt/cmb-1.html [More results from www.tias.com]

  • Collectible Glass **MUSIC BOXES**
    myevents468. fis1.gif (46499 bytes). Glass MUSICAL BOXES. logo.jpg (3883 bytes). WEB BROWSER'S COLLECTION ...
    http://www.sell-free.com/WBC/glass_musicals.html

  • music boxes
    ... boxes. The Man The Moon. unique **music boxes**. Beautiful and unique **music boxes** certainly
    are highly **collectible**. These **music boxes** are expertly crafted and some ...
    http://www.themaninthemoon.com/musicbox.html [More results from www.themaninthemoon.com]

  • Bidder's Edge - Search Results for "All items in **Collectible** ...
    ... Search Results: All items in **Collectible Music Boxes**, Collectibles > Music Boxes, Matching Categories: click on a category to narrow your search, ...
    http://www.biddersedge.com/search.jsp?c=1363 [More results from www.biddersedge.com]

Figure 10.9 Web Page Matches (contrasted with Site Matches) come from the Google database. The terminology is a bit confusing at first, but you'll get the hang of it.

Searching with Yahoo

Now let's try an actual Yahoo search to see how it works and how the search results are presented. Start by going to the Yahoo home page (www.yahoo.com).

To search with Yahoo:

1. Type a word or phrase in the Yahoo search form (**Figure 10.7**) and click on the Search button to submit it.

   Yahoo ignores the words AND, OR, and NOT. Therefore, to do an AND search, put a plus sign (+) directly in front of each word or phrase you want to include in your search results.

   For OR searches, type each word or phrase separated by a space.

   For NOT searches, put a minus sign (-) in front of the word or phrase you want to exclude.

   Phrases should be enclosed in double quotes.

2. Yahoo will search its database for both topic categories and Web sites that match your query. Category Matches (if any) will be listed first, followed by Site Matches (**Figure 10.8**). Your search terms will be displayed in bold to make them easier to spot.

3. If Yahoo doesn't find any matching categories or Web sites in its database, it will automatically display matches from the Google database (**Figure 10.9**). Yahoo refers to these results as Web Page Matches (contrasted with Site Matches or Web Sites, which both refer to sites in the Yahoo database).

continues on next page

4. To explore any category or Web site on the results page, simply click on it. Web site links, of course, take you directly to the site. Category links take you to the next level down in the Yahoo Web directory, where you're given a chance to do another search or explore more links.

5. If you choose to do another search while you're on a category page, you have the option of limiting it to the category you're currently exploring. Simply key in one or more search terms and click on the radio button labeled just this category (**Figure 10.10**).

6. To look for news articles or Internet events that match your search request, go back to the results page and click Related News or Events in the menu bar (**Figure 10.11**).

✔ Tips

■ Plain-English queries aren't recommended with Yahoo. You're more likely to find Category Matches and Site Matches if you limit your Yahoo queries to a couple of words or phrases rather than a complete question.

■ Case doesn't count with Yahoo, so you can use uppercase, lowercase, or a combination when you type your queries in the Yahoo search form and you'll get the same results.

■ To search the Yahoo directory for recently added categories and Web sites, click on the link for advanced search on the Yahoo home page, enter your query, and use the drop-down menu to select a timeframe ranging from one day to four years.

Figure 10.10 Yahoo gives you the option of limiting your directory search to the category you're currently exploring, a neat feature that comes in handy for refining a query.

Figure 10.11 The menu bar on the results page allows you to direct your search to Yahoo's database of news articles and Internet events.

Figure 10.12 This tutorial, available at howto.yahoo.com, does a great job of introducing new users to the Internet and Yahoo searching.

■ Yahoo allows two types of field searching: titles and URLs. To limit your search to the titles of Web pages, use t: followed by a word or phrase t:"Victorian furniture", for example, to find Web pages with the phrase *Victorian furniture* in the title. The term u:antiques would find sites with the word *antiques* in the URL.

■ For wildcard searches, type at least three letters of the word followed by an asterisk: classic*, for example, would find references to *classic*, *classics*, and *classical*. (Yahoo doesn't support the use of asterisks at the beginning or in the middle of a word.)

■ If you create a search that you expect to run again periodically, you might want to save it using Yahoo's Saved Searches feature. For more on this feature, see "Customizing Yahoo" later in this chapter.

■ For a summary of Yahoo search commands and syntax, see the Yahoo Quick Reference (**Table 10.1**).

■ For Yahoo's online help information, click on the Help link located at the top of the Yahoo home page and on all search results pages. Or go to howto.yahoo.com, where you'll find a delightful "Tutorial for Web Surfers" (**Figure 10.12**). The tutorial includes search tips, an Internet glossary, sample searches, and more.

Table 10.1

Yahoo Quick Reference		
FOR THIS TYPE OF SEARCH:	DO THIS:	EXAMPLES:
Plain-English Question	Not recommended.	
Phrase Search	Type the phrase as a sequence of words surrounded by **double quotes.**	`"Russian lacquer boxes"`
AND Search (multiple words and phrases, each of which must be present)	Use a **plus sign (+)** in front of a word or phrase that *must* appear in the results.	`+antiques +Victorian`
OR Search (multiple words and phrases, any one of which may be present)	Type words or phrases separated by a space, without any special notation.	`eggs "Carl Faberge"`
NOT Search (to exclude a word or phrase)	Use a **minus sign (-)** in front of a word or phrase you want to exclude from your results. To find software Easter eggs, for example, you might want to exclude the word *Fabergé*.	`"Easter eggs" -Faberge`
Case-Sensitive Search	Not available.	
Date Search	Not available. However, you *can* search for categories and Web sites that have been added to the Yahoo directory within a certain time frame.	
	To do that, click on `advanced search` on the Yahoo home page and use the drop-down menu to select a timeframe (1 day to 4 years).	
Field Search	To search titles of Web page documents, use **t :** directly in front of a word or phrase.	`t:"oriental rugs"`
	To search Web page URLs, use **u :** directly in front of the word you want to find. To search for multiple words, use multiple u: search terms with **plus signs (+).**	`u:carpeting` `+u:oriental +u:rug`
Nested Search	Not available.	
Proximity Search	Not available.	
Wildcard Search	Use an **asterisk (*)** with at least the first three letters of your search term. The example would find references to *lacquer* as well as *lacquered* and *lacquerware*.	`lacq*`
	(Note: You *cannot* search for wildcard characters at the beginning or in the middle of a word.)	

Figure 10.13 Yahoo's Search Options page offers several "advanced search" features not available on the home page.

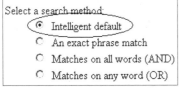

Figure 10.14 Click *advanced search* on the Yahoo home page to get to the Search Options page.

Figure 10.15 Leave the search method set to Intelligent default to search just as you would on the Yahoo home page, using +/- signs to include/exclude words and double quotes for phrases.

Using Advanced Search

Yahoo offers a second search form on what it calls the Search Options page (**Figure 10.13**). This form gives you three "advanced search" capabilities not available on the Yahoo home page:

◆ You can limit your search of the Yahoo directory to categories or Web sites added within a specified time frame ranging from one day to four years.

◆ You can change the number of matches that are displayed on each page of your search results following the initial summary page.

◆ You can specify that you want to search Usenet newsgroup postings rather than the Yahoo directory.

Let's take at look at how you might use the form on the Search Options page to search the Yahoo directory and Usenet postings.

To search the Yahoo directory:

1. Go to the Yahoo home page (www.yahoo.com) and click on the advanced search link (**Figure 10.14**) to the right of the Search button.

2. Type your query in the search box, just as you would on the Yahoo home page, and select a search method (**Figure 10.15**). If you leave the search method set to Intelligent default, you can use double quotes to indicate a phrase search and plus and minus signs to include (+) or exclude (-) terms. Alternatively, you can use one of the other settings to do a phrase, AND, or OR search, in which case you don't need to use any special punctuation.

continues on next page

3. If you want to limit your search to Web sites (rather than categories) in the Yahoo directory, click on the Web Sites radio button (**Figure 10.16**). To search both categories *and* Web sites, leave the search area set to Yahoo Categories.

4. To restrict your search to categories or sites that have been added to the Yahoo directory within a certain time frame, use the drop-down menu (**Figure 10.17**) to select from choices ranging from one day to four years.

5. Finally, if you want to change the number of matches displayed per page, use the drop-down menu (**Figure 10.18**) to choose a number from 10 to 100. The new setting applies only after the first page of results. (The layout for the first page is fixed.)

6. Click on the Search button to submit your query.

Figure 10.16
Use the Web Sites radio button if you prefer not to have Yahoo Categories included in your results.

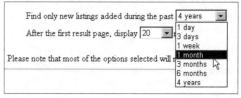

Figure 10.17 This menu lets you limit your search to categories and Web sites added to the Yahoo directory within a certain time frame.

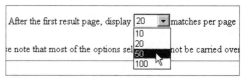

Figure 10.18 Yahoo typically displays search results 20 to a page, but this menu lets you increase the number to 100.

Figure 10.19 You can search newsgroups from the Search Options page by clicking on the Usenet radio button.

To search Usenet newsgroups:

1. Type your query in the search form and click on the Usenet radio button (**Figure 10.19**.)

2. Then click on the Search button and your query will be directed to a database of newsgroup postings maintained by Deja (www.deja.com).

   For more sophisticated searches of Usenet newsgroup postings, see Chapter 15 on Deja and its newsgroup search offerings.

✔ Tips

- ■ The options for search method, time frame, and results per page don't apply to Usenet searches.

- ■ For a summary of Yahoo search commands and syntax, see the Yahoo Quick Reference (Table 10.1) presented earlier in this chapter. The same rules apply to using the search forms on the Yahoo home page and the Search Options page.

- ■ For additional search tips and examples, click Search Tips or Advanced Search Syntax in the menu bar on the Search Options page.

Using Yahoo's Web Directory

As we've said before, when it comes to organizing the Web by topic, Yahoo has set the standard. All the major engines offer Web directories of some sort, often provided by third parties like the Open Directory or LookSmart. But Yahoo offers three advantages over most of its competitors:

◆ You can simultaneously search both its human-compiled Web directory and a gigantic database of more than a billion Web pages, and the combined results will be presented to you in a well-organized and readable format.

◆ You can easily avoid (or zero in on) business or shopping Web sites, or sites that are of regional interest, because Yahoo makes a distinction in its directory between commercial *vs.* non-commercial sites, and between sites that are of global interest *vs.* those that are only relevant to a specific geographic region.

◆ If you find a category in the Yahoo directory that looks promising, you can search again within just that category to find the exact information that you're after.

Think of Yahoo's directory as an incredibly detailed outline of what's available on the Web. And the outline itself, as well as a 25-word description of each site, can be searched. So you can usually zero in on just the information you need, without having to wade through descriptions of hundreds, if not thousands, of irrelevant sites.

The best way to understand what we're talking about is to simply go to the Yahoo home page (www.yahoo.com) and choose a category from the Web directory (**Figure 10.20**). Then explore (or "drill down") through the resulting pages that offer subtopics and sub-subtopics of greater and greater specificity.

Arts & Humanities Literature, Photography...	**News & Media** Full Coverage, Newspapers, TV...
Business & Economy B2B, Finance, Shopping, Jobs...	**Recreation & Sports** Sports, Travel, Autos, Outdoors...
Computers & Internet Internet, WWW, Software, Games...	**Reference** Libraries, Dictionaries, Quotations...
Education College and University, K-12...	**Regional** Countries, Regions, US States...
Entertainment Cool Links, Movies, Humor, Music...	**Science** Animals, Astronomy, Engineering...
Government Elections, Military, Law, Taxes...	**Social Science** Archaeology, Economics, Languages...
Health Medicine, Diseases, Drugs, Fitness...	**Society & Culture** People, Environment, Religion...

Figure 10.20 Yahoo's Web directory is organized into 14 major topic categories.

Categories

- Business to Business *(258921)* NEW!
- Shopping and Services *(354306)* NEW!

- Business Libraries *(20)*
- Business Schools@
- Chats and Forums *(24)*
- Classifieds *(3631)* NEW!
- Consortia *(42)*
- Consumer Advocacy and Information@
- Conventions and Conferences *(37)*
- Cooperatives *(24)*
- Directories *(342)* NEW!
- Economics@
- Education *(807)* NEW!
- Electronic Commerce *(202)* NEW!
- Employment and Work *(1706)* NEW!
- Ethics and Responsibility *(44)*
- Finance and Investment *(1648)* NEW!
- Global Economy *(269)*
- History *(21)*

- Intellectual Property@
- Labor *(716)* NEW!
- Law@
- Magazines *(127)*
- Management Science *(193)* NEW!
- Marketing and Advertising *(329)*
- News and Media@
- Organizations *(11762)* NEW!
- Quality Standards@
- Real Estate *(365)* NEW!
- Small Business Information *(290)*
- Statistics and Indicators *(5)*
- Taxes@
- Television@
- Trade *(416)*
- Transportation *(2038)* NEW!

Figure 10.21 Here's what you see when you click on Business & Economy in the Yahoo Web directory—almost two dozen subtopics, presented alphabetically.

- **Business Libraries** *(20)*
- **Business Schools@**
- **Chats and Forums** *(24)*
- **Classifieds** *(3631)* NEW!
- **Consortia** *(42)*

Figure 10.22 The numbers in parentheses show how many Web sites are in that subtopic. The @ symbol indicates a cross-reference. Recently added categories are marked *NEW!*

Counsel By Request - temporary and permanent attorney staffing for law firms and companies in the Greater New York City area.

Figure 10.23 The Web site descriptions in the Yahoo directory are brief but informative.

Most Popular Sites

- German Academic Exchange Service (DAAD) - organizes international exchange for students, professors, researchers, scholarships and funding.
- Gates Millennium Scholars - a 20-year plan to provide financial assistance to high-achieving minority students who are in severe financial need and otherwise would be excluded from higher education.
- Siemens Foundation - awards students who show excellence in science and mathematics.
- Rhodes Scholarship Trust - official site for information from the American Secretary of the Rhodes Scholarship Trust.
- College Fund/UNCF - an educational assistance organization with 40 private, historically black, member colleges and universities.
- International Education Financial Aid - provides a searchable database of scholarship information.

Figure 10.24 For categories with a large number of Web sites, Yahoo often provides guidance on the ones that are most popular.

To browse the Web by topic:

1. Click on one of the 14 topic categories on the Yahoo home page (www.yahoo.com) to display the subtopics for that category (**Figure 10.21**), along with some helpful information about each one (**Figure 10.22**):

   The **numbers in parentheses** tell you how many entries are categorized under a particular subtopic.

   An **@ symbol** means that the topic's primary location is located elsewhere in the Yahoo directory. (Clicking on one of these links will take you to the topic's primary location.)

   The word *NEW!* (highlighted in yellow) identifies topic categories that have been added recently to the Yahoo Web directory. Yahoo's 14 main topics haven't changed in some time, but new subtopics and sub-subtopics are being added all the time.

2. As you work your way down through the Yahoo directory, you'll eventually reach a page that includes a set of links for specific Web sites, presented alphabetically, along with a brief description of each one (**Figure 10.23**). Written by each site's owner or creator and approved by Yahoo editors, these descriptions will give you a quick handle on the nature and purpose of the Web site—something you don't always get when you use a search engine whose database is created by a spider or crawler program.

3. If the list includes an exceptionally large number of Web sites, it will often be preceded by a section labeled "Most Popular Sites" (**Figure 10.24**).

   continues on next page

4. You may also encounter a section called "Inside Yahoo!" (**Figure 10.25**), which includes links for message boards, clubs, special events, and subject matter created and maintained by Yahoo itself.

5. A pair of sunglasses (**Figure 10.26**) is used to identify Web sites that Yahoo editors consider to be "especially noteworthy resources" in their particular subject areas. Only non-commercial sites qualify for the sunglasses designation.

   Why sunglasses? It only makes sense if you know that, in the early Yahoo days, sites were chosen to "wear the sunglasses" because they were considered to be "cool."

6. As you're working your way through the Yahoo directory, you can stop at any point and perform a search, using a form (**Figure 10.27**) that allows you to specify whether you want to search all of Yahoo! or just this category that you're currently exploring.

✔ Tips

- If you have a subject in mind but aren't sure what topic to choose from the Yahoo Web directory, do a search first. For example, type collectibles in the Yahoo search form and you'll be presented with categories within four major topics in the Web directory: Business & Economy, Entertainment, Recreation, and Regional.

- As you move around the Yahoo directory, the category you're exploring will always be presented at the top of the page, with each subtopic separated by a greater-than symbol (>) (**Figure 10.28**). You can go directly to any subtopic by simply clicking on it.

Inside Yahoo!

- **Yahoo! Small Business** - features, news, how-to, tools, and more.
- Join a Chat, Start or Join a Club   • Live Net Events
- Post a Message   • Classifieds

Figure 10.25 Topic-related features created by Yahoo are presented in a section of the results page called "Inside Yahoo!"

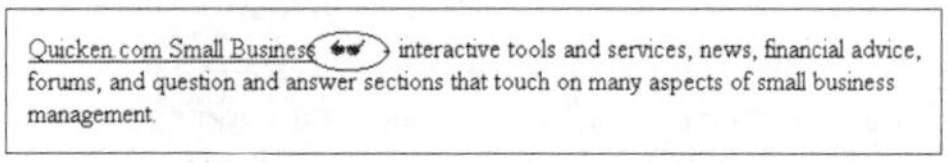

Figure 10.26 Yahoo uses the sunglasses icon to call your attention to exceptionally good (i.e. "cool") Web sites.

Figure 10.27 We've chosen to look for our search phrase in the "Conventions and Conferences" subtopic instead of the entire Yahoo directory.

Figure 10.28 Yahoo helps you keep track of where you are in the directory by displaying your location. To go back to, say, Antiques and Collectibles, click on its link.

Welcome to My Yahoo!

Figure 10.29 My Yahoo is a customized version of the Yahoo home page, tailored to your particular interests.

Figure 10.30 Use the Personalize link on the Yahoo home page to access My Yahoo.

Figure 10.31 Signing up for My Yahoo involves choosing an ID and password. Note that capitalization matters for your password!

Customizing Yahoo

If you like Yahoo and decide to make it your primary search tool, how about creating your own special version of the Yahoo home page, tailored to your personal interests and information needs? That's what My Yahoo (**Figure 10.29**) is all about.

You can't change anything having to do with the way Yahoo searches and displays your results. But once you've signed up for My Yahoo—by selecting a user ID and password and providing some personal information—you can control the content, layout, and color scheme for the Yahoo home page.

More importantly, you can take advantage of three search-related features not available on the Yahoo home page:

◆ **Saved Searches**. Allows you to save frequently used searches and run them again with a single click.

◆ **News Clipper**. Similar to Saved Searches, but instead of running your query against the directory of Web sites, you'll be searching Yahoo's database of news articles.

◆ **Web Site Tracker**. Alerts you to the latest additions to your favorite categories in the Yahoo directory.

To customize Yahoo:

1. Click on the Personalize link (**Figure 10.30**) at the top of the Yahoo home page.

2. Then click Sign me up! and complete the form (**Figure 10.31**). You'll be asked to choose a user ID and password and to provide some personal information—name, birth date, e-mail address, zip code, gender, occupation, and industry affiliation.

continues on next page

One word of warning on selecting your My Yahoo password: case counts! So whatever combination of uppercase and lowercase letters you use when you select your password, that's what Yahoo will expect when you access your My Yahoo page.

3. Once you've completed the questionnaire and submitted the information, continue on to your new My Yahoo page, which you can now personalize to your liking by clicking on the Content and Layout buttons (**Figure 10.32**).

4. You can display up to 20 features on your My Yahoo page. To add a feature, click on the box next to it so that a check mark appears (**Figure 10.33**). If you change your mind, click again and the check mark will disappear. Once you've selected the features you want (and removed the ones you don't want), click Finished.

5. The next step is to tailor things further by using the Edit button that appears with each feature. For example, if you've chosen to include Saved Searches on your My Yahoo page, click on its Edit button (**Figure 10.34**) to access the form that allows you to create and save a query. Then click on Finished. (The News Clipper feature works the same way.)

Once you've added a search to Saved Searches (or News Clipper), you can run it from your My Yahoo page by simply clicking on it (**Figure 10.35**).

Figure 10.32 You can personalize both the content and layout of your My Yahoo page using these buttons.

Figure 10.33 Saved Searches is one of many features you can add to your My Yahoo page.

Figure 10.34 Click Edit to further customize a feature (in this case, Saved Searches) on your My Yahoo page.

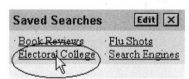

Figure 10.35 Having edited Saved Searches to include several queries, we can run any one by simply clicking on it.

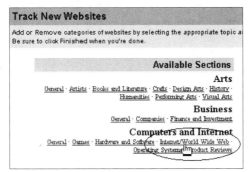

Figure 10.36 To track the addition of new Yahoo categories and Web sites dealing with the Internet, click on that link on the Web Site Tracker page.

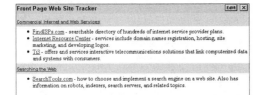

Figure 10.37 Web Site Tracker has identified four new sites in the Yahoo directory dealing with the Internet and Web searching.

6. To track new Web sites in a particular category, add the Web Site Tracker feature to your My Yahoo page and then click on its Edit link to display the list of available topics (**Figure 10.36**). Make your selections and then click Finished.

   If new Web sites have been added recently to your chosen Web Site Tracker categories, you'll see them immediately on your My Yahoo page (**Figure 10.37**). If not, the Web Site Tracker section will be empty—you won't even see the category names. Rest assured, however, that the categories *will* be tracked (and new Web sites displayed) until you choose to remove them.

7. To make My Yahoo your browser's default home page, use its complete address (http://my.yahoo.com) when you specify your home page or startup location. For specific instructions, see the section in Chapter 4 called "Customizing Your Web Browser."

✔ Tips

■ You can switch back and forth between the standard Yahoo home page and your personalized page using the links for Yahoo! (to get back to standard Yahoo from your personalized page) and My Yahoo! (to get to your personal page from the Yahoo home page).

■ If you have trouble setting up your personalized version of Yahoo, click on Help at the top of the My Yahoo page for step-by-step instructions and answers to frequently asked questions.

CUSTOMIZING YAHOO

PART 3

OTHER GENERAL-PURPOSE SEARCH ENGINES

Other General-Purpose Search Engines

In Part 2 we introduced you to six of the very best search engines and showed you how to use them to maximum advantage. In our view, you could pick any two of these "Big Six" engines, learn their ins and outs, and henceforth rely on them almost exclusively whenever you need to find information on the Web.

There *are* other options, however. In this part of the book, we'll tell you about the search capabilities offered by four of the most popular Internet portal sites:

- ◆ **America Online (AOL)**
- ◆ **Excite**
- ◆ **Microsoft Network (MSN)**
- ◆ **Netscape**

If you're currently using AOL, Excite, MSN, or Netscape as your gateway to the Internet— and you're generally happy with the services the site offers—read the relevant chapter in this part of the book to learn how to search more effectively. Then choose at least one of the Big Six engines in Part 2 to use as a backup when you can't find what you're looking for with your primary search engine.

If you're *not* wedded to any of these portal sites and are simply "shopping around" for a couple of good search engines, skip this part of the book completely and make your selections from the Big Six engines described in Part 2. The search features offered by AOL, Excite, MSN, and Netscape are adequate, but they're no match for the Big Six.

✔ Tip

- ■ If you haven't done so already, be sure to read the chapters on search basics in Part 1 of this book. The next four chapters include references to search techniques and terminology that are explained in more detail in Part 1.

AOL SEARCH

Good to Know

- AOL Search is the default search engine for America Online (AOL).

- Its main benefit is that it allows you to search both the Web and AOL's proprietary content—assuming you're an AOL subscriber.

- If you're *not* a subscriber, you can use AOL Search, but your results will be limited to information found on the Web.

- AOL Search's Web results come from the Open Directory Project, supplemented by Inktomi's relatively small 110-million-page database.

- You can use Boolean operators and wildcards in your queries, but AOL Search offers little else in the way of "power search" features.

AOL Search is the creation of America Online (AOL), the world's largest online service. If you're one of AOL's 28 million subscribers—and you use the service not only for Internet access but also for its special proprietary content—you'll definitely want to learn some AOL Search basics. Why? It's the only search engine that allows you to simultaneously explore both the Web *and* AOL content.

Unfortunately, that's about all AOL Search has going for it. The search tools it offers leave a lot to be desired—a full assortment of Boolean operators, but little else to help you focus your queries. And the Inktomi database that it relies on to supplement its Web directory is the smallest of the top search engines covered in this book.

Another major complaint we have about AOL Search is that its search results page, though nicely organized, is very poorly documented. Unlike most of its competitors, AOL Search provides no explanation of what is meant by "Recommended Sites" or "Most Popular Sites." Nor do they explain the distinction between "Matching Sites" and "Matching Web Pages."

Our advice, therefore, is this:

◆ **If you're *not* an AOL subscriber.**
Don't bother reading this chapter. There's
simply no point in even considering AOL
Search as an option for finding information on the Web. Choose instead from
among the "Big Six" engines covered in
Part 2 of this book, or the other general-
purpose engines described in Part 3.

◆ **If you *are* an AOL subscriber.** Read on!
In just a few short pages, we'll tell you
what you need to know in order to use
AOL Search to best advantage. We'll also
try to shed a bit of light on exactly what
it is that you're searching, and how to
interpret AOL's confusing terminology
on the search results page.

As you may recall from the chapters in
Part 1 of this book, it's important—no matter
which search engine you use most of the
time—to have one or two others that you can
fall back on for a "second opinion." That goes
double for AOL Search, because its database
is so small (relative to others) and its search
tools are so limited.

AOL SEARCH

Contact Information

America Online (AOL)
Dulles, Virginia
703-265-1000 (voice)
703-918-1400 (fax)
www.aol.com (AOL portal)
search.aol.com (AOL Search)

Table 11.1

How AOL Search Stacks Up Against the Leading Search Engines

SEARCH ENGINE	NUMBER OF WEB PAGES INDEXED
Google	1.2 billion
Netscape Search (powered by Google)	1.2 billion
Yahoo (powered by Google)	1.2 billion
Lycos (powered by FAST)	575 million
HotBot (powered by Inktomi GEN3)	500 million
AltaVista	350 million
Northern Light	330 million
Excite	250 million
AOL Search (powered by Inktomi)	110 million
MSN Search (powered by Inktomi)	110 million

Note: Search engine sizes are based on figures reported as of January 2001 by Search Engine Watch (www.searchenginewatch.com).

Figure 11.1 You'll find press releases and other information about AOL Time Warner at the company's Web site.

✔ Tips

■ To see how AOL Search measures up against the leading search engines when it comes to database size, see **Table 11.1**.

■ In late 1998, AOL bought Netscape Communications, so AOL Search and Netscape Search are now owned by the same company.

■ For news and information about AOL and its parent company, AOL Time Warner, visit www.aoltimewarner.com/press (**Figure 11.1**).

AOL SEARCH

The AOL Search Home Page

Nicely designed and refreshingly clutter-free, the AOL Search home page (**Figure 11.2**) provides you with three different ways of finding information. You can search the Web by entering a query in a very basic search form, browse the Web by topic, or use a set of specialized tools for some of the most common day-to-day search tasks.

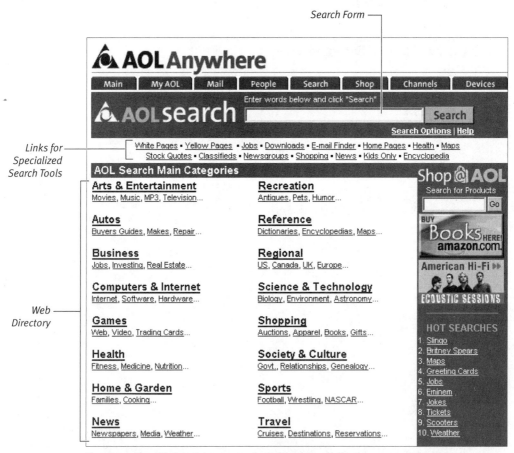

Figure 11.2 The AOL Search home page looks like this, whether you access it via AOL or the Web.

Figure 11.3 AOL subscribers can use the AOL toolbar's Internet/Search the Web option to get to the AOL Search home page.

Figure 11.4 There's nothing complicated about the AOL Search form—just type your query in the text box and click the Search button.

As mentioned previously, anyone with Internet access can use AOL Search, which is located on the Web at search.aol.com. Subscribers to AOL's online service can also get to the AOL Search home page by signing on to AOL and then clicking the toolbar's Internet/Search the Web option (**Figure 11.3**).

Search form

The search form for AOL Search (**Figure 11.4**) includes a box for entering your query and a Search button to submit it. AOL Search defaults to doing an AND search, looking for *all* the words and phrases you type, so it's not necessary to use plus signs (+) or the Boolean operator AND, but you can if you wish. (AOL Search supports a full range of Boolean operators, including proximity operators and parentheses for nested searches.)

✔ Tip

■ AOL Search automatically looks for your search words in both AOL content and the Web. But what if you want to limit your search to one or the other?

You might try the Search Options link, right below the Search button. It takes you to a page offering "Where should we look?" radio buttons for AOL Only or On the Web Only. Unfortunately, it doesn't seem to work. We did more than a dozen "AOL Only" searches for features that we know AOL offers (games, horoscopes, and photography, among others), and got "no results found" messages every time.

THE AOL SEARCH HOME PAGE

Web directory

AOL Search's Web directory (**Figure 11.5**) comes from the Open Directory Project (dmoz.org), a human-compiled guide to the best Web sites, organized in outline fashion, with 16 main topics and hundreds of subtopics and sub-subtopics. You can click on any topic (or subtopic) that appears on the AOL Search home page and then "drill down" through the various levels of the directory (**Figure 11.6**) to locate Web sites that might be of interest.

✔ Tips

- Unlike Yahoo (www.yahoo.com), AOL Search doesn't give you the option of limiting your search to topic categories in the Web directory. But it *does* include matching Web-directory topic categories in your search results.

- The Open Directory Project is owned by AOL, which acquired it along with Netscape Communications in 1998. Despite the change in ownership, the process for building the directory remains the same— volunteer editors from around the world who are knowledgeable on a particular topic take responsibility for reviewing Web sites and selecting the best ones for inclusion in the directory.

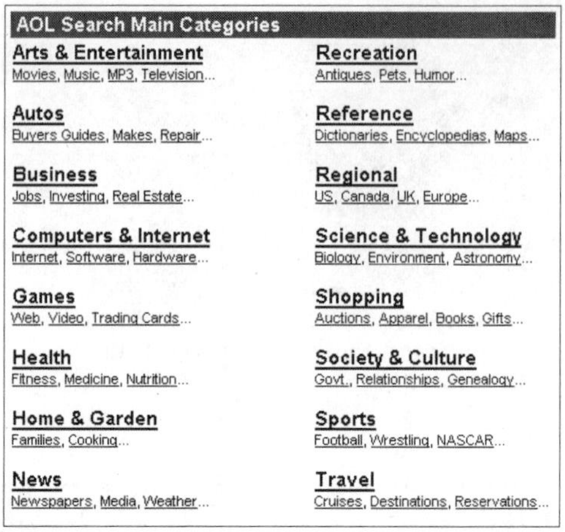

AOL Search Main Categories

Arts & Entertainment	**Recreation**
Movies, Music, MP3, Television...	Antiques, Pets, Humor...
Autos	**Reference**
Buyers Guides, Makes, Repair...	Dictionaries, Encyclopedias, Maps...
Business	**Regional**
Jobs, Investing, Real Estate...	US, Canada, UK, Europe...
Computers & Internet	**Science & Technology**
Internet, Software, Hardware...	Biology, Environment, Astronomy...
Games	**Shopping**
Web, Video, Trading Cards...	Auctions, Apparel, Books, Gifts...
Health	**Society & Culture**
Fitness, Medicine, Nutrition...	Govt., Relationships, Genealogy...
Home & Garden	**Sports**
Families, Cooking...	Football, Wrestling, NASCAR...
News	**Travel**
Newspapers, Media, Weather...	Cruises, Destinations, Reservations...

Figure 11.5 The Web directory is organized into 16 main categories, shown here in bold.

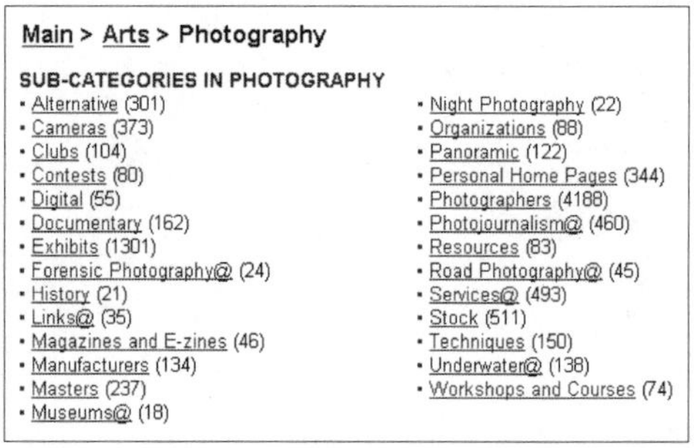

Main > Arts > Photography

SUB-CATEGORIES IN PHOTOGRAPHY
- Alternative (301)
- Cameras (373)
- Clubs (104)
- Contests (80)
- Digital (55)
- Documentary (162)
- Exhibits (1301)
- Forensic Photography@ (24)
- History (21)
- Links@ (35)
- Magazines and E-zines (46)
- Manufacturers (134)
- Masters (237)
- Museums@ (18)
- Night Photography (22)
- Organizations (88)
- Panoramic (122)
- Personal Home Pages (344)
- Photographers (4188)
- Photojournalism@ (460)
- Resources (83)
- Road Photography@ (45)
- Services@ (493)
- Stock (511)
- Techniques (150)
- Underwater@ (138)
- Workshops and Courses (74)

Figure 11.6 The Arts & Entertainment category includes Photography, which is further broken down into more than two dozen sub-categories. The numbers tell you how many Web sites you'll find by clicking on each link.

Figure 11.7 Often one of these specialized tools can get you the answer you need faster than a regular Web search.

AOLsearch

Figure 11.8 Clicking this logo takes you back to the AOL Search home page.

Specialized search tools

The AOL Search home page includes links for a set of specialized tools that come in handy for everyday search tasks—looking up e-mail addresses and phone numbers in yellow pages and white pages directories, checking stock prices, getting maps and driving directions, locating product information, and so forth (**Figure 11.7**).

✔ Tips

■ To make AOL Search your Web browser's default home page, see "Customizing Your Web Browser" in Chapter 4.

■ You can return to the AOL Search home page at any time by clicking the AOL Search logo (**Figure 11.8**) that appears on every page.

Searching with AOL Search

There are two important points to keep in mind when searching with AOL Search:

◆ AOL's overall goal is to help you find what it considers to be the *best* information related to your search. Consequently, it favors its own proprietary content and Web sites that have been selected by AOL editors (and the Open Directory Project's volunteer subject experts) over Web sites from the spider-created Inktomi database. You won't even be shown Web pages from Inktomi if matches are found in these other sources.

◆ Anyone with Internet access can use AOL Search, but unless you're an AOL subscriber and you have signed in with your screen name and password, you won't be shown AOL content.

To enter a query:

1. If you're an AOL subscriber, sign on to AOL and use the toolbar's Internet/ Search the Web option to go to the AOL Search home page. Subscribers and non-subscribers alike can access the home page by going directly to search.aol.com.

2. Type your query—expressed as a plain-English question or one or more unique keywords—in the search form (**Figure 11.9**). If you type a question, leave off the question mark at the end because that's one of the symbols AOL Search uses for a wildcard character.

3. To look for an exact phrase, enclose the words in double quotes: "digital photography".

Figure 11.9 AOL Search defaults to doing an AND search, so it would interpret a query like this to mean you want to find items with all three words.

4. You can use the Boolean operators AND and OR (uppercase *not* required) to combine words and phrases. AND isn't really necessary, however, because AOL Search defaults to doing an AND search.

You can also use plus signs (+) in front of required words and phrases.

5. If you want to *exclude* a word or phrase from your results, use the Boolean operator NOT: photography NOT fashion.

✔ Tips

■ Instead of going to the AOL Search home page, AOL subscribers can simply enter a query in the AOL navigation bar's text box and click Search to submit it (**Figure 11.10**).

■ AOL Search is *not* case sensitive, so you'll get the same results whether you type your queries in uppercase, lowercase, or a mix of the two.

■ Two types of wildcard characters can be used in AOL Search queries.

To match *multiple* characters anywhere in a word (beginning, middle, or end), use an asterisk: photog* would find references to *photograph*, *photographer*, and *photographic*.

To match a *single* character, use a question mark (?): adapt?r would find references to both *adapter* and *adaptor*. Fran? would find both *Frans* and *Franz*.

Figure 11.10 AOL subscribers don't have to go to the AOL Search page. They can type a query in the AOL navigation bar's text box and click Search to submit it.

To view your search results:

1. Click the Search button (or hit Enter) to submit your query.

2. Your search results (**Figure 11.11**) will be organized into as many as four sections:

   ▲ **Recommended Sites**. The items here include AOL's proprietary content, "official" Web sites for companies and celebrities, and other Web sites selected by AOL's editorial staff.

   ▲ **Sponsored Links**. These are paid listings for sites offering products and services related in some way (often quite loosely) to your search words.

   ▲ **Matching Sites**. Typically the largest section, this includes AOL content and Web sites from the Open Directory Project. You can scroll through the entire list or click the Show Me link for AOL Only or Most Popular Sites (**Figure 11.12**).

   ▲ **Matching Categories**. These are topic categories from the Open Directory Project that may be relevant to your search (**Figure 11.13**).

RECOMMENDED SITES
• **Kodak Digital Cameras** - Find products and compare prices at Shop@AOL

SPONSORED LINKS
The search results below are provided by a third party and are not necessarily endorsed by AOL
• **Shop4tech.com: Kodak DC240 - $369**
• **Don't Buy It Before You PriceSCAN It!**
• **Kodak Digital Sale! at CameraClub.com**

MATCHING SITES
Show Me: AOL and the Web | AOL Only | Most Popular Sites
Results from the WorldWideWeb may contain objectionable material that AOL doesn't endorse.

Kodak Digital Science
The DVC323, Kodak's USB desktop video camera.
http://www.kodak.com/cgi-bin/webCatalog.pl?product=KODA...
Show me more like this

Kodak Digital
Comprehensive guide to digital cameras with how to use guides, price comparisons
http://www.kodak.com/US/en/nav/digital.shtml
Show me more like this

Digital Camera Now
Clear and concise information and reviews about digital cameras.
http://www.digital-camera-now.com
Show me more like this

MATCHING CATEGORIES
1. Computers > Hardware > Peripherals > **Desktop Video Cameras**
2. Arts > Photography > **Digital**
3. Shopping > Photography > **Digital**
4. Arts > Photography > Alternative > **Infrared**
5. Arts > Photography > Cameras > **Advanced Photo System**

Figure 11.11 Here's an example of how AOL Search presents results. You may not be able to read the individual items here, but you'll get a sense of how a typical results page is organized.

MATCHING SITES
Show Me: AOL and the Web | AOL Only | Most Popular Sites

Figure 11.12 You can view a subset of your Matching Sites results by clicking the link for AOL Only or Most Popular Sites.

MATCHING CATEGORIES
1. Computers > Hardware > Peripherals > **Desktop Video Cameras**
2. Arts > Photography > **Digital**
3. Shopping > Photography > **Digital**
4. Arts > Photography > Alternative > **Infrared**
5. Arts > Photography > Cameras > **Advanced Photo System**

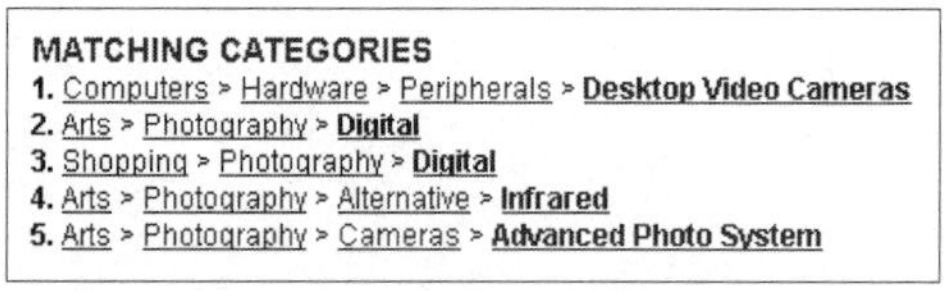

Figure 11.13 Matching Categories come from the Open Directory Project. For recommendations on the best Web sites on a particular topic, just click its link.

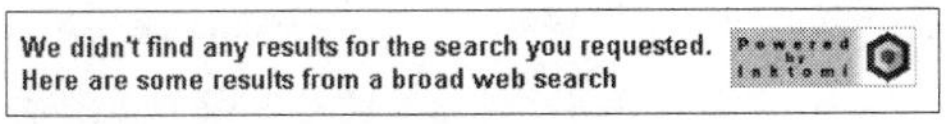

We didn't find any results for the search you requested.
Here are some results from a broad web search

Figure 11.14 AOL Search displays this message to alert you that the results that follow are from the Inktomi database.

Figure 11.15 Click the Web Pages tab to display results from the Inktomi database. (AOL Search uses *Web Sites* to refer to its original set of results and *Web Pages* for results that come from Inktomi.)

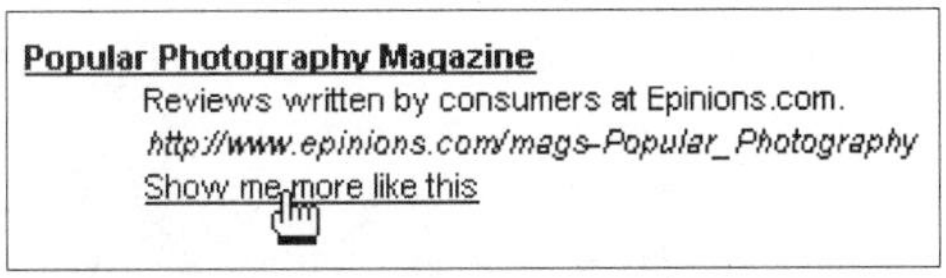

Popular Photography Magazine
   Reviews written by consumers at Epinions.com.
   http://www.epinions.com/mags-Popular_Photography
   Show me more like this

Figure 11.16 Until the technology is perfected, the Show me more like this option is likely to be a waste of time.

In addition to these four sections, your results may include two additional sets of results:

▲ **Matching Web Pages.** These results come from the Inktomi database. They are displayed automatically (**Figure 11.14**) if no results are found for any of the other four sections. Otherwise, you have to click the Web Pages tab (**Figure 11.15**).

▲ **Matching News Articles.** Displayed only if you click the Related News tab that may appear at the top of your search results page, these items come from *The New York Times*, major news wires (Associated Press, Reuters, and Bloomberg), and other news sources.

3. You can visit any item on the search results page by clicking its link.

✔ Tips

■ You can increase the likelihood of being presented with all six categories of AOL Search results by limiting the number of words you type in the search box.

■ The Show me more like this link (**Figure 11.16**) for Web sites on the search results page is a neat idea, but the technology isn't quite there yet. Ask for more sites like the one for *Popular Photography* magazine, for example, and you'll be presented with a list of other magazines starting with the letter *P*.

In most cases, you'll probably have better luck using the Matching Categories section to find similar sites.

■ AOL Search doesn't give you any control over how your results are displayed.

To refine an AOL Search query:

1. One way to refine a query is to simply add another unique keyword or phrase and run the search again. AOL Search looks for *all* the words that you type in the search box, so this has the effect of searching *within* your original results (also referred to as *set searching*).

2. Use the Matching Categories section to get ideas for additional keywords. And remember that you can use Boolean operators (AND, OR, NOT, etc.) to combine words and phrases.

3. Another technique you might try is to look for words in close proximity to one another, which can often cut down considerably on the number of irrelevant hits (**Figure 11.17**). AOL Search supports three different proximity operators: ADJ, NEAR, and W/*n*. See the AOL Search Quick Reference (**Table 11.2**) for examples of each.

✔ Tips

- Don't struggle too much with refining your search. Instead, try another search engine that offers a larger database of Web pages and better tools for refining a query (field searching, case sensitivity, limiting a search to a specific language, etc.). AltaVista, Google, or one of the other "Big Six" engines covered in Part 2 of this book would be a good place to go for a "second opinion."

- For a summary of search rules and examples for AOL Search, see the AOL Search Quick Reference (**Table 11.2**).

- For AOL Search's own help information, click the Help link that appears below the Search button (**Figure 11.18**).

Figure 11.17 A proximity search using the Boolean operator NEAR may produce better results than simply typing kodak digital camera in the search box.

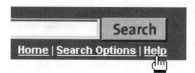

Figure 11.18 To learn more about AOL Search, including new features that may have been added, click the Help link.

Table 11.2

AOL Search Quick Reference		
FOR THIS TYPE OF SEARCH:	**DO THIS:**	**EXAMPLES:**
Plain-English Question	Type a question that expresses the idea or concept, using as many words as necessary. Don't include a question mark, because it may be interpreted as a wildcard character.	Does Norm Abram have a Web site
Phrase Search	Type the phrase enclosed in **double quotes**.	"New Yankee Workshop"
AND Search (multiple words and phrases, each of which *must* be present)	Type words or phrases separated by a space. You can also use the Boolean operator AND (uppercase or lowercase) to connect two or more search terms, or put plus signs (+) directly in front of required search terms. All three examples will produce the same results.	"paint shaver" clapboard "paint shaver" AND clapboard +"paint shaver" +clapboard
OR Search (multiple words and phrases, any one of which may be present)	Use the Boolean operator **OR** (uppercase or lowercase) to combine words and phrases.	woodworking OR cabinetry
NOT Search (to exclude a word or phrase)	Use the Boolean operator **NOT** (uppercase or lowercase) to exclude a word or phrase.	"custom windows" NOT software
Case-Sensitive Search	Not available.	
Date Search	Not available.	
Field Search	Not available.	
Nested Search	Use **parentheses** to group search expressions into more complex queries.	hardware AND (antique OR reproduction)
Proximity Search	AOL Search offers three different proximity operators, which you can type in uppercase or lowercase:	
	ADJ to find words next to each other. The example would find *paint stripping* and *stripping paint*.	paint ADJ stripping
	NEAR or **NEAR**/n to find one search term within a specified distance (*n* is number of words) from another. The example would find *moss* within five words of *roof*.	moss NEAR/5 roof
	W/n to find one search term within a specified distance (*n* is number of words) *after* another. The example would find *roof* within three words after *moss*.	moss W/3 roof
Wildcard Search	Use an **asterisk (*)** to match *multiple* characters anywhere in a word (beginning, middle, or end). The example would find *cabinetmaker*, *cabinetry*, and *cabinets*.	cabinet*
	Use a **question mark (?)** to match a *single* character.	"anders?n windows"

EXCITE

Like many successful high-tech ventures, Excite was conceived in the garage of a suburban California home. It was the brainchild of six young software developers, fueled by burritos and a strong desire to "work together and do something entrepreneurial." They launched their service in 1995, went public a year later, and in 1999 merged with @Home, a leader in broadband "always-on" cable Internet services.

Now one of the most popular Internet portals, Excite supports the use of Boolean operators and nested searches for creating complex queries. It also offers some nice features for locating multimedia files and for searching and tracking news stories.

On the downside, Excite lacks many of the "power search" features that Internet users have come to expect, like searching Web page titles and other fields, doing case-sensitive searches, and incorporating wildcards in their queries.

Another drawback to Excite is the relatively small size of its database. Currently 250 million pages, Excite's database is more than twice the size of the one used by AOL Search and MSN Search. (Both are powered by Inktomi's 110-million-page database.) But it's substantially smaller than the 1.2-billion-page Google database—which is also used by Netscape Search and Yahoo—and the databases of the other Big Six engines.

Good to Know

◆ One of the original Web search engines, Excite is now part of Excite@Home, a company that provides Internet portal features and high-speed cable service.

◆ Excite supports the use of Boolean operators and makes it easy to search for news and multimedia files.

◆ But its database is relatively small (250 million pages) and it lacks "power search" options like field searching, case sensitivity, and wildcards.

◆ If you don't like Excite's cluttered home page, you can "personalize" it, or enter your queries on a page devoted to searching.

Consequently, if your Excite search is unsuccessful—or whenever thoroughness counts—be sure to try Google (www.google.com) or one of the other Big Six engines.

✔ Tips

■ To see how Excite's database stacks up against all the leading search engines covered in this book, see **Table 12.1**.

■ For more information about Excite and its parent company, Excite@Home, scroll down to the bottom of the Excite home page (www.excite.com) and click Press Releases. In addition to news stories, you'll find a brief company history, Q&A, and a short broadband tutorial (**Figure 12.1**).

Figure 12.1 You can learn more about the Excite search engine and its parent company by clicking Press Releases on the home page.

Table 12.1

How Excite Stacks Up Against the Leading Search Engines	
SEARCH ENGINE	NUMBER OF WEB PAGES INDEXED
Google	1.2 billion
Netscape Search (powered by Google)	1.2 billion
Yahoo (powered by Google)	1.2 billion
Lycos (powered by FAST)	575 million
HotBot (powered by Inktomi GEN3)	500 million
AltaVista	350 million
Northern Light	330 million
Excite	250 million
AOL Search (powered by Inktomi)	110 million
MSN Search (powered by Inktomi)	110 million

Note: Search engine sizes are based on figures reported as of January 2001 by Search Engine Watch (www.searchenginewatch.com).

Contact Information

Excite@Home
Redwood City, California
650-556-5000 (voice)
650-556-5100 (fax)
www.excite.com

The Excite Home Page

The first thing you'll notice when you visit the Excite home page (www.excite.com) is that it's without a doubt the most cluttered and disorganized Web page imaginable. Like a teenager's room, there's stuff strewn everywhere. And depending on the season, you may even find that the site has been "decorated" for Halloween, or that snowflakes are drifting across the screen.

The good news is that, with Excite's Personalize feature, you can get rid of the clutter and create your own version of the Excite home page that's more conducive to searching (**Figure 12.2**). Once you've done that (we'll tell you how later in this section), you'll find it much easier to focus on the most important search-related features—the Excite search form and Quick Tools.

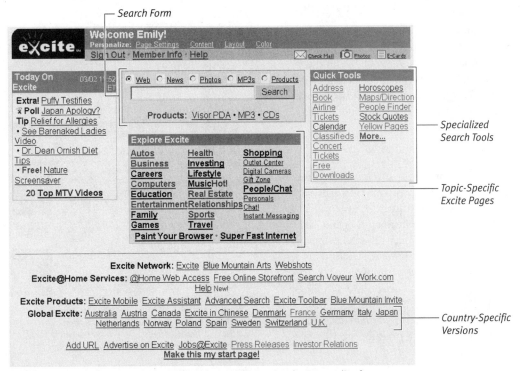

Figure 12.2 The Excite home page, optimized for searching using the Personalize feature.

Search form

Excite's search form (**Figure 12.3**) makes it easy to focus your search on a specific type of information. Just type your query in the search box and click the appropriate radio button to indicate whether you want to search the Web, news articles, photo archives, MP3 files, or product information.

You can search for phrases in quotes, or use the Boolean operators AND, OR, AND NOT, and parentheses to combine words and phrases.

Quick Tools

A section called Quick Tools (**Figure 12.4**), conveniently located to the right of the search form on our personalized Excite home page, provides links to a number of *specialized* reference tools—airline farefinder, searchable classifieds, concert and sporting events locator, maps and driving directions, yellow pages, people-finding tools, and so forth.

The Quick Tools section is a standard feature of every personalized Excite home page. The same set of tools is available on the regular (cluttered) version of the home page, but you might very well miss it because it's buried in a section called Explore Excite under the heading "Tools."

✔ Tips

■ The Explore Excite section of the Excite home page (**Figure 12.5**) looks like a traditional Web directory, organized by topic, but it's really not. Each link takes you to a special page devoted to a single broad subject area—Autos, Business, Careers, etc. The content varies by topic, but typically includes pointers to the best Web sites, news headlines, specialized search tools, and (of course) advertisements for related products and services (**Figure 12.6**).

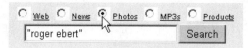

Figure 12.3 Excite's search form lets you specify whether you want to search the Web or another database, such as a photo archive.

Figure 12.4 You can use this collection of reference tools for many common day-to-day searches, like getting stock quotes or looking up phone numbers and e-mail addresses.

Figure 12.5 Excite has created a set of topic-specific Web pages that you can get to with these links.

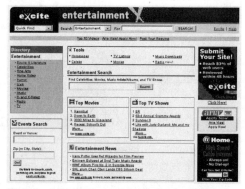

Figure 12.6 Here's an example of what you'll find if you click the Explore Excite Entertainment link: a topic directory, special search forms, top movies and TV shows, entertainment news, and more.

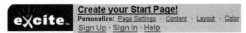

Figure 12.7 The links for Excite's Personalize feature are next to the logo on the home page. Until you go through the sign-up process, Page Settings, Content, Layout, and Color are inactive.

Figure 12.8 For Excite searches without the portal interface, use this search-only page at www.excite.com/search.

■ Excite is offered in several country-specific versions that you can access from a set of links on the home page labeled "Global Excite."

■ To use Excite's Personalize feature for creating your own customized home page, click Sign Up or Create your Start Page! (**Figure 12.7**) and complete the form. Once you've done that, you can pick and choose the content for your page, move features around on the screen, and even change the color scheme if you're so inclined.

■ If you'd rather not bother with the Personalize feature, here's another solution to the home-page clutter problem: Go to www.excite.com/search and do your Excite queries from that page (**Figure 12.8**). It's devoted exclusively to searching.

■ To make Excite your Web browser's default home page, use these URLs in your browser's home-page setup Address or Location box:

http://www.excite.com
(for the Excite home page)

http://www.excite.com/search
(for the special Excite search page)

If you're not sure how to access your Web browser's home-page setup feature, see "Customizing Your Web Browser" in Chapter 4.

■ To get back to the Excite home page from anywhere within the site, click the Excite logo that appears at the top of every page.

Searching with Excite

Whether you use the search form on the Excite home page (www.excite.com), or the one on the page devoted exclusively to searching (www.excite.com/search), the process for entering a query is the same. Here are the key points to keep in mind:

Figure 12.9 It's a good idea to use plus signs (or the Boolean operator AND) in your searches, because Excite defaults to looking for *any* of the words (OR search).

◆ You can express your query as a plain-English question, one or more unique keywords, or a phrase in quotes.

◆ By default, Excite performs an OR search, looking for *any* of the words in your query.

◆ For more precise searches, you can use plus and minus signs to require (+) or exclude (-) words and phrases, or use the Boolean operators AND, OR, AND NOT, and parentheses. Full caps are *required* for Boolean operators.

◆ Except for Boolean operators, Excite searches are *not* case sensitive. You'll get the same results whether you use upper-case, lowercase, or a mix of the two.

To enter a query:

1. Type a question, several unique keywords, a phrase in quotes, or a Boolean expression in the search form text box (**Figure 12.9**).

2. If you want to tell Excite to search a database other than the Web, click the appropriate ratio button above the search form text box. Options include News, Photos, MP3s, and Products.

✔ Tip

■ For a description of the non-Web data-bases that Excite searches, click Help on the Excite home page and then select Search Help from the Directory/Info menu.

Figure 12.10 Here's an example of how Excite presents search results. The total number of matches appears in the upper left.

Figure 12.11 The Show Titles Only display option lets you quickly scan page titles for information that might be of interest.

Figure 12.12 Using the View by URL display option, it's easy to see that the *Chicago Sun-Times* Web site is the place to go for Roger Ebert movie reviews.

To view your search results:

1. Click the Search button (or hit [Enter]) to submit your query.

2. Your results will be presented 10 to a page, with the best matches listed first, along with a count of the total number of matches found (**Figure 12.10**).

3. To get a quick handle on your search results, try one of Excite's alternate display options:

   Show Titles Only presents your results *without* the descriptions (**Figure 12.11**).

   View by URL organizes the titles by Web address (**Figure 12.12**)—a neat way to find out if there's a particular site that has lots of pages devoted to the information you're looking for.

4. You can view any item listed on your results page by clicking its title link.

continues on next page

5. To find related items, click the Web Directory link (**Figure 12.13**) at the top of your search results list. Web Directory matches (**Figure 12.14**) come from LookSmart (`www.looksmart.com`), a human-compiled guide to the best sites on the Web.

LookSmart is organized in hierarchical fashion, with major topics, subtopics, and sub-subtopics. To help you understand where a particular item in your search results fits in the LookSmart Directory, Excite includes the main topic category, and each level of subtopics, separated by a greater-than symbol (>).

Figure 12.13 To find Web pages in the LookSmart Directory with content related to your query, click this link, located at the top of your search results list.

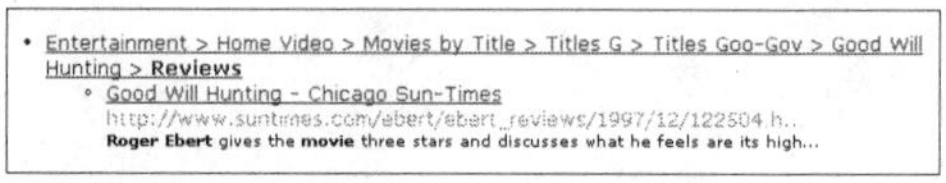

Figure 12.14 The first two lines in this Web Directory listing tell you where the item is categorized by LookSmart. A greater-than symbol (>) separates each topic from the next level down.

✔ Tips

■ Many of the leading search engines "cluster" search results and show only one or two pages from any given Web site. The idea is to present you with as much variety as possible, especially in the first couple of pages of your search results.

■ Excite takes a different approach. They give you *all* the matching pages. But they also provide you with the View by URL display option, which you can use to get a bird's-eye view of where your results are coming from.

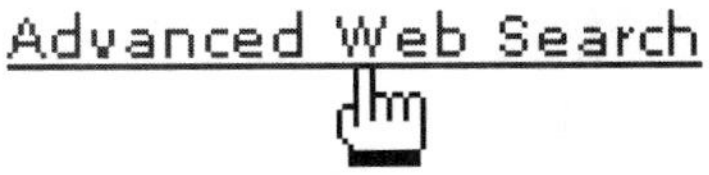

Advanced Web Search

Figure 12.15 This link gives you access to Excite's Advanced Web Search page.

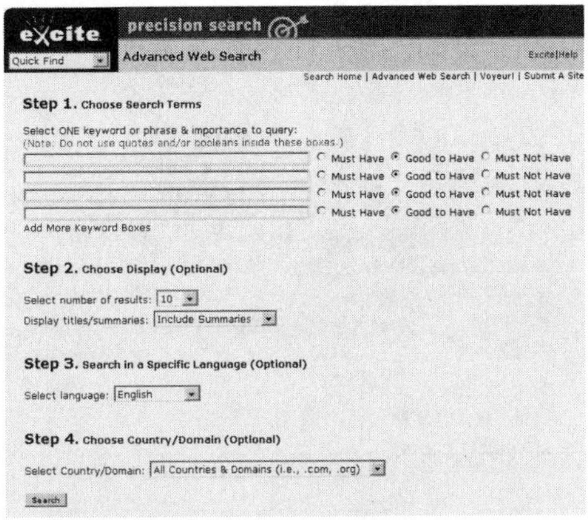

Figure 12.16 If you want to limit your search to a specific language, domain type, or country, use this search form. You can also boost the number of search results per page from 10 to 50.

To refine an Excite query:

1. Try adding another search term, and be sure to use the Boolean operator AND or plus signs (+) to tell Excite that each word or phrase in your query *must* appear in the results.

   Remember that by default, Excite searches for *any* of the words. So if you type multiple words in the search box without using AND or plus signs, you're sure to get a huge number of irrelevant results.

2. You might also try clicking Advanced Web Search (**Figure 12.15**) on the search results page and re-entering your query in the form presented there (**Figure 12.16**).

   With the Advanced Web Search form, you can limit your search to Web pages written in a specific language, and focus on a particular domain type (com, edu, gov, etc.) or country.

   You can also boost the number of search results that are presented on each page from 10 to 50.

3. If you're not successful finding what you're looking for after a couple of attempts with Excite's search forms, try another search engine that has a larger database and more sophisticated search tools.

continues on next page

✔ Tips

- For a summary of Excite search terms and how to use them, see the Excite Quick Reference (**Table 12.2**).

- You can learn more about Excite features, including new ones that may have been added, by clicking Help on the Excite home page. Then pick a topic from the Directory/Info menu (**Figure 12.17**).

  The two menu options that you're likely to find most useful are Search Help (for descriptions of Excite databases and general and advanced search tips) and NewsTracker (to learn how to set up a your own personal "news clipping service").

Directory
Info
· Add URL
· Channels Help
· Classifieds 2000
· Download Center
· Excite Assistant
· Excite Chat
· Excite Inbox
· Excite Messenger
· Excite Mobile
· Excite Planner
· Excite Voice Chat
· FreeLane
· Getting Listed
· My Excite Help
· New to the Net
· NewsTracker
· PAL Instant Messaging
· Registration Sign In
· Search Help
· Shopping
· Toolbar

Figure 12.17 This menu on the Help page leads to information on a variety of Excite features and services. NewsTracker and Search Help are the most important from a searcher's perspective.

Table 12.2

Excite Quick Reference		
FOR THIS TYPE OF SEARCH:	DO THIS:	EXAMPLES:
Plain-English Question	Simply type a phrase or question that expresses the idea or concept. Use as many words as necessary.	thoroughbred racing in Kentucky Where can I find information about thoroughbred racing in Kentucky?
Phrase Search	Type the phrase enclosed in **double quotes**.	"Kentucky Derby"
AND Search (multiple words and phrases, each of which *must* be present)	Use a **plus sign (+)** in front of each word or phrase that *must* appear in the results. Alternatively, you can use **AND** (full caps required) between the words or phrases.	+racing +"Churchill Downs" racing AND "Churchill Downs"
OR Search (multiple words and phrases, any one of which may be present)	Type words or phrases separated by a space. Alternatively, you can use **OR** (full caps required) between each word or phrase.	Derby Preakness Derby OR Preakness
NOT Search (to exclude a word or phrase)	Use a **minus sign (-)** directly in front of the word or phrase you want to exclude from your results. (Note that there's no space between the minus sign and the search word.)	"horse race" –Derby
	Or use NOT or AND NOT (all caps) in front of the word or phrase you want to exclude.	"horse race" NOT Derby "horse race" AND NOT Derby
Case-Sensitive Search	Not available.	
Date Search	Not available.	
Field Search	Not available.	
Nested Search	Use **parentheses** to group Boolean expressions into more complex queries.	racing AND (horse OR thoroughbred)
Proximity Search	Not available.	
Wildcard Search	Not available.	

SEARCHING WITH EXCITE

Figure 12.18 We can periodically check for reviews of our books—on the Web and in various news sources—by clicking a link in the My Searches box.

- Excite's NewsTracker feature isn't as easy to set up and use as Northern Light's Search Alert Service (covered in Chapter 9). But it's worth considering if you plan to make Excite your primary search engine and you'd like to be able to monitor news stories.

- You can do the same thing for both Web and news searches—enter a search once and save it so that you can run it again from time to time—with an Excite feature called Saved Searches.

  You'll first have to use the Personalize feature to create a customized version of the Excite home page, as described earlier in this chapter. Then click Content on the Excite home page and select Saved Searches from the Content menu. Click Done and a My Searches box will appear on your personalized Excite page.

  Once you've added your searches using the edit button in the My Searches box, you can run them any time you wish by simply clicking the appropriate link (**Figure 12.18**).

MSN Search

MSN Search is among the most heavily used search sites on the Internet. But its popularity is due in large measure to the fact that it has a built-in audience—the four million subscribers to the Microsoft Network (MSN) Internet service, plus the tens of millions of brand-new computer users each year whose systems come equipped with the Microsoft Internet Explorer (IE) Web browser.

The vast majority of these MSN subscribers and new computer users have no idea that they can change IE's default home page from MSN (www.msn.com) to some other Web site of their choosing. Consequently, they leave it set the way it is, and whenever they click the MSN or IE Search button, they're presented with an MSN Search form.

Fortunately, it's possible to get fairly good results with MSN Search, using the simplest of queries. The creators of the site have chosen to emphasize quality *vs.* quantity of search results. (Their objective is to present a small number of highly relevant Web pages on the very first results page.) And they discourage the use of "power search" capabilities—Boolean expressions, field searching, limiting a query by date and language—by relegating these features to the Advanced Search form.

Good to Know

◆ MSN Search is the default search engine for Internet Explorer (IE) and Microsoft Network (MSN).

◆ It's powered by Inktomi's 110-million-page database (the smallest of the top search engines covered in this book) and uses LookSmart for its Web directory.

◆ MSN Search encourages you to keep your queries simple. Boolean operators and most other "power search" features are available only with Advanced Search.

◆ Despite its relatively small database and limited search options, MSN Search does a surprisingly good job of returning high-quality results.

◆ For more precise searching of a larger database, use Google or one of the other "Big Six."

MSN Search even tries to accommodate poor spellers and those prone to typing errors with what it calls a "what you mean is what you get" approach to searching. They've designed their software to recognize common misspellings, so that a search for, say, `Brittany Spears` or `Britney Speers` will nevertheless return Web pages featuring teen singing idol Britney Spears (**Figure 13.1**).

Like its rival America Online (AOL), MSN uses Inktomi's 110-million-page database for its Web-page results. That makes them tied for last place among the major search engines covered in this book when it comes to database size. (See **Table 13.1** for specifics.)

But the relatively small size of the MSN Search database isn't necessarily a problem. Unless you're looking for some very obscure piece of information, or when thoroughness is absolutely essential, it probably doesn't really matter whether you search 110 million Web pages, or 1.2 billion.

The biggest drawback to MSN Search, in our opinion, is that it doesn't allow you to search with much precision. And features like the "what you mean is what you get" approach to common misspellings may work most of the time. But what if you're looking for information on a business associate named *Britt Speers*? Try as you might, MSN Search will insist that "what you mean" is *Britney Spears*!

Figure 13.1 Spelling and typing errors are often not a problem for MSN Search. Even though we spelled the name incorrectly, the search engine located several "official" Britney Spears fan pages.

Table 13.1

How MSN Search Stacks Up Against the Leading Search Engines

SEARCH ENGINE	NUMBER OF WEB PAGES INDEXED
Google	1.2 billion
Netscape Search (powered by Google)	1.2 billion
Yahoo (powered by Google)	1.2 billion
Lycos (powered by FAST)	575 million
HotBot (powered by Inktomi GEN3)	500 million
AltaVista	350 million
Northern Light	330 million
Excite	250 million
AOL Search (powered by Inktomi)	110 million
MSN Search (powered by Inktomi)	110 million

Note: Search engine sizes are based on figures reported as of January 2001 by Search Engine Watch (www.searchenginewatch.com).

Contact Information

Microsoft Network
Redmond, Washington
800-386-5550 (customer service)
877-635-7019 (technical support)
www.msn.com (MSN home page)
search.msn.com (MSN Search)

✔ Tips

- Out of curiosity, we did an MSN Search for the "what you mean is what you get" acronym WYMIWYG (which could be pronounced "why-me-wig," but we're just guessing!). Turns out the acronym has been used since the mid-1990s in educational measurement circles to refer to "What You Measure Is What You Get."

  An obscure fact and a relatively small database, but we found it quickly and easily by simply typing wymiwyg in the MSN Search form.

- You won't find an About link on the MSN Search page, but if you're interested in reading up on the latest Microsoft and MSN corporate news and information, visit www.microsoft.com/mscorp.

MSN SEARCH

The MSN Search Home Page

If you're an MSN or IE user, you've probably already figured out that clicking any button labeled "Search"—on the MSN home page (www.msn.com) or on the IE toolbar—takes you to the MSN Search home page (**Figure 13.2**) or some version of the MSN Search form.

You can also go to MSN Search directly, of course, by typing the Web address search.msn.com in your browser's Address or Location box.

The MSN Search home page is devoted exclusively to searching. The key features to zero in on are the search form, Web directory, and Advanced Search option.

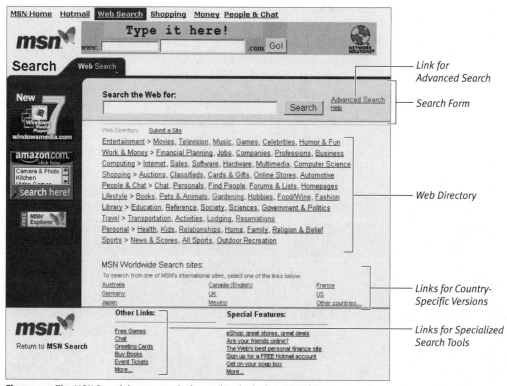

Figure 13.2 The MSN Search home page is devoted exclusively to searching.

Figure 13.3 MSN Search would interpret this query to mean that you want to find Web pages with *both* words, even though you haven't used plus signs.

Web Directory   Submit a Site

Entertainment > Movies, Television, Music, Games, Celebrities, Humor & Fun
Work & Money > Financial Planning, Jobs, Companies, Professions, Business
Computing > Internet, Sales, Software, Hardware, Multimedia, Computer Science
Shopping > Auctions, Classifieds, Cards & Gifts, Online Stores, Automotive
People & Chat > Chat, Personals, Find People, Forums & Lists, Homepages
Lifestyle > Books, Pets & Animals, Gardening, Hobbies, Food/Wine, Fashion
Library > Education, Reference, Society, Sciences, Government & Politics
Travel > Transportation, Activities, Lodging, Reservations
Personal > Health, Kids, Relationships, Home, Family, Religion & Belief
Sports > News & Scores, All Sports, Outdoor Recreation

Figure 13.4 The Web directory on the MSN Search home page comes from LookSmart, a human-compiled guide to the best Web sites, organized by topic.

Web Directory > Lifestyle > Books

Web Directory
• Guides & Directories   • Authors A-Z   • Bestsellers   • Bookstores   • By Country
• Chat & Events   • Drama   • Genres   • Periods & Movements   • Poetry   • Publications
• Theory & Criticism   • Writing & Publishing

Figure 13.5 We clicked on the Web directory's Lifestyle category and found a subcategory called Books, which is further broken down into the subcategories shown here.

Search form

The MSN Search form (**Figure 13.3**) is about as simple as they get—a box for entering your query and a Search button to submit it. MSN Search automatically looks for *all* the words in your query, so it's not necessary to put plus signs (+) in front of required terms.

✔ Tip

■ Boolean operators aren't allowed on this search form. In fact, if you combine search terms with AND or OR (in full caps) on the MSN Search home page, you'll get a "no results found" message. Use lowercase and the Boolean operators will simply be ignored.

Web directory

The Web directory (**Figure 13.4**) on the MSN Search home page is created and maintained by LookSmart (www.looksmart.com), a company that employs a staff of editors to identify the best Web sites and organize them into meaningful categories.

When you do an MSN Search, your results include matches from the LookSmart Web directory as well as the Inktomi database of Web pages. But you can also *browse* the directory by clicking the link for one of the 10 major categories (Entertainment, Work and Money, Computing, etc.) or the dozens of subcategories, and then "drill down" through topics of greater specificity (**Figure 13.5**).

✔ Tip

■ Unlike Yahoo (www.yahoo.com), MSN Search doesn't give you the option of limiting your search to the Web directory. But you can increase the likelihood of finding Web directory matches by using a fairly general word or phrase as your search term.

THE MSN SEARCH HOME PAGE

Advanced Search option

When you want to search with more precision, or exercise some control over how your results are presented, click Advanced Search (**Figure 13.6**) and use the form presented there.

With Advanced Search, you can enter Boolean expressions, boost the number of results per page from 15 to 50, change the sort order, do field searches (titles, links, and domains), and limit your queries in a variety of ways— by language, date modified, and multimedia file type, among others.

✔ Tips

■ For a set of specialized tools called Quick Links (**Figure 13.7**) that will help you with common day-to-day search tasks (looking up e-mail addresses and phone numbers, getting maps and driving directions, checking stock market perform- ance, etc.), click More in the Other Links section of the MSN Search home page.

■ MSN Search is offered in several country- specific versions that you can access from the home page (**Figure 13.8**). In addition to being presented in the country's native language, the content is also tailored to the country.

■ To make MSN Search your Web browser's default home page, see "Customizing Your Web Browser" in Chapter 4.

■ You can get back to the MSN Search home page by clicking the Web Search link (**Figure 13.9**) that appears at the top of most pages within the site.

Figure 13.6
The Advanced Search link takes you to a page that gives you access to "power search" features not available on the MSN Search home page.

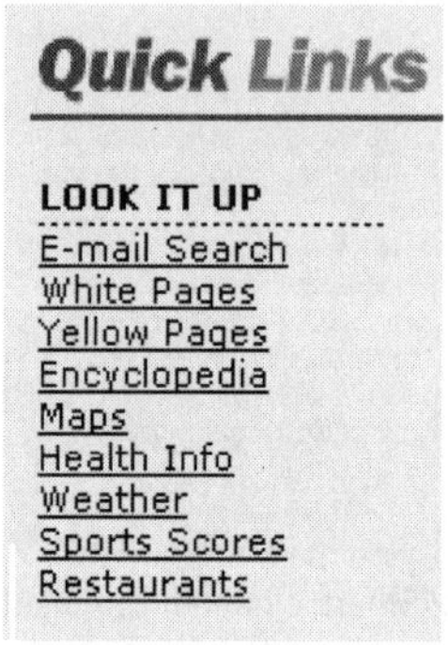

Figure 13.7 These are just a few of the many specialized search tools you'll find on the Quick Links page.

Figure 13.8 If you live outside the United States— or you simply want to explore the Web from the perspective of another country—try one of MSN Search's country-specific versions.

Figure 13.9 Use this link, which you'll find at the top of most pages within the site, to get back to the MSN Search home page.

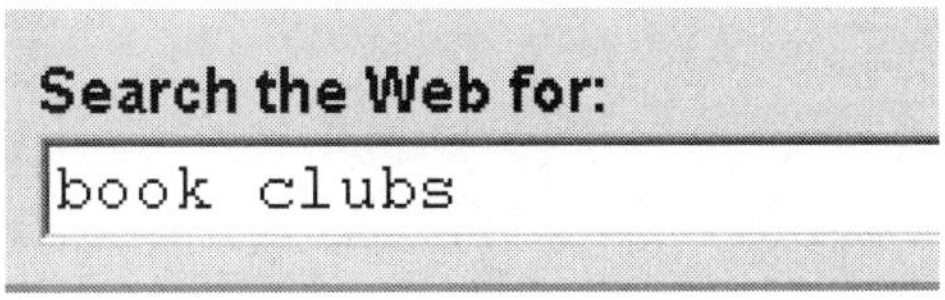

Search the Web for:

book clubs

Figure 13.10 With MSN Search, it's often best to start with a simple query like this.

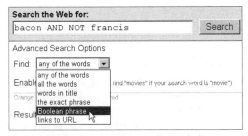

Figure 13.11 For searches that involve *excluding* a word, we've found that using AND NOT on the Advanced Search form works better than using a minus sign (-) on the regular search form.

✔ Tip

■ A more effective way to exclude a word or phrase from your search results is to go to the Advanced Search page, type your query in the search box using the Boolean operator AND NOT (in full caps), and choose Boolean phrase from the Find menu (**Figure 13.11**).

Searching with MSN Search

As we've said, the search form on the MSN Search home page is quite simple to use and offers very few options. There are just a few basic rules to keep in mind:

◆ You can type up to 150 characters in the search form's text box.

◆ There's no need to use plus signs (+) to combine words and phrases, because MSN Search automatically looks for *all* the words in your query.

◆ Boolean operators aren't allowed, and including them is likely to result in a "no results found" message.

◆ Searches are *not* case sensitive, so you'll get the same results whether you type your search terms in uppercase, lowercase, or a combination of the two.

To enter a query:

1. Go to MSN Search (search.msn.com) and type a plain-English question or several unique keywords in the search form (**Figure 13.10**).

2. To look for an exact phrase, enclose the words in double quotes: "reading maketh a full man".

3. If you want to *exclude* a word or phrase from your search results, try putting a minus sign (-) in front of it: bacon -francis (no space between the minus sign and the search word).

   This may or may not actually eliminate the word from your search results, but it's likely to push pages containing the excluded word farther down in the list.

To view your search results:

1. Click the Search button (or hit (Enter))
   to submit your query.

2. Your results will be presented 15 to a page,
   along with a count of the total number of
   matches found (**Figure 13.12**). They'll be
   organized into as many as five categories:

   ▲ **Popular Search Topics** are designed
   to help you refine your query by sug-
   gesting search words or phrases that
   might be related (**Figure 13.13**).

   ▲ **Featured Sites** are Web sites from
   MSN.com and MSN sponsors, some of
   whom pay for appearing in this section.
   A special icon is used to identify the
   official Web site of a company, brand,
   or product (**Figure 13.14**).

   ▲ **Web Directory Sites** come from the
   human-compiled LookSmart Directory
   (the Web directory that's featured on
   the MSN Search home page).

   ▲ **Top 10 Most Popular Sites** are
   generated by Direct Hit (**Figure 13.15**),
   a "popularity engine" that ranks Web
   sites based on how often users click
   on them at the Direct Hit Web site
   (www.directhit.com).

   ▲ **Web Pages** come from the 110-million-
   page Inktomi database. MSN Search
   does *not* "cluster" search results, so if
   multiple pages within a Web site
   match your query, they will all be
   included in your results.

3. You can visit any Web site on the search
   results page by clicking its title link.

Figure 13.12 Here's an example of how MSN Search presents results. The total number of matches appears in the line right below the shaded box.

Figure 13.13 The Popular Search Topics section for our book clubs search suggests four topics we might want to explore.

🔊 Audio Book Club

Figure 13.14 Links tagged with the special icon shown here lead to the *official* Web site for a company, brand, or product. Microsoft is part owner of RealNames, the company that registers names and authorizes use of the icon.

Figure 13.15 MSN Search gets its "Top 10 Most Popular Sites" from a company called Direct Hit.

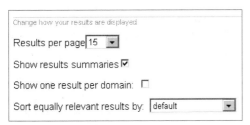

Figure 13.16 To make changes in the way your results are displayed, use these options on the Advanced Search form. Unfortunately, you have to make the changes each time you search.

Figure 13.17 The Advanced Search form offers a number of "power search" capabilities that can help you refine a query.

✔ Tips

- If you want to increase the likelihood of being presented with all five categories of MSN Search results, don't enter a long phrase or a plain-English question in the search box. MSN Search's objective is to direct you to the "most popular" or "best" Web sites on a given topic, and the search engine has been designed to do that most effectively when you enter just a couple of search words.

- If you want to be able to control how your results are presented, click Advanced Search and use the form presented there. The Advanced Search display options (**Figure 13.16**) let you boost the number of results per page from 15 to 50, suppress Web-page descriptions, "cluster" results so that you'll only be shown one page per Web site, and sort equally relevant results by date, title, or page depth (how far "down" in the Web site the page is located).

To refine an MSN Search query:

1. Start by reviewing the list of Popular Search Topics (if any) to see if there's one that seems appropriate. If so, click on it to generate a new search.

2. You can also refine an MSN Search by simply adding another unique keyword or phrase to your original query. Since MSN Search looks for *all* the words, this has the effect of searching *within* your original results (also referred to as *set searching*).

3. You might also try clicking Advanced Search on the results page and using the fill-in-the-blanks form (**Figure 13.17**) to refine your query. Advanced Search offers a number of "power search" features not available on the MSN Search home page:

continues on next page

▲ **Boolean Operators**. You can use AND, OR, AND NOT, and parentheses in your queries to create Boolean expressions and nested searches. Just be sure to type the Boolean operators in *uppercase* and select `Boolean phrase` in the Find menu (**Figure 13.18**).

▲ **Field Search**. You can look for words in Web page titles and links using the Find menu's `words in title` and `links to URL` options. For links, be sure to type the *complete* URL (including `http://`) in the Advanced Search form's search box: `http://www.bartleby.com`.

To limit a search to a specific domain or domain type (`com` for commercial, `edu` for education, `org` for non-profit organization, etc.), enter that information in the Domain section (**Figure 13.19**)

▲ **Language Option**. You can limit your search to Web pages written in a specific language.

▲ **Date Search**. You can focus on Web pages modified within a range of dates.

▲ **Multimedia/File Search**. You can search for Web pages that include specific types of files (images, audio, video, VBScript, etc.).

▲ **Stemming**. You can turn on *stemming* (a type of wildcard searching), so that MSN Search will automatically look for both *root* words and *variations*.

If you haven't found what you're looking for after a couple of attempts with MSN Search's regular and Advanced Search forms, try another search engine that has a larger database and more sophisticated search tools.

✔ Tips

■ A set of tabs (**Figure 13.20**) at the top of the search results page lets you do a follow-on search for news articles, shopping sites, and yellow-pages listings related to your query.

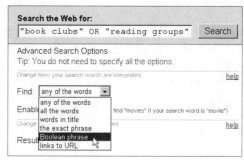

Figure 13.18 You can use Boolean operators on the Advanced Search form. Just remember to type them in *uppercase* and set the Find menu to `Boolean phrase`.

Figure 13.19 Typing `edu` in the Domain search box tells MSN Search to limit the query to education Web sites (sites whose domain names end in `.edu`).

Figure 13.20 You can use these tabs to do a quick search of news, shopping, and yellow-pages information, without having to retype your query.

Figure 13.21 The MSN Search help information is accurate and searchable, but we're not crazy about the way it's presented, in a skinny frame like this.

- For a summary of search rules and examples, see the MSN Search Quick Reference for the regular (**Table 13.2**) and Advanced Search (**Table 13.3**) forms.

- MSN Search's own help information, which you can access by clicking Help on the home page and the Advanced Search form, is rather skimpy and difficult to use. It appears in a frame on the right side of your screen (**Figure 13.21**), and you have to *right-click* in the frame order to print a topic ([Control]-click on the Macintosh).

- On the plus side, the help information is searchable and, for the most part, accurately describes MSN Search features. The only topic we encountered that didn't work as advertised was wildcard searching using an asterisk (*) on the Advanced Search page. (Every wildcard search we tried resulted in a "no results found" message.)

Table 13.2

MSN Search Basic Search Quick Reference*

FOR THIS TYPE OF SEARCH:	DO THIS:	EXAMPLES:
Plain-English Question	Simply type a question that expresses the idea or concept, using as many words as necessary.	What's the best place for cross-country skiing in Minnesota?
Phrase Search	Type the phrase enclosed in **double quotes.**	"Gunflint Lodge"
AND Search (multiple words and phrases, each of which *must* be present)	Type words or phrases separated by a space. MSN Search automatically searches for *all* the words, so **plus signs (+)** aren't necessary.	skiing snowboarding
OR Search (multiple words and phrases, any one of which may be present)	Not available. Use Advanced Search.	
NOT Search (to exclude a word or phrase)	Use a **minus sign (-)** directly in front of the word or phrase you want to exclude from your results. (Note that there's no space between the minus sign and the search word.)	skiing -downhill
Case-Sensitive Search	Not available.	
Date Search	Not available. Use Advanced Search.	
Field Search	Not available. Use Advanced Search.	
Nested Search	Not available. Use Advanced Search.	
Proximity Search	Not available.	
Wildcard Search	Not available. Use Advanced Search.	

Note: This table applies to searches using the form on the MSN Search home page. For Advanced Search, see **Table 13.3.*

Table 13.3

MSN Search Advanced Search Quick Reference*		
FOR THIS TYPE OF SEARCH:	DO THIS:	EXAMPLES:
Plain-English Question	Type a question that expresses the idea or concept and choose all the words on the Find menu.	When was the Mir space station launched"?
Phrase Search	Type the phrase without any special punctuation and choose the exact phrase on the Find menu.	Hubble space telescope
AND Search (multiple words and phrases, each of which *must* be present)	Type words or phrases separated by a space and choose all the words on the Find menu.	"space camp" scholarships
	Alternatively, you can combine words and phrases with the Boolean operator **AND** (full caps required) and choose Boolean phrase on the Find menu.	"space camp" AND scholarships
OR Search (multiple words and phrases, any one of which may be present)	Type words or phrases separated by a space and choose any of the words on Find menu.	NASA "space program"
	Alternatively, you can combine words and phrases with the Boolean operator **OR** (full caps required) and choose Boolean phrase on the Find menu.	NASA OR "space program"
NOT Search (to exclude a word or phrase)	Use the Boolean operator **AND NOT** (full caps required) with the word or phrase you want to exclude and choose Boolean phrase on Find menu.	shuttle AND NOT challenger
Case-Sensitive Search	Not available.	
Date Search	Specify range of dates in the **Modified between** section of the search form, using the format dd/mm/yyyy.	Modified between: 01/01/2001 and: 30/06/2001
Field Search	Three types of field searches are possible:	
	Titles. Type search words or phrases in the search box and choose words in title on Find menu.	astronaut hall of fame
	Links. Type complete URL (including http://) in search box and choose links to URL on Find menu.	http://www.astronaut.org
	Domain. Use Domain section of form to limit your search by domain type (com, edu, gov, org, etc.) or to a specific domain.	Domain: com Domain: nasa.gov
Nested Search	Combine search terms with **Boolean operators** and **parentheses**, and choose Boolean phrase from the Find menu.	(NASA OR "space program") AND budget AND 2001
Proximity Search	Not available.	
Wildcard Search	Use **Enable stemming** option to automatically search for both *root* words and *variations*. With stemming enabled, a search for budget would also find references to *budgets*, *budgetary*, and *budgeting*.	budget

*Note: This table applies to searches using MSN Search's Advanced Search form. For searches using the form on the MSN Search home page, see **Table 13.2**.*

SEARCHING WITH MSN SEARCH

NETSCAPE SEARCH

If you use Netscape Navigator as your Web browser, you're probably at least somewhat familiar with the Netscape home page and its various "portal features," chief among them Netscape Search, for finding information on the Web. When you install Netscape for the first time, or upgrade to a new version, the Netscape home page loads automatically. The hope is that you'll leave it that way and begin all your online sessions—and do all your Web searches—from home.netscape.com.

As you may recall from the section in Chapter 4 on "Customizing Your Web Browser," you can make *any* Web site your default "home page" location. But if you're currently using the Netscape home page and you're happy with the features it offers, by all means stick with it. This chapter will help you understand what Netscape's search function is all about and how to use it to best advantage.

Good to Know

- Netscape Search is the default search engine for the Netscape portal site, and it's one of several search options for Netscape Navigator.

- Search results come from three main sources: Netscape's Smart Browsing database of "official" Web sites, the Open Directory Project, and the gigantic Google database.

- You can use Boolean operators, plus and minus signs, and wildcards with Netscape Search, but the site offers little else in the way of "power search" features.

- Where it really shines is in locating Web sites for companies, brand-name or trademarked products, and sites that have been identified as the best on a particular topic.

Toward that end, there are two things you need to know up front:

◆ **What are you searching?** The creators of Netscape Search have decided to emphasize *quality* over *quantity*. When you do a search, your results come from several different sources, including the 1.2 billion-page Google database (`www.google.com`). But whenever possible, Netscape Search *first* presents you with Web sites from its Smart Browsing database, and a manageable number of related topic categories and Web sites from the Open Directory Project (`dmoz.org`).

◆ **What search tools are available?** The search tools that are offered with Netscape Search are quite limited. You can use Boolean operators (AND, OR, and ANDNOT), plus and minus signs, and wildcards, but that's about it. You can't search by date or language, focus on specific fields, do case-sensitive searches, or control the way your results are displayed.

Despite the lack of "power search" tools, Netscape Search is a good choice when your objective is to find some of the *best* Web sites on a particular topic, or when you're looking for brand-name products and therefore want to be able to zero in on the official company site.

Contact Information

Netscape Communications
Mountain View, California
650-254-1900 (voice)
650-528-4124 (fax)
home.netscape.com (Netscape portal)
search.netscape.com (Netscape Search)

Table 14.1

How Netscape Search Stacks Up Against the Leading Search Engines	
SEARCH ENGINE	NUMBER OF WEB PAGES INDEXED
Google	1.2 billion
Netscape Search (powered by Google)	1.2 billion
Yahoo (powered by Google)	1.2 billion
Lycos (powered by FAST)	575 million
HotBot (powered by Inktomi GEN3)	500 million
AltaVista	350 million
Northern Light	330 million
Excite	250 million
AOL Search (powered by Inktomi)	110 million
MSN Search (powered by Inktomi)	110 million

Note: Search engine sizes are based on figures reported as of January 2001 by Search Engine Watch (www.searchenginewatch.com).

Figure 14.1 *Estée Lauder* is an Internet keyword, so with Netscape 6 and IE 5, you can use that instead of www.elcompanies.com to get to the company's Web site.

✔ Tips

- The Google database of Web pages used by Netscape Search is the largest of the leading search engines. (See **Table 14.1** for a comparison.)

- Netscape's Smart Browsing database of company and product Web pages is similar to the RealNames database used by Google, MSN Search, and others. Both are designed to enable you to access a Web site by typing an *Internet keyword* (instead of a complicated URL) in your browser's Address or Location box (**Figure 14.1**).

  RealNames (www.realnames.com) charges companies for the privilege of "owning" an Internet keyword, while inclusion in Netscape's Smart Browsing database is free.

- The Open Directory Project, a volunteer effort to identify the best Web sites and organize them into meaningful topic categories, was acquired by Netscape in 1998. Some 20,000 volunteer editors from around the world—people who are passionate about a particular subject—contribute to the directory.

- Close on the heels of Netscape's acquisition of the Open Directory Project, America Online (AOL) bought Netscape. To read about this and other Netscape developments dating back to 1994, go to home.netscape.com/company.

The Netscape Search Home Page

Located at search.netscape.com, the Netscape Search home page (**Figure 14.2**) is nicely organized and designed exclusively for searching and browsing the Web. It includes a search form, Web directory, and links for a set of specialized tools for handling common search tasks.

Figure 14.2 The Netscape Search home page gives you two ways to look for information on the Web: using a search form or browsing by topic.

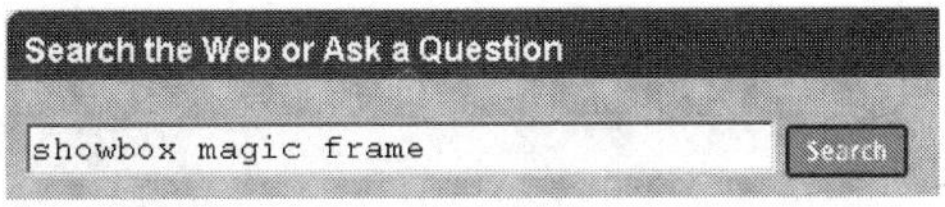

Search the Web or Ask a Question

```
showbox magic frame          Search
```

Figure 14.3 Type a query like this and Netscape Search will look for all three words, even though we haven't used AND or plus signs.

Arts & Entertainment
Literature, Movies, Music
Radio, TV, Celebrities

Business
Investing, Jobs, Consulting
Small Business

Computing & Internet
Hardware, Software, WWW
Programming, Web Authoring

Games
Board, Console, PC, Online
Video, RPGs, Gambling

Health
Women's, Men's, Children's
Diseases, Fitness, Medicine,
Nutrition

Home & Family
Kids, Teens, Seniors, Pets
Improvement, Real Estate

Netscape
Shareware, Small Business

News
Tech, Magazines
Newspapers, Weather

Recreation
Travel, Outdoors, Collecting
Gardening, Crafts, Food

Reference
Colleges & Universities, K-12
Maps, Dictionaries, Translation

Regional (in English)
USA, UK, Australia, Canada,
Europe, South America, Africa,
Asia

Science & Technology
Astronomy, Biology, Chemistry
Earth, Environment

Shopping
Autos, Antiques, Auctions
Clothing, Gifts, Electronics

Society & Lifestyles
Genealogy, Relationships
History, Law, Politics, Religion

Sports
Baseball, Basketball, Football
Golf, Hockey, Soccer

World (in native language)
Deutsch, Español, Français,
Japanese, Chinese, Italiano,
Português, Russian, Polska, Indonesia

Figure 14.4 Netscape owns the Open Directory Project, so that's the Web directory that appears on the Netscape Search home page.

- **Adoption** *(4)*
- **Chat and Message Boards** *(13)*
- **Directories** *(68)*
- **Heraldry** *(19)*
- **Immigration** *(134)*
- **Magazines and Ezines** *(10)*
- **Medical** *(6)*
- **Military** *(16)*

- **Obituaries** *(24)*
- **Personal Pages** *(487)*
- **Products and Services** *(338)*
- **Religions** *(58)*
- **Resources** *(133)*
- **Reunions** *(24)*
- **Royalty** *(49)*
- **Surnames** *(3,409)*

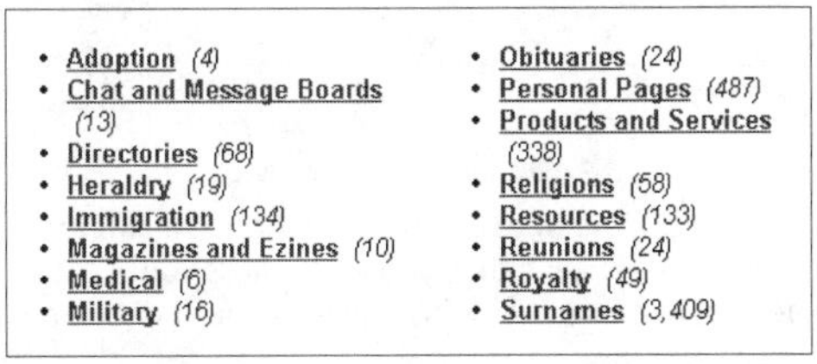

Figure 14.5 We clicked on Society & Lifestyles and then Genealogy to reach this set of sub-subtopics. The numbers in parentheses tell you how many reviewed Web sites you'll find for each one.

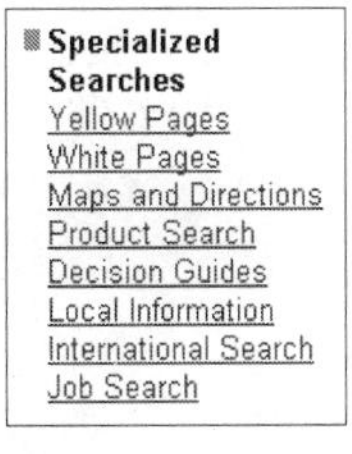

Specialized Searches
Yellow Pages
White Pages
Maps and Directions
Product Search
Decision Guides
Local Information
International Search
Job Search

Figure 14.6 Often one of these specialized tools can get you the answer you need faster than a regular Web search.

Search form

The search form for Netscape Search is very straightforward—a box for entering your query and a Search button to submit it (**Figure 14.3**). Netscape Search defaults to doing an AND search, looking for *all* the words that you type in the search box, so it's not necessary to use the Boolean operator AND or to put plus signs (+) in front of required terms, although you can if you wish.

Web directory

The Web directory (**Figure 14.4**) on the Netscape Search home page comes from the Open Directory Project (dmoz.org) and is similar in concept to Yahoo (www.yahoo.com). You can click on any one of the 16 major topic categories and then "drill down" through the various subtopics and sub-subtopics (**Figure 14.5**).

The Web sites you'll encounter in the directory are generally among the best available on a given topic, because they've been hand-selected by knowledgeable editors—not rounded up by an automated spider program.

✔ Tip

- Unlike Yahoo, Netscape Search doesn't give you the option of limiting your search to the Web directory. But you can increase the likelihood of finding Web directory matches (rather than Web pages from the Google database) by using a fairly general word or phrase as your search term.

Specialized search tools

The Netscape Search home page includes links for a set of specialized tools for common day-to-day search tasks—looking up e-mail addresses and phone numbers in yellow pages and white pages directories, getting maps and driving directions, locating product information, and so forth (**Figure 14.6**).

continues on next page

You'll also find a link for International Search, which gives you access to versions of Netscape Search designed for specific countries and for languages other than English.

✔ Tips

■ The links in the Learn More and Get Involved sections of the home page provide details on Netscape's Internet keywords, the Smart Browsing feature, and the Open Directory Project (including how to become an editor yourself).

■ To make Netscape Search your Web browser's default home page, see "Customizing Your Web Browser" in Chapter 4.

■ If you use Netscape Navigator as your browser, its Search button (shown in **Figure 14.7** for Netscape 6 and **Figure 14.8** for earlier versions) takes you to a multi-option search page called Net Search (**Figure 14.9**).

Each time you visit Net Search, one of nine search engines will be chosen for you at random—not a good idea in our opinion, because they all work a bit differently, and who wants to master all nine?

Fortunately, you're given the option of setting a default search engine. Just click its name and then click the "Keep" checkbox.

■ Whatever browser you use, you can return to the Netscape Search home page at any time by clicking the Search button with the magnifying-glass icon (**Figure 14.10**) that appears at the top of most pages within the site. (Note that this is different from the Search buttons shown in Figures 14.7 and 14.8.)

Figure 14.7 With Netscape 6, the Search button's Search the Web option takes you to the Net Search page shown in **Figure 14.9**.

Figure 14.8 With older versions of Netscape, use the Search button shown here to get to the Net Search page.

Figure 14.9 The Net Search page features a different search engine each time you visit unless you designate a favorite by clicking its name and then the Keep checkbox.

Figure 14.10 Click this button, which you'll find at the top of most pages within the Netscape Search site, to get back to the home page.

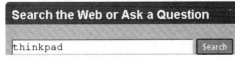

Figure 14.11 With Netscape Search, it's often best to start with a simple query like this one, especially if you're looking for product information or a company-sponsored Web site.

Figure 14.12 You can also enter a Netscape Search query using this form on the Netscape home page (home.netscape.com).

Searching with Netscape Search

Even though the search tools available to you with Netscape Search are quite limited, you can get very good results as long as you keep a few general concepts in mind:

◆ Netscape Search is designed to help you find what it considers to be the *best* information related to your search, so it favors Web sites from its Smart Browsing database and the Open Directory Project over those from the spider-created Google database.

◆ You won't even be shown Web pages from Google if matches are found in these other sources.

◆ You can increase the likelihood of finding Web sites in Netscape Search's non-Google sources by limiting the number of words in your query and avoiding the use of plus signs (+).

◆ Conversely, you can virtually assure that your results will come from Google by using three or more unique keywords and putting plus signs in front of each of them.

To enter a query:

1. Go to the Netscape Search home page at search.netscape.com (or the Netscape home page at home.netscape.com) and type your query—expressed as a plain-English question or one or more unique keywords—in the search form (**Figures 14.11** and **14.12**). If you're looking for a company or a brand-name or trademarked product, use that as your search term.

2. To look for an exact phrase, enclose the words in double quotes: "pentium processor upgrade".

continues on next page

SEARCHING WITH NETSCAPE SEARCH

3. You can use the Boolean operators AND and OR (uppercase *not* required) to combine words and phrases. AND isn't really necessary, however, because Netscape Search defaults to doing an AND search.

You can also use plus signs (+) in front of required words and phrases, but if you do, you're not likely to find Smart Browsing and Open Directory Project Web sites in your search results.

4. If you want to *exclude* a word or phrase from your results, put a minus sign (-) in front of it: `sherlock -holmes` (no space between the minus sign and the search word) to find information on the Macintosh Sherlock application rather than the fictional detective (**Figure 14.13**).

Or use the Boolean operator ANDNOT (one word, uppercase *not* required): `sherlock ANDNOT holmes`.

✔ Tips

■ Netscape Search is *not* case sensitive, so you'll get the same results whether you type your queries in uppercase, lowercase, or a mix of the two.

■ You can use an asterisk (*) as a wildcard character to look for multiple characters at the end of a word: `spam*` to find references to *spam*, *spamkiller*, *spammer*, and *spamming*.

To view your search results:

1. Click the Search button (or hit Enter) to submit your query.

2. Your results (**Figure 14.14**) will be organized into as many as five sections:

▲ **Partner Search Results**. Similar to what other search engines refer to as "sponsored links," these are paid listings from GoTo (www.goto.com), a pay-for-placement search site.

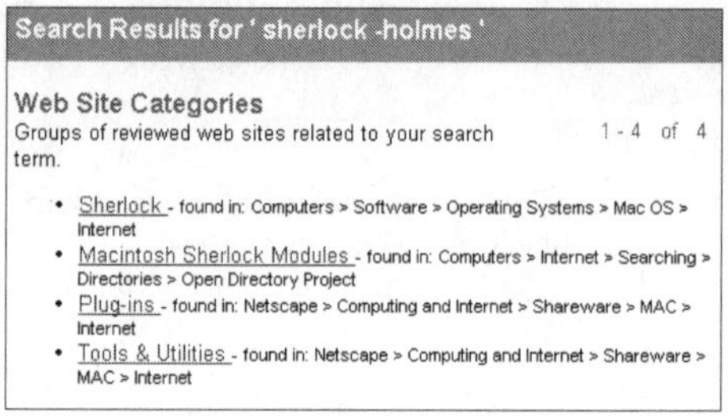

Figure 14.13 A search for `sherlock -holmes` proved to be just the ticket for finding Web-site topic categories dealing with Macintosh software.

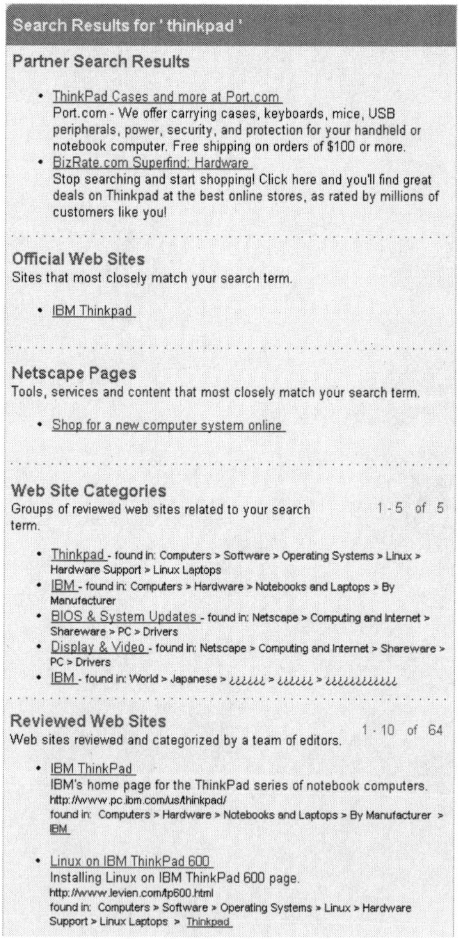

Figure 14.14 Here's an example of how Netscape Search presents results. Don't worry about trying to read the individual items. Our point is simply to show you how the results page is organized.

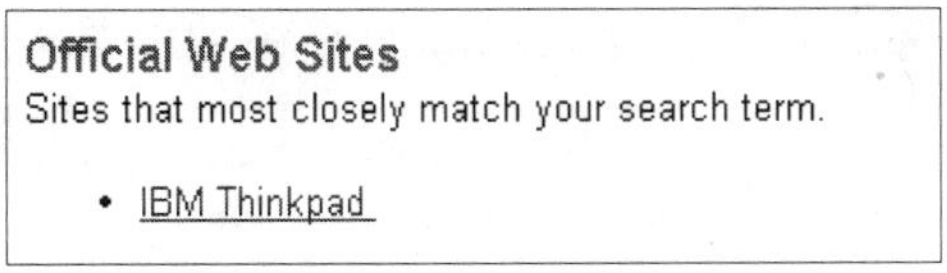

Official Web Sites

Sites that most closely match your search term.

- IBM Thinkpad

Figure 14.15 Clicking this link (or typing the *Internet keyword* ibm thinkpad in your browser's Address or Location box) will take you to the official company Web site for IBM's Thinkpad computer.

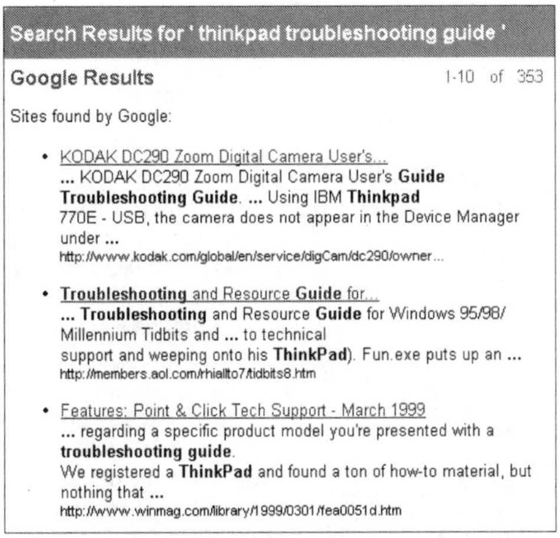

Search Results for ' thinkpad troubleshooting guide '

Google Results   1-10 of 353

Sites found by Google:

- KODAK DC290 Zoom Digital Camera User's...
  ... KODAK DC290 Zoom Digital Camera User's **Guide Troubleshooting Guide**. ... Using IBM **Thinkpad** 770E - USB, the camera does not appear in the Device Manager under ...
  http://www.kodak.com/global/en/service/digCam/dc290/owner...

- Troubleshooting and Resource **Guide** for...
  ... **Troubleshooting** and Resource **Guide** for Windows 95/98/ Millennium Tidbits and ... to technical support and weeping onto his **ThinkPad**). Fun.exe puts up an ...
  http://members.aol.com/rhiallto7/tidbits8.htm

- Features: Point & Click Tech Support - March 1999
  ... regarding a specific product model you're presented with a **troubleshooting guide**. We registered a **ThinkPad** and found a ton of how-to material, but nothing that ...
  http://www.winmag.com/library/1999/0301/fea0051d.htm

Figure 14.16 A search for thinkpad troubleshooting guide was automatically forwarded to Google because no matches were found in Netscape Search's other databases.

▲ **Official Web Sites**. The sites listed here come from Netscape's Smart Browsing database, described earlier in this chapter (**Figure 14.15**).

▲ **Netscape Pages**. Created by Netscape, each page presented here offers a collection of tools, services, and content related (sometimes rather loosely) to your search words.

▲ **Web Site Categories**. These are topic categories from the Open Directory Project that may be relevant to your search.

▲ **Reviewed Web Sites**. Also from the Open Directory Project, these are specific Web sites that have been reviewed and categorized by volunteer editors.

If no results are found for any of these sections, Netscape Search will check the Google database and report what it finds there (**Figure 14.16**).

3. You can visit any Web site on the search results page by clicking its title link.

✔ Tips

- Don't forget that you can increase the likelihood of being presented with all five categories of Netscape Search results by limiting the number of words you type in the search box.

- Netscape Search doesn't give you any control over how your results are displayed.

To refine a Netscape Search query:

1. Scroll down to the bottom of the search results page, where you'll find the Search Again form (**Figure 14.17**) with your original query.
2. One way to refine a query is to simply add another unique keyword or phrase and run the search again. Netscape Search looks for *all* the words that you type in the search box, so this has the effect of searching *within* your original results (also referred to as *set searching*).
3. You might also try adding a word or phrase that you want Netscape Search to *exclude* from your results, using a minus sign (-) or the Boolean operator ANDNOT.

✔ Tips

- Netscape Search makes it easy to get a "second opinion" from another search engine. Using the links that appear right above the Search Again form (**Figure 14.18**), you can do the same search with a variety of leading engines.
- If your original set of results came from sources other than Google, you'll find a `Search again` link (**Figure 14.19**) that you can click on to send your query to the Google database.
- For more precise Google searching, go to `www.google.com` and perform your search there. At the Google site, you can use field-search terms to limit your query to Web page titles, domains, links, and URLs. (See Chapter 6 for more on searching with Google.)

Search Again or Ask a Question
thinkpad
Search

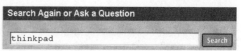

Figure 14.17 You'll find this form, with your original query entered for you, at the bottom of your search results page.

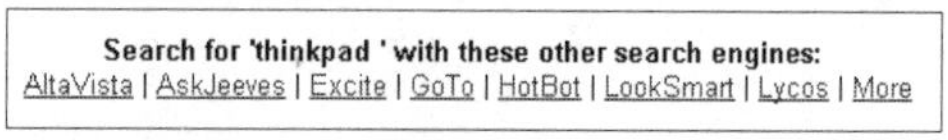

Search for 'thinkpad ' with these other search engines:
AltaVista | AskJeeves | Excite | GoTo | HotBot | LookSmart | Lycos | More

Figure 14.18 You can use these links to send your query to another search engine for a "second opinion."

Search again for 'thinkpad ' using
Google

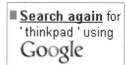

Figure 14.19 To forward your search to Google, use this link, which you'll find in the left column of your search results whenever Google wasn't included the first time around.

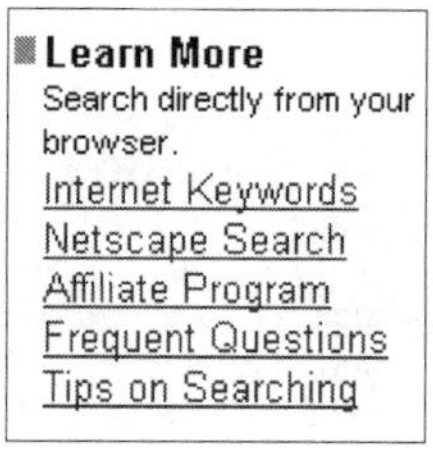

Learn More
Search directly from your browser.
Internet Keywords
Netscape Search
Affiliate Program
Frequent Questions
Tips on Searching

Figure 14.20 In addition to search tips, this set of links will provide you with more details on Internet keywords, the Open Directory Project, and other "behind-the-scenes" aspects of Netscape Search.

- For a summary of search rules and examples, see the Netscape Search Quick Reference (**Table 14.2**).
- For Netscape Search's own help information, use the Learn More links on the home page (**Figure 14.20**), and the `Help` link that appears at the bottom every page within the site.

Table 14.2

Netscape Search Quick Reference		
FOR THIS TYPE OF SEARCH:	DO THIS:	EXAMPLES:
Plain-English Question	Simply type a question that expresses the idea or concept, using as many words as necessary.	Where can I buy accessories for my IBM Thinkpad?
Phrase Search	Type the phrase enclosed in **double quotes**.	"thinkpad accessories"
AND Search (multiple words and phrases, each of which *must* be present)	Type words or phrases separated by a space, or use the Boolean operator AND (uppercase or lowercase) to connect two or more search terms. Both examples would produce the same results.	IBM thinkpad IBM AND thinkpad
	You can also put **plus signs (+)** directly in front of required search terms, in which case your results will be limited to Partner Search Results (paid listings from GoTo) and Web pages from Google.	+IBM +thinkpad
OR Search (multiple words and phrases, any one of which may be present)	Use the Boolean operator **OR** (uppercase or lowercase) to combine words and phrases.	notebook OR laptop
NOT Search (to exclude a word or phrase)	Use a **minus sign (-)** directly in front of the word or phrase you want to exclude from your results. (Note that there's no space between the minus sign and the search word.)	notebook -thinkpad
	Alternatively, you can use the Boolean operator **ANDNOT** (one word, uppercase or lowercase) followed by the word you want to exclude.	notebook ANDNOT thinkpad
Case-Sensitive Search	Not available.	
Date Search	Not available.	
Field Search	Not available.	
Nested Search	Not available.	
Proximity Search	Not available.	
Wildcard Search	Use an **asterisk (*)** to search for multiple characters at the end of a word only. The example would find references to *technological*, *technologies*, and *technology*.	technolog*

SEARCHING WITH NETSCAPE SEARCH

PART 4

SPECIALIZED
SEARCH ENGINES

Specialized Search Engines

Good as they are, the all-purpose search engines presented in Parts 2 and 3 of this book aren't the best tools for every job. Sometimes the fastest, easiest way to find a particular type of information is with a special-purpose search engine. For example:

- **Deja** for searching Usenet newsgroups.

- **Topica** for searching Internet mailing lists.

- **Argus Clearinghouse** for finding topical guides to Internet resources, written by experts in a particular field.

- **InfoSpace** for tracking down e-mail addresses, home addresses, and phone numbers.

- **Zip2** for finding businesses, whether they're on the Internet or not.

Chapters 15 through 19 focus on these five search engines. You'll find step-by-step examples and Quick Reference guides, similar to the ones for the all-purpose search engines in Parts 2 and 3.

Chapter 20 takes a slightly different approach. Here you'll find brief descriptions of 29 of the best *single-subject* search tools. In most cases, they are so specialized that using them is as easy as filling in the blanks. The most difficult thing about these search tools is remembering to use them.

✔ Tip

- Sooner or later, you're bound to need a specialized search engine for a subject that we haven't covered in this part of the book. When that happens, try one of these sites, which offer searchable directories of specialized search tools:

Invisible Web
invisibleweb.com

Search Engine Guide
searchengineguide.com

Search Engine Watch
www.searchenginewatch.com/links

DEJA FOR NEWSGROUP SEARCHES

What You Can Search

◆ Recent Usenet newsgroup postings (one month's worth)

◆ Usenet newsgroup archives (older postings dating back to May 1999)

Contact Information

Deja, Inc.
Austin, Texas
512-343-6397 (voice)
512-502-8889 (fax)
www.deja.com

The World Wide Web gets most of the press coverage, but for many people, Usenet newsgroups are the best thing about the Internet. Think of them as "electronic-word-of mouth" —millions of people from all over the world sharing information, ideas, and personal experiences. Some 35,000 newsgroups are out there, each devoted to a specific topic. And unlike Web sites, nobody owns or controls newsgroups, so people are free to say anything they wish—rants, raves, and tirades included.

You have to take a lot of it with a grain of salt, of course. But the fact is, newsgroups can be an excellent source of information— especially if you use a search engine like Deja to find the really good stuff. Deja also makes it relatively easy to avoid the "Get Rich Quick," "Free Horoscope Reading," and other widely distributed junk-mail postings—generally known as *spam*—that have made browsing and subscribing to newsgroups (as opposed to targeted searching) practically intolerable. Some general-purpose search engines (AOL Search, HotBot, and Yahoo, among others) give you the option of searching newsgroups as well as the World Wide Web. In fact, most of them actually use Deja to handle newsgroup queries made from their search forms. So why bother learning more about Deja? Why not simply master a couple of general-purpose search engines and rely on them whenever you want to explore newsgroups?

The main reason is that the Deja search capabilities offered by HotBot and other general-purpose search engines are but a *subset* of what's available at the Deja Web site (**Figure 15.1**). To take full advantage of this incredible resource—especially if you're an active participant in newsgroups— you'll want complete access to the full range of Deja databases and search capabilities, including the following:

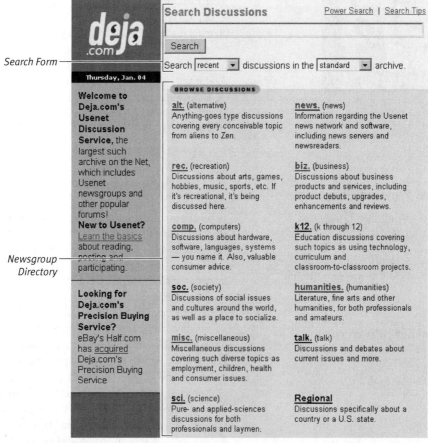

Search Form

Newsgroup Directory

Figure 15.1 The Deja home page includes a basic search form and newsgroup directory.

Figure 15.2 The search form on the Deja home page is fine for quick newsgroup queries.

◆ **Newsgroup Archives**. Deja has the largest collection of indexed, archived Usenet newsgroup postings available anywhere. The search form on the Deja home page (**Figure 15.2**) allows you to search the current database for recent postings (one month's worth). Or you can search for older material dating back as far as May 1999. (Eventually, the service hopes to archive postings all the way back to March 1995.)

◆ **Power Search**. Deja is *optimized* for searching newsgroups. You can do a quick search on a couple of keywords. But for even better results, and to avoid being swamped with irrelevant hits, use the Power Search page.

◆ **Query Language**. The Deja query language is quite sophisticated and well documented, with all the standard types of searches (AND, OR, NOT, and phrase searching), as well as more advanced features like proximity and field searching.

In short, the Deja Web site is superb, and for serious newsgroup searching, it just can't be beat.

✔ Tips

- If you'd like to know more about Internet history, terminology, and slang, look for *The Internet Glossary and Quick Reference Guide*, published by AMACOM. We wrote the *Internet Glossary* in collaboration with Alan Freedman, author of *The Computer Desktop Encyclopedia* and *The Computer Glossary* (also from AMACOM).

- For more information about the company behind Deja, click on About Deja.com at the bottom of the Deja home page.

- *Usenet* (short for *Usenet Network*), is a program that was created in 1979 to help foster communication and the exchange of ideas among people interested in the UNIX operating system. The program was designed to use the Internet to automatically transmit news about UNIX. That's why, to this day, the features Usenet offers are called *newsgroups*. But these days, of course, news about the UNIX operating system can be found in only a tiny fraction of the 35,000 or so newsgroups in existence.

- Deja was founded in 1995 as a service called *Deja News*, a pun on the phrase *déjà vu*—that odd sensation we all get from time to time of having heard or seen something before.

Understanding Newsgroup Names

The Deja site (www.deja.com) is so well designed and well documented that you'll have newsgroup searching mastered in no time. But before you plunge in, you need to know a couple of things about the terminology associated with Usenet newsgroups.

First, in recognition of the possible confusion over the term *Usenet newsgroups*, Deja often refers to them instead as *discussions* or *discussion forums*.

Second, the names of specific newsgroups (or discussions) don't make much sense until you understand the concept of *newsgroup hierarchies*—the system used on the Internet to organize the groups into general areas, topics, and subtopics. The most popular top-level newsgroup hierarchies are alt, biz, comp, misc, news, rec, sci, and soc (**Table 15.1**).

Specific topics and subtopics under these main areas are designated by the addition of a *period* (or *dot*) and an identifying word: for example, misc.health (pronounced "miss-dot-health"), misc.health.arthritis, and so forth.

One of the best ways to get a handle on Usenet newsgroup names and hierarchies is to spend a few minutes browsing newsgroups with Deja's Browse Discussions feature.

To browse newsgroups:

1. Click on one of the top-level newsgroup hierarchies in the Browse Discussions area (**Figure 15.3**) of the Deja home page.

Table 15.1

Popular Newsgroup Hierarchies	
alt	Alternative newsgroups—everything from sexy stuff to the truly offbeat.
biz	Business-related newsgroups that welcome advertising and marketing messages.
comp	Computer-related newsgroups.
misc	Grab-bag category, including the popular misc.jobs and misc.forsale.
news	Groups concerned with the Usenet network (not current affairs, as you might think).
rec	Recreation and hobbies.
sci	Science-related newsgroups.
soc	Groups devoted to social issues, often related to a particular culture.

BROWSE DISCUSSIONS

alt. (alternative)
Anything-goes type discussions covering every conceivable topic from aliens to Zen.

rec. (recreation)
Discussions about arts, games, hobbies, music, sports, etc. If it's recreational, it's being discussed here.

comp. (computers)
Discussions about hardware, software, languages, systems — you name it. Also, valuable consumer advice.

soc. (society)
Discussions of social issues and cultures around the world, as well as a place to socialize.

misc. (miscellaneous)
Miscellaneous discussions covering such diverse topics as employment, children, health and consumer issues.

sci. (science)
Pure- and applied-sciences discussions for both professionals and laymen.

news. (news)
Information regarding the Usenet news network and software, including news servers and newsreaders.

biz. (business)
Discussions about business products and services, including product debuts, upgrades, enhancements and reviews.

k12. (k through 12)
Education discussions covering such topics as using technology, curriculum and classroom-to-classroom projects.

humanities. (humanities)
Literature, fine arts and other humanities, for both professionals and amateurs.

talk. (talk)
Discussions and debates about current issues and more.

Regional
Discussions specifically about a country or a U.S. state.

Figure 15.3 Deja's Browse Discussions feature lets you explore newsgroups by *hierarchy*, the system used on the Net to name and organize discussion groups.

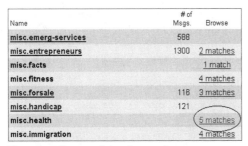

Figure 15.4 The misc (miscellaneous) newsgroup hierarchy includes misc.health, which, according to information in the Browse column, is further broken down into five additional newsgroups.

Figure 15.5 As you're browsing newsgroups with Deja, you can always stop and do a search of the category you're exploring.

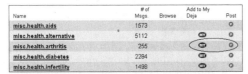

Figure 15.6 To subscribe or post a message to a specific newsgroup, click on the My button (to subscribe) or the P button (to post). The first time around, you'll also have to register with Deja.

2. Continue working your way down through the resulting pages until you find the specific newsgroup that you're looking for. At each point along the way, the Browse column (**Figure 15.4**) alerts you to the existence of additional subtopics.

3. You can stop at any point and do a keyword search of a specific topic or the entire Deja database (**Figure 15.5**).

✔ Tips

- In addition to browsing newsgroups, you can also use Deja to post messages and subscribe to newsgroups (**Figure 15.6**).

- For more on Usenet newsgroup hierarchies, see Appendix C.

UNDERSTANDING NEWSGROUP NAMES

Searching Newsgroups

Browsing newsgroups is okay for starters, but Deja's real power lies in its newsgroup search capabilities. Your best bet is to skip the form on the Deja home page, which is likely to produce too much information to be very useful. Instead, use the Power Search form for your Deja newsgroup searches.

To search with Power Search:

1. Click on Power Search (**Figure 15.7**) on the Deja home page to access the Power Search form (**Figure 15.8**).

2. Type your search terms in the text box and use the drop-down menu to specify whether you want to search for all or any of the keywords (**Figure 15.9**).

   Because the Deja archives are so vast (more than 1.5 terabytes of data), you may sometimes want to limit your search to a specific database using the Archive drop-down menu (**Figure 15.10**). Choices include:

   Complete. The entire archive.

   Standard. Everything *except* Adult, Jobs, and For Sale.

   Adult. Messages suitable only for adult readers because of explicit sexual content.

   Jobs. Job openings and resume postings.

   For Sale. Classified ads and advertising messages.

3. The Results Type menu (**Figure 15.11**) allows you to specify whether your search results page displays discussions (a list of newsgroup *messages*), forums (a list of newsgroup *names*), or Deja Classic (an older display format that dates back to when the service was called Deja News).

   Many longtime newsgroup searchers prefer the Deja Classic format and have prevailed upon Deja to continue to offer it. If you're using the service for the first time, you'll probably find that the discussions and forums options are perfectly acceptable.

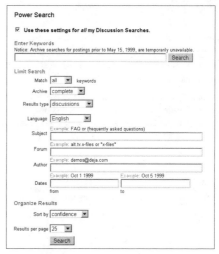

Figure 15.7 Most of the time, you'll want to use this link on the Deja home page to go directly to Power Search.

Figure 15.8 The Power Search form is easy to use and gives you a great deal of control over your newsgroup searches.

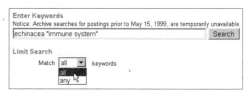

Figure 15.9 Selecting all on this menu tells Deja to do an AND search for the keywords typed in the text box. For an OR search, click on any.

Figure 15.10 Use the Archive menu to limit your search a specific Deja database.

Figure 15.11 This menu tells Deja whether you want to locate newsgroup *messages* (discussions) or *names* (forums). It also includes the Deja Classic option.

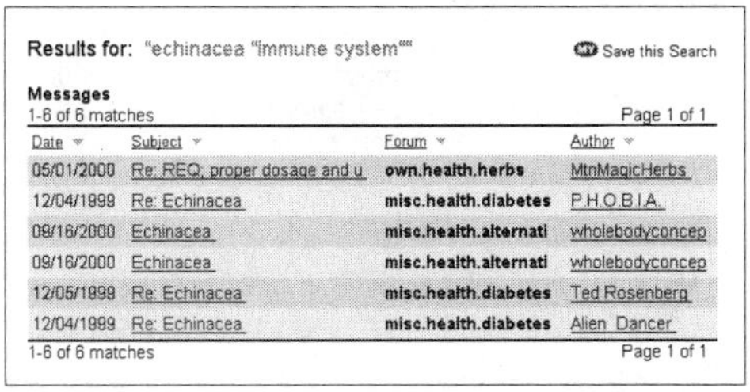

Figure 15.12 Here's an example of how Deja presents newsgroup search results.

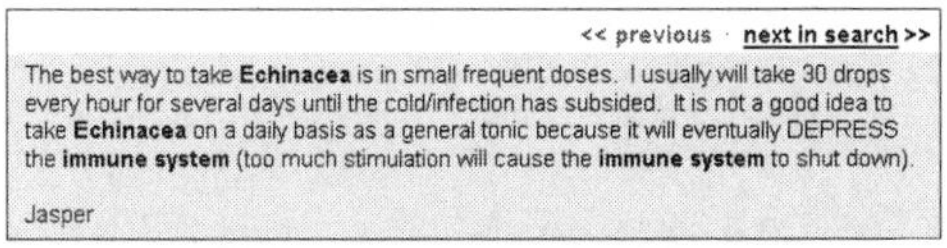

Figure 15.13 When you display a specific message, your search terms will be presented in bold to make them easy to spot.

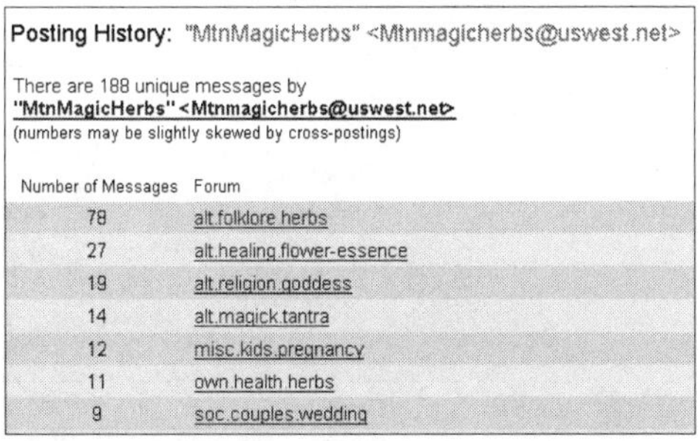

Figure 15.14 Clicking on an Author link shows you the person's *posting history*—the specific newsgroups in which the person participates and the number of messages posted.

4. Next you'll be given the option to specify these search options:

Language. You can limit your results to a specific language, or set the Language option to ANY for the widest possible search.

Field Search. You can search the Subject, Forum (i.e., newsgroup name), and Author fields of newsgroup messages by simply typing search terms in the spaces provided on the Power Search form.

Date Search. You can search for messages posted within a certain range of dates going back to May 1999. Be sure to specify dates in the format MMM D YYYY or MMM DD YYYY (for example, Jan 1 2000 or Mar 24 2001).

5. Power Search also lets you choose to have your results sorted by confidence (how well it matches your search terms), subject, forum, author, or date. And you can specify how many search results will be displayed per page (25, 50, or 100).

6. Once you've made all your search selections, click the Search button to submit your query and view your results (**Figure 15.12**).

7. To view the complete text of any message (**Figure 15.13**), click on its Subject link. Once you're on a message page, you can scroll back and forth through other messages, use the Thread link to view the complete *message thread* (original message and all subsequent replies), and post messages of your own.

8. You can also click on the Author link to learn about the person's other newsgroup interests and activities. Though by no means foolproof, checking a person's posting history (**Figure 15.14**) can help you assess the reliability of a source.

continues on next page

SEARCHING NEWSGROUPS

✔ Tips

- Deja supports phrase searching; the Boolean operators AND, OR, AND NOT, and NEAR; nested searches; field searches; and wildcards. For details, see the Deja Quick Reference (**Table 15.2**).

- Searches are *not* case-sensitive, so you can type search terms in uppercase or lowercase, or a combination, and you'll get the same results.

- Don't expect to find images, program listings, and other encoded binary files among Deja postings. They're simply too large and can't be easily indexed.

- The Deja help information is very thorough and well written. It even includes the service's list of *stopwords*—common words that the Deja search engine ignores (**Figure 15.15**).

- To access Deja's help information, click on Search Tips on the Deja home page. Then click on Boolean connectors for more details.

1995	do	may	s
1996	for	message-id	sender
a	from	newsgroups	subject
an	gmt	nntp-posting-host	t
and	have	of	that
any	i	on	the
are	if	or	there
as	in	organization	this
be	is	path	to
but	it	re	with
can	lines	references	you
date			

Figure 15.15 Unlike most search engines, Deja includes its list of stopwords along with the help information for the site.

Table 15.2

Deja Quick Reference

FOR THIS TYPE OF SEARCH:	DO THIS:	EXAMPLES:
Plain-English Question	Not recommended. Use a phrase or AND search instead.	
Phrase Search	Type the phrase as a sequence of words surrounded by **double quotes**. **Restrictions:** Phrases must contain at least two words that are not Deja stopwords. For a list of *stopwords*, see **Figure 15.15**.	"forensic medicine"
AND Search (multiple words and phrases, each of which must be present)	Use AND or & to connect two or more words or phrases. Or simply type the words or phrases separated by a space. All three of the examples would produce the same results.	cholesterol AND exercise cholesterol & exercise cholesterol exercise
OR Search (multiple words and phrases, any one of which may be present)	Use OR or I (**pipe symbol**) to connect two or more words or phrases. Both examples would find newsgroup postings that mention either *fitness* or *nutrition*.	fitness OR nutrition fitness I nutrition
NOT Search (to exclude a word or phrase)	Use AND NOT or &! in front of a word or phrase you want to exclude from your results. To look for postings about vitamins but not multi-level marketing deals, for example, you might want to exclude *mlm*.	vitamins AND NOT mlm vitamins &! mlm

SEARCHING NEWSGROUPS

Table 15.2

Deja Quick Reference *continued*		
FOR THIS TYPE OF SEARCH:	DO THIS:	EXAMPLES:
Case-Sensitive Search	Not available.	
Date Search	Use the Power Search form and specify a range of dates in the fill-in-the-blanks form. Use the format MMM D YYYY (for single-digit days of the week) or MMM DD YYYY (for double-digit days).	Oct 1 2000 Apr 15 2001
	Alternatively, you can use the date-search operator ~dc (for *date created*) right on the search form, in which case the date format must be YYYY/MM/DD.	~dc 2001/03/24
Field Search	Use the Power Search form for fill-in-the blank searching of newsgroup Author, Subject, and Forum (i.e., newsgroup name) fields.	
	Alternatively, you can use the following field-search operators on the search form itself:	
	Author: ~a Subject: ~s Group name: ~g	~a bjones@nih.edu ~s "lyme disease" ~g sci.med.diseases.*
Nested Search	Use **parentheses** to group search expressions into more complex queries. The example would find postings that mention *clinical study* or *clinical trial*.	clinical AND (study OR trial)
Proximity Search	Use NEAR or ^ (**carat symbol**) to find words that appear in close proximity to each other. The default distance is 5 characters, but you can change that by including a number along with the carat symbol.	infertility NEAR treatment
	The second example would look for the two words within 30 characters of each other.	infertility ^ treatment
	Restrictions: Phrases aren't allowed with Deja proximity searches. Also, neither search term can be on the Deja stopwords list. (See **Figure 15.15** for stopwords.)	infertility ^30 treatment
Wildcard Search	Use an **asterisk (*)** to search for wildcard characters. The example would find *therapeutic, therapist,* and *therapy*.	therap*
	You can also use **braces** ({ }) to search for a range of words. The example would find all words that fall alphabetically between *therapeutic* and *therapy*.	{therapeutic therapy}
	Restrictions: Wildcards cannot be used in phrases.	

TOPICA FOR MAILING LIST SEARCHES

Internet mailing lists are groups of people who regularly exchange e-mail on a subject that interests them. As with newsgroups, there are tens of thousands of mailing lists covering every conceivable topic. The vast majority of them are private—university professors discussing scholarly subjects, clubs and associations communicating with their members, families doing genealogical research or planning reunions. But there are plenty of general-interest mailing lists that welcome subscribers. The trick is to find them.

Topica (pronounced "TOP-i-kuh") is designed to help you do just that. Having acquired Scotty Southwick's highly regarded Liszt database of over 90,000 public and private mailing lists, Topica is now the premier site on the Net for doing mailing-list searches.

Once you find a list that sounds interesting, you can click on a link to subscribe (or to request more information if it's a members-only group for which you might qualify). From that point on, you'll receive all the group's postings automatically by e-mail.

Mailing lists aren't as freewheeling and interactive as newsgroups, and it takes some effort to locate and subscribe to the right ones. Furthermore, once you subscribe to a mailing list, you have to deal with the postings as they come into your mailbox.

What You Can Search

- Directory of over 90,000 mailing lists
- Message archives for public lists and lists to which you subscribe

Contact Information

Topica
San Francisco, California
415-344-0800 (voice)
415-344-0900 (fax)
info@get.topica.com (general info)
support@get.topica.com (tech support)
www.topica.com

But on the plus side, they aren't nearly as likely as newsgroups to be polluted with advertisements and get-rich-quick solicitations, because many list owners go to the trouble of making sure that such junk never reaches your mailbox. There's also the fact that people who have taken the time to seek out and subscribe to a particular mailing list are likely to be genuinely (perhaps passionately) interested in the subject, so they can be an incredible information resource.

✔ Tips

■ Mailing lists vary widely in what they offer and how they operate. Some maintain searchable archives. Some give you the option of reading "digests" instead of complete messages. Some lists are quite interactive, while others are designed primarily to distribute a newsletter or magazine and do little to encourage interaction with or among members.

■ One of the neat things about Topica is that, before subscribing to a mailing list, you often have the option of reading not only a *description* of the list but also the *archive* of messages that have been posted to it. Reading some actual messages is the best way of determining whether a mailing list will be interesting and worthwhile for you.

■ Scotty Southwick's Liszt directory is still available at www.liszt.com. But in a letter posted at the site, Southwick advises his fans that "Basically [Topica] will do everything I did for Liszt (except with a great big support and technical staff)."

■ There are three other widely used and respected mailing-list directories available on the Web. Though not as comprehensive and easy to use as Topica and Liszt, they're worth knowing about, if only to get a different perspective on the mailing-list phenomenon:

CataList
www.lsoft.com/lists/listref.html

Publicly Accessible Mailing Lists (PAML)
paml.net

Tile.Net
tile.net/lists

Searching for Mailing Lists

The Topica home page (**Figure 16.1**) gives you two ways of locating Internet mailing lists (or "Newsletters and Discussions" as they are called at the Topica site):

◆ You can click on one of several broad categories—like Art & Design or Sports & Recreation—to display a special page devoted to mailing lists on that topic.

◆ You can use the search form to do a keyword search of all the mailing lists in the Topica database.

continues on next page

Mailing List Topic Categories

Search Form

Figure 16.1 The Topica home page includes a search form and a directory of mailing lists organized into several broad topics.

SEARCHING FOR MAILING LISTS

In our opinion, however, the best way to search for mailing lists at Topica is to forget the home page completely. There's another location within the site that offers a more detailed subject directory and better search features. That's what we'll focus on here. But first you'll have to become a registered user of the site.

To register with Topica:

1. Go to the Topica home page at www.topica.com and click on sign up now (**Figure 16.2**) in the navigation bar.

2. Complete the short registration form and follow the prompts for confirming your registration via e-mail. It only takes a couple of minutes.

3. Once you've logged in as a registered Topica user, the navigation bar will include several new options, including one that will provide you with more and better search capabilities (**Figure 16.3**).

To search for mailing lists:

1. Go to the Topica home page at www.topica.com and click on search in the navigation bar. (If you don't see the search link, click on login and enter your e-mail address and password.)

2. To browse for mailing lists by subject, click on one of the topics or subtopics in the List Directory (**Figure 16.4**).

3. To do a search, type one or more keywords (or a phrase in quotes) in the space provided on the Topica search form.

   Topica supports the Boolean operators AND, OR, and NOT, as well as parentheses for more complex queries. Searches are *not* case-sensitive, so you can use uppercase or lowercase and you'll get the same results.

4. Use the search form's drop-down menu (**Figure 16.5**) to tell Topica whether you want to search Lists or Messages. In most

Figure 16.2 To take full advantage of all that Topica offers, you'll need to become a registered user. It's free and only takes a couple of minutes.

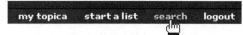

Figure 16.3 Once you're logged in, use this link to access Topica's expanded search capabilities.

Figure 16.4 The mailing-list directory for registered users is much more detailed than the one offered on the Topica home page.

Figure 16.5 The search form for registered users lets you specify whether you want to search Lists or Messages.

Figure 16.6 Search results are presented like this, with matching categories followed by matching lists.

Figure 16.7 Mailing lists with readable archives are identified by a magnifying-glass icon.

> MysticVisions ([MysticVisions])
>
> A list for writers of Fantasy, Futuristic, Science Fiction, Time Travel and Paranormal Romance. Whether you are published, just beginning, or anywhere in-between, short story, novelette, novella or novel length, please think about joining. There aren't many lists for fantasy, futuristic, science fiction, time travel & paranormal romance writers, so we hope you will find a home here. We want everyone to feel they can contribute and are a part of this writing list. We will share tips, URLs, contests, information on submitting, books, etc, and most of all encouragement and support for each other.
>
> Mystic Visions also offers a free email newsletter. Visions & Voices Monthly contains Mystic Visions news, updated information, market news, publisher interviews, articles, fiction and poetry. Sign up today on our website at Mystic Visions

Figure 16.8 Here's the description of a mailing list called MysticVisions, aimed at writers of fantasy, science fiction, and paranormal romance.

Website URL:	http://www.mysticvisions.com
List Type:	Unmoderated discussion
Subscription:	Does not require owner approval
Archive:	Readable by subscribers only
Created:	Jul 31, 2000
Owners:	Mary Kay, Owner 2, Owner 3
To Join:	Subscribe here, or send an email to MysticVisions-subscribe@topica.com
To Post:	Send mail to 'MysticVisions@topica.com'
Stats:	147 subscribers / 10 messages per day
Categories:	Humanities	Social Science	Communications	Writing	Organizations

Figure 16.9 Along with the mailing-list description, you'll find other useful information, like the availability of a message archive, number of subscribers, and message volume.

Figure 16.10 Topica makes it quite easy to join a mailing list and to read the list's archives.

cases, your best bet is to start by searching for lists, since not all mailing lists include message archives.

5. Click on Search to submit your query and view your results (**Figure 16.6**). Category matches, if any, will be presented first, followed by mailing-list matches. A magnifying-glass icon (**Figure 16.7**) identifies lists that include readable message archives.

6. Clicking on the name of a mailing list will take you to its description in the Topica database. Prepared by the list owner, the description typically includes a brief explanation of the list (**Figure 16.8**) and details on how to subscribe, unsubscribe, communicate with the list owner, and access other features like archives and digests (**Figure 16.9**).

7. In many cases, you can subscribe to a list or read the archives by simply clicking the appropriate button (**Figure 16.10**).

continues on next page

SEARCHING FOR MAILING LISTS

✔ Tips

- Before joining or even sending an e-mail message to a mailing list, do your homework. Use Topica to find out what the group is all about and whether new members are welcome.

- Mailing lists almost always have a special e-mail address for subscribing and unsubscribing. (When you use that address, your request is handled automatically, without any intervention on the part of the list's owner.) Don't make the classic new-user mistake of sending a subscription-related message to the address designated for posting messages to the mailing list (**Figure 16.11**).

- For a summary of Topica search syntax, see the Topica Quick Reference (**Table 16.1**).

- To access Topica's search tips and to find out about new features that may have been added, click on the `Help` link that appears on most Topica pages.

| To Join: | Subscribe here, or send an email to MysticVisions-subscribe@topica.com |
| To Post: | Send mail to 'MysticVisions@topica.com' |

Figure 16.11 Be sure to pay careful attention to the address used for *joining* vs. *posting to* a mailing list. Other list subscribers won't take kindly to receiving your subscription request in their mailboxes.

Table 16.1

Topica Quick Reference

FOR THIS TYPE OF SEARCH:	DO THIS:	EXAMPLES:
Phrase Search	Type the phrase as a sequence of words enclosed in **double quotes**.	"book reviews"
AND Search (multiple words and phrases, each of which *must* be present)	Use AND to connect two or more words and phrases.	authors AND mystery
OR Search (multiple words and phrases, any one of which may be present)	Use OR to connect two or more words and phrases.	grisham OR turow
NOT Search (to exclude a word or phrase)	Use NOT in front of a word or phrase you want to exclude from your results.	"genre fiction" NOT romance
Nested Search	Use **parentheses** to group words and phrases into more complex queries.	(fantasy OR SF) AND writers
Wildcard Search	Use an **asterisk (*)** to search for wildcard characters. The example would find references to *literacy*, *literature*, and *literary*.	litera*

ARGUS CLEARINGHOUSE SUBJECT GUIDES

The Internet's Premier Research Library
A Selective Collection of Topical Guides

We can't do a book about online searching without covering one of our all-time favorite information-finding resources, the Argus Clearinghouse. The quick handle on the Argus Clearinghouse is this: It's designed to make it as easy as possible for you to find "master" subject-specific Web sites or *guides*, as the Argus Clearinghouse calls them.

Guides are assembled and maintained by experts in a particular subject—not by robots and spider programs. They offer links—selected, organized, and annotated—to the most important Internet resources devoted to that subject.

What You Can Search

◆ Directory of subject-specific guides to Internet resources, prepared by subject-matter experts and reviewed and rated by information and library studies professionals.

Contact Information

Argus Associates, Inc.
Ann Arbor, Michigan
734-913-0010
clearinghouse@argus-inc.com
www.clearinghouse.net

To fully appreciate this incredible resource, a little history is in order. The Clearinghouse (its original name) was created in 1993 as an academic venture at the University of Michigan's School of Information and Library Studies (SILS). As part their Master's Degree program, SILS students would choose a topic and prepare a guide to Internet resources. The guides were critiqued and evaluated by professors and fellow classmates, and the best ones were made available on the Internet.

Graphical Web browsers like Microsoft's Internet Explorer and Netscape Navigator hadn't been invented yet, nor had Web search engines and directories like AltaVista and Yahoo. So the Clearinghouse was a most welcome addition to the Internet. But in the beginning, it was simply a plain-text menu (or *Internet Gopher*) site, and the guides themselves were ASCII text files that you could read or download.

The Clearinghouse has since moved to the Web, of course. It is now owned and operated by Argus Associates, a consulting firm that specializes in information architecture design for complex Web sites and Intranets. Students and graduates of the SILS Master's Degree program are still very much involved, but the guides are now created by subject-matter experts from all over the world. Clearinghouse staff members set rigorous standards and will only accept guides that rate high on content, design, and organization. More than 90 percent of the guides that are submitted for consideration are rejected for one reason or another.

The Argus Clearinghouse doesn't claim to be comprehensive—so you may or may not find the guide you need among its collection. But it's the perfect *first* stop for any in-depth Web research project.

✔ Tips

■ For details on how the Argus Clearinghouse evaluates subject guides, visit the site's home page and click on `Ratings System`.

■ Another link that's worth checking is the `Digital Librarian's Award`. It's sort of a Clearinghouse Hall of Fame—guides recognized by the staff as being truly exceptional.

■ If you don't find the guide you need at the Argus Clearinghouse, try one of these sites:

Virtual Library (`vlib.org`). The oldest collection of Web guides, VL was started by Tim Berners-Lee, the creator of HTML and the World Wide Web. Volunteers run the site, and the subject guides presented there—prepared by experts in a particular field—are highly regarded by academics and professional searchers.

About (`www.about.com`). This site takes the idea of Internet subject guides one step further—by hiring people who are knowledgeable in a particular field to not only create and maintain subject guides but also to interact with visitors to the site via newsletters, e-mail, discussion groups, and chat rooms.

Finding Subject Guides

To experience the Argus Clearinghouse for yourself, go to the site's home page at www.clearinghouse.net (**Figure 17.1**). Once there, you can click your way through menus or search for guides by keyword.

The menu system organizes Clearinghouse guides into 13 major categories—Arts & Humanities through Social Sciences & Social Issues. Click on any one of them and you'll be presented with a half dozen or so subcategories that lead, in turn, to a set of keywords. Click on a keyword and you'll be presented with all the guides for that subject.

By all means, take a walk through the menus. But if you have something specific in mind, you may find it's faster to use the keyword search feature.

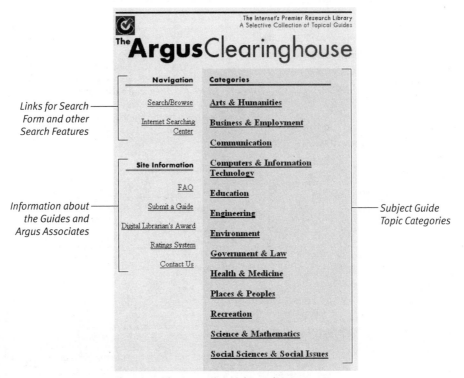

Links for Search Form and other Search Features

Information about the Guides and Argus Associates

Subject Guide Topic Categories

Figure 17.1 The Argus Clearinghouse home page includes a menu of 13 major subject categories.

To search for guides by keyword:

Navigation

1. Click on Search/Browse (**Figure 17.2**) on the Argus Clearinghouse home page to get to the search page.

Figure 17.2 The Search/Browse link in the upper left corner of the home page takes you to the search form and a more detailed subject outline.

2. Type your query in the search form text box (**Figure 17.3**). Coming up with the right search terms might take some trial and error. Keep in mind that what you are searching is a directory of guide descriptions (the Clearinghouse calls them *information pages*), not the guides themselves, so general search terms are likely to produce better results than very specific ones.

Figure 17.3 Here's the Argus Clearinghouse search form with a sample query you might use to locate guides dealing with children's literature.

3. Click the submit search button to display your results (**Figure 17.4**), which will include the name of each guide, along with its associated keywords and overall rating (one to five check marks).

Figure 17.4 Search results are presented like this, with several keywords along with each guide's overall rating—in this case 5, 4, and 3, as shown by the number of bold checkmarks.

4. Click on the name of any guide to display its information page (**Figure 17.5**), with the guide's title, Web address, author and professional affiliation, scores on five Argus Clearinghouse criteria, and descriptive keywords.

5. From there, you can click on the Web address to view the guide itself (**Figure 17.6**).

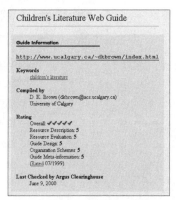

Figure 17.5 This is the information page for the award-winning "Children's Literature Web Guide" created by D. K. Brown at the University of Calgary.

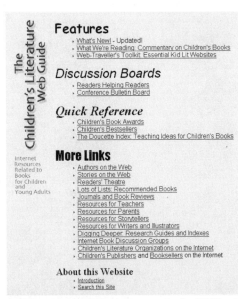

Figure 17.6 And here's the home page for the "Children's Literature Web Guide" itself, well-organized and full of useful information—just what you'd expect from a top-rated Clearinghouse guide.

✔ Tips

■ You can search for a single word or use some very basic search operators: AND, OR, parentheses, and wildcards.

■ Your best bet with the Argus Clearinghouse is to try to think of some very general search words that are likely to appear on the guide's information page. Searching for `Dr. Seuss AND Beatrix Potter` would be a great way to find children's literature Web pages with a search engine like AltaVista or Google, but *not* with the Argus Clearinghouse. For a Clearinghouse search, you'll have better luck searching with, say, `childrens literature` or `children AND books`.

■ The Argus Clearinghouse search software ignores case, so you'll get the same results whether you use uppercase, lowercase, or a combination. Punctuation marks (apostrophes, dashes, hyphens, quotation marks, etc.) are ignored as well, so it's recommended that you leave them out of your searches.

■ See the Argus Clearinghouse Quick Reference (**Table 17.1**) for search syntax and examples.

Table 17.1

Argus Clearinghouse Quick Reference*		
FOR THIS TYPE OF SEARCH:	DO THIS:	EXAMPLES:
Word or Phrase Search	Type the word or phrase without any special punctuation.	`news media`
AND Search (multiple words and phrases, each of which *must* be present)	Use AND to connect two or more words or phrases. The example would find guides whose titles or keywords include both words.	`Asia AND business`
OR Search (multiple words and phrases, any one of which may be present)	Use OR to connect two or more words or phrases, either one of which may appear in the guide's title or keywords.	`justice OR judicial`
Wildcard Search	Use an **asterisk (*)** to search for wildcard characters at the end of a word. The example would find *biology* as well as *biological* and *biologist*.	`biolog*`
Nested Search	Use **parentheses** to group search expressions into more complex queries. The example would find references to *art museum*, *art gallery*, and *art galleries*.	`art AND (museum OR galler*)`

*Note: *Argus Clearinghouse searches are not case-sensitive. Also, punctuation marks (apostrophes, dashes, hyphens, etc.) are ignored, so it's recommended that you leave them out when searching.*

INFOSPACE PEOPLE-FINDING TOOLS

What You Can Search

- Worldwide e-mail directory

- Telephone directory for residential listings in U.S., Canada, and Europe

- Reverse lookup directories (phone, address, e-mail, and area code)

- Celebrity directory (athletes, authors, journalists, movie stars, etc.)

Contact Information

InfoSpace, Inc.
Bellevue, Washington
425-201-6100 (voice)
425-201-6150 (fax)
information@infospace.com
www.infospace.com

Sending and receiving e-mail is without a doubt the most popular of all online and Internet features. Newsgroups, mailing lists, and chat rooms all have their devoted fans, and most online users venture at least occasionally onto the World Wide Web. But virtually *everyone* who's online sends and receives e-mail on a regular basis and counts it among their top two or three reasons for being online in the first place.

That being the case, it's no wonder that Web sites specializing in e-mail directories and other *people-finding* tools consistently rank among the Internet's 100 most frequently visited sites. We'll take a look here at InfoSpace, one of several excellent directory sites.

If InfoSpace doesn't have what you're looking for (and that's bound to happen from time to time), try one of these sites:

AnyWho	www.anywho.com
Switchboard	www.switchboard.com
WhoWhere?	www.whowhere.com
Yahoo! **People Search**	people.yahoo.com

There's simply no single, comprehensive source for all the world's e-mail addresses. Nor will there be any time soon. InfoSpace and these other e-mail directory sites provide a great service, but they currently list only a fraction of the millions of e-mail addresses that are out there.

✔ Tips

- InfoSpace and similar people-finding sites are often referred to as *white pages* because their databases typically include residential telephone numbers and street addresses—just like you'd find in your local telephone directory white pages. The difference is that you can search for anyone, anywhere in the United States.

- When we say "anyone, anywhere," we mean it quite literally. You can use InfoSpace and other such sites to find parents, grand-parents, neighbors, and friends who have never so much as touched a computer keyboard, let alone gone online.

- Because they allow you to cast such a wide net, white pages are terrific for locating former classmates, tracking down long-lost military buddies, and doing genealogical research. Yahoo! People Search (people.yahoo.com) is attempting to make the process even easier by allowing you to add descriptive keywords when you add or update your listing.

- Learn to use at least a couple of white pages Web sites. But keep in mind that sometimes the best way to find out a person's e-mail address is to do it the "old-fashioned" way: Pick up the tele-phone and call!

Finding E-mail Addresses

There are just a few things you need to know to take full advantage of InfoSpace's people-finding features. Start by going to the InfoSpace home page (www.infospace.com), where you'll find a menu of directory options (**Figure 18.1**). The section to zero in on is White Pages, which includes links for Phone & Address, Email, Reverse Lookup, and World Directories.

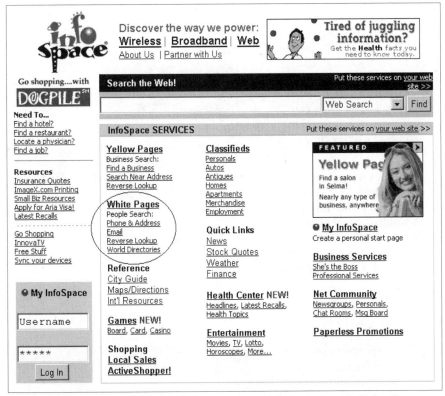

Figure 18.1 The InfoSpace home page includes a set of people-finding tools under the heading *White Pages*.

To search for e-mail addresses:

1. Click on Email on the InfoSpace home page to display the E-mail Search form (**Figure 18.2**). For relatively unusual names, you can probably get by with completing just the Last Name and First Name fields. For common names like Smith or Jones, go ahead and complete the City, State/Province, or Country fields as well, using the drop-down menus to make your selections.

2. Click on Find Email to submit your query. If InfoSpace finds a match, that information will be presented (**Figure 18.3**). If it comes up empty, you'll be given the opportunity to refine your search.

3. If a follow-up search is unsuccessful, try another directory site. See page 253 for other sites.

✔ Tips

- Unlike its competitors, InfoSpace doesn't actually provide you with e-mail addresses at its Web site. Instead, you're given a clickable link that you can use to send a message to a person you've located in the e-mail directory. The recipient can then decide whether or not to reveal his or her e-mail address by responding to your message.

- It's usually best to start with a name-only search. If you get too many hits, complete additional fields one at a time. If your search returns nothing, try a variation on the person's first name (Margaret instead of Meg, for example). Or use a single letter in the First Name field (E to find *Ed* or *Edward* or *Edwin*.)

- If you're not sure of the spelling of a last name, make your best guess, and then try a couple of variations. Unfortunately, InfoSpace doesn't support truncation or the use of wildcards in the Last Name field. So a search for Meyer will find listings for that name only, and you'll have to do a second search to look for Meyers.

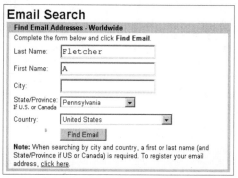

Figure 18.2 Here's the InfoSpace search form for locating e-mail addresses worldwide.

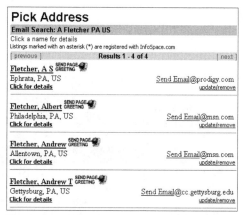

Figure 18.3 Results of an e-mail search are presented in this format. Instead of giving you the actual e-mail address, InfoSpace provides a link you can click on to send the person a message.

■ InfoSpace offers a feature called Reverse Lookup that allows you to search for the *owner* of an e-mail address. You can also use Reverse Lookup to find all the people in the InfoSpace directory who work at a particular company. For example, a Reverse Lookup search for @microsoft.com would bring up the names of all the Microsoft employees in the directory.

To use this feature, just click on Reverse Lookup in the White Pages section of the InfoSpace home page.

■ For Celebrity e-mail addresses, click on White Pages on the InfoSpace home page. Then scroll down the page and click on Celebrity Search. No telling what you'll find—some searches return e-mail addresses, some land addresses, some nothing at all. But it's worth checking.

■ You'll find a summary of InfoSpace search features in the InfoSpace Quick Reference (**Table 18.1**).

FINDING E-MAIL ADDRESSES

Table 18.1

InfoSpace Quick Reference	
FOR THIS TYPE OF SEARCH:	**DO THIS:**
E-mail Address Search (worldwide)	Click on Email in the White Pages section of the InfoSpace home page to display the search form. Start by completing just the Last Name and First Name fields.
	To narrow a search, complete additional fields one at a time, in this order: Country, State/Province, City.
	To broaden a search, try a partial entry in the First Name field. Searching for **A** in the First Name field and **Fletcher** in the Last Name field would find listings for *Albert, Al,* and *A. S. Fletcher.*
Phone Number and Address Search (U.S., Canada, and Europe)	Click on **Phone&Address** in the White Pages section of the InfoSpace home page to display the search form. Start by completing the Last Name, First Name, and State/Province fields.
	To narrow a search, complete the City field.
	To broaden a search, try a partial entry in the First Name field. Searching for **Jo Anderson** would find listings for *Joe Anderson* as well as *Joseph Anderson.*
	Another way to broaden a search that includes a City field is to select the **Including SurroundingRegion** option.
Reverse Lookup (phone and fax numbers, street addresses, e-mail addresses, and area codes)	Click on **ReverseLookup** in the White Pages section of the InfoSpace home page.

Finding Phone Numbers and Addresses

FINDING PHONE NUMBERS AND ADDRESSES

InfoSpace allows you to look for e-mail addresses worldwide. But what if the person you're trying to find doesn't have an e-mail address? (Lots of people don't.) And let's say you can't call Directory Assistance because you're not even sure what city the person lives in. What then?

The solution: Use the InfoSpace Phone & Address Search feature. If the person lives in the United States, Canada, or Europe, chances are you can find both an address (including zip code for U.S. addresses) and telephone number.

To search for phone numbers and addresses:

1. From the InfoSpace home page (www.infospace.com), click on Phone & Address in the White Pages section (**Figure 18.4**).

2. Enter the person's name in the spaces provided on the Phone & Address Search form (**Figure 18.5**). It's generally a good idea to start with a broad search, completing just the Last Name, First Name, and State/Province. If the name you're looking for is quite common, you might want to take your best guess at completing the City field as well.

3. Click on Find to display your results (**Figure 18.6**). If InfoSpace locates multiple entries in its database, you'll be presented with a list of all the matches. For details on a specific listing, just click on the name.

White Pages
People Search:
Phone & Address
Email
Reverse Lookup
World Directories

Figure 18.4 To search for home addresses and telephone numbers, click on Phone & Address in the White Pages section of the InfoSpace home page.

Figure 18.5 The Phone & Address Search form lets you look for residential phone numbers and addresses in the United States, Canada, and Europe.

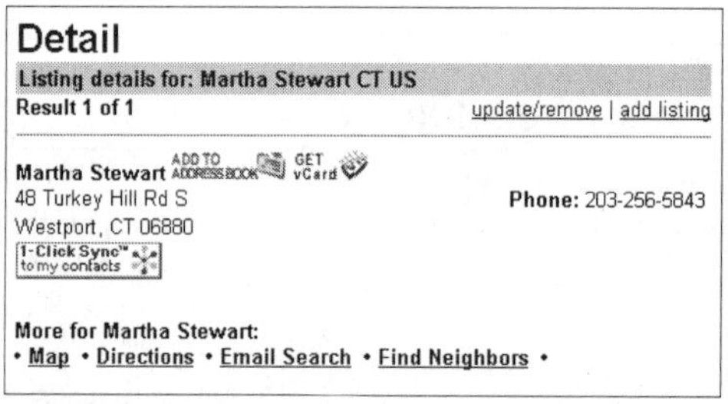

Detail

Listing details for: Martha Stewart CT US
Result 1 of 1   update/remove | add listing

Martha Stewart ADD TO ADDRESS BOOK   GET vCard
48 Turkey Hill Rd S   Phone: 203-256-5843
Westport, CT 06880
1-Click Sync™ to my contacts

More for Martha Stewart:
• **Map** • **Directions** • **Email Search** • **Find Neighbors** •

Figure 18.6 The search results include street address, city, state, zip code, phone number, and links for getting maps and driving directions.

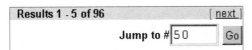

Figure 18.7 Instead of paging through dozens of listings, you can skip ahead by entering a number in the Jump to # box.

Find Neighbors

Figure 18.8 Click on this link to find all the other residents of a particular street—your own or someone else's!

4. If you get an exceptionally large number of hits, you can use the Jump feature (**Figure 18.7**) to advance more quickly through the list. Alternatively, you can go back and narrow the search. (Try adding a city, for example.)

5. If you get too few hits (or none at all), check your spelling. Or try typing just an initial in the First Name field.

   For United States searches that include a City field, you might also try the Including Surrounding Region option, so that your search will be expanded to include the outlying suburbs for a major metropolitan area.

✔ Tips

- InfoSpace gets home addresses and telephone numbers from companies that compile the information published in regional phone books. The InfoSpace database is updated about four times a year. If the person you're looking for has moved recently, it may take several months or so for the new information to make its way into the InfoSpace database.

- Keep in mind that many people list themselves in the phone book with a first initial instead of a full name. If your search for, say, Janet Parker is unsuccessful, try searching for J Parker.

- Once you've located a specific address that's of interest, you can use InfoSpace's Find Neighbors feature (**Figure 18.8**) to get the names, addresses, and phone numbers of all the other residents on that street.

To do reverse lookups of phone numbers and addresses:

1. Click on Reverse Lookup in the White Pages section of the InfoSpace home page.

2. Use the Reverse Phone Number form (**Figure 18.9**) to find out who "owns" a particular phone number. You can even search for a partial number as long as you know the area code and first few digits.

3. To find out who lives at a certain address, use the Reverse Address form (**Figure 18.10**). Fill in the House Number, Street Name, and City fields, and select a State from the drop-down menu.

✔ Tips

- The one caveat when using the Reverse Address form is that you may have to go through a couple of iterations on Street Name. The search software isn't very sophisticated and requires that you use "standard postal abbreviations." Consequently, if you type, say, River Road in the Street Name field, you won't find listings for *River Rd* and will have to try again using River Rd (no period).

- InfoSpace's Reverse Phone Number form allows you to search for partial numbers only if you know the area code. If that's the part of the phone number you *don't* know, try AnyWho (www.anywho.com). Its Reverse Lookup feature lets you look for phone numbers that begin or end with certain numbers.

Figure 18.9 Reverse Lookup of phone numbers is a neat feature. You can even look for a *partial* number—when you can't read your handwriting, for example, or your answering machine garbles the sound.

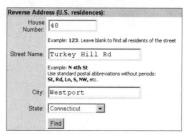

Figure 18.10 The Reverse Address form lets you search for the name and phone number of the residents of a particular street address.

ZIP2 FOR BUSINESS SEARCHES

You can use virtually any Web search engine to find information on businesses like Barnes & Noble, Disney, Federal Express, and Microsoft. Product announcements, catalogs, press releases, stock quotes, earnings reports—all these (and more) are available on the World Wide Web.

But what about the vast numbers of businesses, large and small, that have yet to establish a presence on the Web? The fact is, most companies, like most people, are *not* online.

And what if the information you're looking for is pretty straightforward—you want a street address or phone number so that you can visit the company or call to ask a specific question? Surprisingly, many business Web sites don't even include this information, or they bury it so deep that it's almost impossible to find.

For situations like these, what you need is an online *yellow pages directory*. The one we'll focus on here is the Zip2. It's well designed, easy to use, and extremely fast.

What You Can Search

- Directory of U. S. businesses, searchable by name and type of business

- Database of maps and driving directions

Contact Information

Zip2 Corporation
Mountain View, California
650-429-4400
webmaster@zip2.com
www.zip2.com

With Zip2, you can search for businesses by name or type—a standard feature of all the major yellow pages directories. Zip2 far outshines the competition, however, when it comes to displaying the *results* of a search. Look for, say, `Italian restaurants` or `dry cleaners`, for example, and Zip2 will present you with a list that includes the name, address, and phone number, organized by distance from your home or office (or any other location you specify).

Another Zip2 feature you'll appreciate is the ability to set up a *search profile*. Fill out a simple form with your home and work addresses and tell Zip2 to store the information. From then on, whenever you do a search, you can automatically look for businesses that are "Near My Home" or "Near My Work." No need to worry about specifying multiple cities, zip codes or area codes. Zip2 will present the results in order by distance, with the closest ones listed first.

Good as Zip2 is, you may from time to time have to check another yellow pages directory—either because the site is down or overloaded, or because you need to do a type of search that Zip2 doesn't offer. On those occasions, try one of these sites:

AnyWho   `www.anywho.com`

InfoSpace   `www.infospace.com`

SuperPages   `www.superpages.com`

Switchboard   `www.switchboard.com`

Yahoo! Yellow Pages `yp.yahoo.com`

✔ Tips

- For general searching, SuperPages comes closest to Zip2 in ease of use. AnyWho and InfoSpace offer Reverse Lookup for phone, fax, address, and area code searches, a feature not currently provided by Zip2. AnyWho is also the home of the AT&T Toll-Free Directory.

- As we've said, many business Web sites don't include a phone number or street address—either purposely or because it simply hasn't occurred to them that people might want to reach them that way. Furthermore, some companies operate on the Web using an entirely different business name from the one that's listed in print and online yellow pages directories. But that doesn't mean you can't track them down.

- One way to do so is to consult the Whois database maintained by Network Solutions. Just go to the Network Solutions Web site (www.networksolutions.com), click on Whois Lookup, and enter the *domain name* (for example, xrefer.com or westward.net) for the Web site that you're interested in finding out about. The Whois database will provide you with the name of the company that owns the domain name, along with the mailing address, phone number, and often even a contact person.

Finding Businesses with Zip2

To look for businesses with Zip2, go to the Zip2 home page at www.zip2.com (**Figure 19.1**). On your first visit to the site, scroll down the page, click on Personalize, and complete the form asking for your home and work addresses.

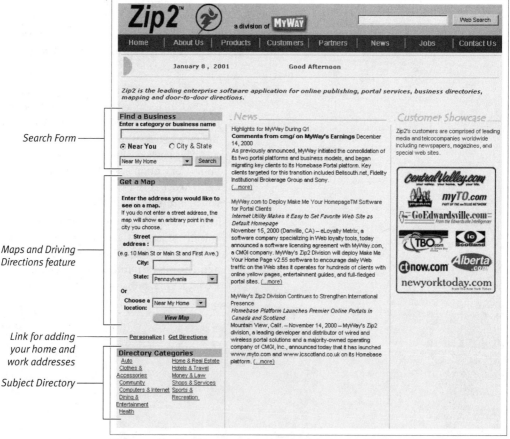

Search Form ——

Maps and Driving Directions feature ——

Link for adding your home and work addresses ——

Subject Directory ——

Figure 19.1 The Zip2 home page lets you search for businesses by type or by company name. And once you've clicked Personalize and entered your home and work addresses, you can search automatically for businesses that are nearby.

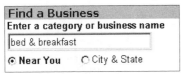

Figure 19.2 You can browse businesses by category using this subject directory on the Zip2 home page.

Figure 19.3 The Zip2 search form makes it easy to locate businesses in a particular area.

Figure 19.4 To search for businesses near your home, office, or some other location, use this drop-down menu.

Once you've done that, you can search automatically for businesses that are near your home or office. You can also browse local businesses by category, selecting from a menu of options (**Figure 19.2**) on the Zip2 home page.

To search for businesses:

1. Enter the type of business or a specific business name in the space provided on the search form (**Figure 19.3**). Then select the radio button to tell Zip2 whether you want to search Near You or by City & State.

2. If you choose the Near You option, you can use the drop-down menu (**Figure 19.4**) to further refine your search. You can look for businesses Near My Home, Near My Work; or near some other address you've entered using the Personalize feature (a vacation house, your parents' home, etc.). Zip2 tailors this menu so that it also includes surrounding towns and geographical areas that you might have occasion to search.

3. Click on the Search button to display your results. If you specified a Near You search and Zip2 finds multiple listings, they'll be presented in order by distance (**Figure 19.5**). City & State searches are presented alphabetically.

continues on next page

FINDING BUSINESSES WITH ZIP2

4. Click on any item on the results page for more information—which typically includes a map and driving directions, along with links for locating related businesses.

   If you're searching for a country inn, for example, the detailed information (**Figure 19.6**) would include a link for other Bed & Breakfast Accommodations— very handy if it turns out that your first choice is booked up. Or you could click on Find Nearby Businesses and search for a list of restaurants or tourist attractions close to a specific inn.

5. To do a new search, use the drop-down menu (**Figure 19.7**) that appears at the top of the page. You can also use this menu to choose other options available at the site—getting maps and driving directions without doing a search, finding a person, personalizing your page, and browsing a directory of businesses organized by type.

✔ Tips

- Zip2 always performs an AND search, looking for business listings that match *all the words* in your query. (There's no way to do an OR search.) Searches are *not* case-sensitive, so you can type your queries using uppercase, lowercase, or a combination and you'll get the same results.

- If you want to look for a particular type of business but aren't sure what search terms to use, start with a single, very general term like pets or roofing or travel. Zip2 will then present you with a list of business categories that you can choose from to focus your query.

Figure 19.5 Here's a sample of Zip2 search results. The icon to the right of each listing leads to maps and driving directions.

Figure 19.6 Details like those shown here for a Bucks County inn called Pineapple Hill Bed & Breakfast are presented when you click on the business's name on the search results page.

Figure 19.7 Use this drop-down menu to do another search or access other features, including the Zip2 business directory organized by subject and the Find a Person feature.

■ In order to show up in a yellow pages directory, companies must have a "business listing" with the telephone company. Many home-based businesses choose not to pay the higher rates for such listings, so you won't find them in the yellow pages. Instead, do a Zip2 Find a Person search using the drop-down menu (**Figure 19.7**) on the search results page. Look for the business owner's name rather than the company name.

■ For a summary of Zip2 search features, see the Zip2 Quick Reference (**Table 19.1**). To find out about new features that may have been added, click on the Feedback or Help link that appears at the bottom of all Zip2 pages.

Table 19.1

Zip2 Quick Reference*	
FOR THIS TYPE OF SEARCH:	DO THIS:
Business Name Search	To search for a specific business, enter its name (or one or two unique words) in the search form text box.
	Click on the radio button to specify whether you want to search NearYou or City& State. If you select NearYou, make sure the drop-down menu is set to NearMyHome, NearMyWork, or whatever location you want to use as a starting point.
Business Category Search	To search for all the businesses in a particular category, type one or two unique words in the search form text box.
	Be sure to specify the area you want to search (NearYou or City&State), as described above.
Point-to-Point Driving Directions and Maps	Click on the Get Directions icon that appears next to every listing in your Zip2 search results. (The Get Directions icon will be either a car in a circle or a double-pointing arrow in a square.)
	To get maps and driving directions without searching, use the Get a Map section of the Zip2 home page.

Note: Zip2 always performs an AND search, looking for all the words in your query. (There's no way to do an OR search.) Also, Zip2 ignores case.

FINDING BUSINESSES WITH ZIP2

OTHER SEARCH TOOLS FROM A TO Z

You've seen what a breeze it can be to use highly specialized search engines like InfoSpace (www.infospace.com) and Zip2 (www.zip2.com). Because they're designed for a single, relatively narrow task—looking for people and businesses in *white pages* and *yellow pages* directories similar to those used by telephone companies—the search forms are simple and there's very little complexity to master. Just fill in the blanks and away you go.

For the most part, that's what you'll find with the 29 special-purpose search engines profiled in this chapter. Each is designed to handle searching for a particular *type* of information really well—whether it's the latest book by a favorite author or Microsoft's Technical Support phone numbers or your Aunt Harriet's zip code. Many offer help pages and search tips, but for most of them, you won't need to learn any special search rules and commands. In our experience, about the only thing that's difficult about special-purpose search engines is remembering to use them.

That being the case, what we'll focus on here is where to find these special-purpose sites and the subject matter or type of information you can search with each one. Read the descriptions and visit some or all of the sites. Then add the ones you think you might use on a regular basis to your Web browser's Bookmarks or Favorites list. That way, you can get to them easily whenever you need them.

Where to Find Specialized Search Engines

When you need a special-purpose search engine for a subject not covered in this chapter, try one of these sites:

Invisible Web
invisible.com

Search Engine Guide
searchengineguide.com

Search Engine Watch
www.searchenginewatch.com/links

amazon.com.

www.amazon.com

Amazon.com

Amazon.com's mission is to sell books, and
they do a superb job of that from their Web
site, also known as "Earth's Biggest Bookstore."
But the Web site (www.amazon.com) is worth
learning about even if you have no intention
of ever placing a book order. Imagine being
able to search a database of some 2.5 million
books by author, title, subject, ISBN, or publisher. You can produce a master list of all
the books by a favorite author, for example,
or search for every book with the word
chocolate in the title.

You can also tap into a rich collection of
reader reviews, current bestseller lists, author
interviews, and book reviews from *The New
York Times*, NPR, Oprah, and elsewhere.

If there's a book you're looking for that's not in
the Amazon.com database (either because
it's out of print or not yet published), let
them know and they'll try to find it for you.

✔ Tips

- You can do a quick search for books from
  the Amazon.com home page. But for more
  precise queries, click on Books and then
  on Search and use the form that allows
  you to specify Author, Title, Subject, etc.

- Barnes & Noble (www.bn.com) and
  Borders (www.borders.com) also offer
  searchable databases of current books.
  For used and out-of-print titles, try
  Alibris (www.alibris.com) or Bibliofind
  (www.bibliofind.com).

www.cdnow.com

CDNOW

Like Amazon.com, CDNOW (www.cdnow.com)
is in the business of selling things—in this
case CDs and videos. To do so, they offer a
searchable database of more than 500,000
CDs and VHS/DVD movies. You can look for
a particular artist, album title, song title,
record label, video title, or actor/director.

But what if some elusive melody keeps going
through your head and you can't think of the
artist or song title? CDNOW has that covered
as well. You can send an e-mail message to
managerfb@cdnow.com and the company's
crackerjack team of music experts will try to
track the song down for you. Just give them
as much information as you can—bits of
lyrics, style of music, approximate release
date, and so forth.

The CDNOW site also includes Top 20 lists,
buyer's guides, sound clips, biographies, and
entertainment news.

www.cdc.gov

Centers for Disease Control and Prevention

There's enough medical and health-related information on the Internet to make your heart race and your head spin. So it's no wonder that the Web site operated by the Centers for Disease Control and Prevention (CDC) has become such a popular destination for people seeking reliable and timely information about healthcare issues.

You can do a keyword search of the entire CDC database, or limit your query to the health department for a particular state. Other highlights of the CDC Web site (www.cdc.gov) include the following:

◆ **Health Topics A-Z**. A directory of fact sheets on specific diseases and medical conditions.

◆ **In the News**. CDC press releases and current health news.

◆ **Travelers' Health**. Advice for international travelers on disease outbreaks and other health-related matters.

◆ **Hoaxes and Rumors**. Official responses from the CDC on health-related misinformation circulating via the Internet and other forms of mass communication.

✔ Tips

■ Other reliable sources often cited by medical professionals include Health A to Z (www.healthatoz.com), Healthfinder (www.healthfinder.gov), and the National Library of Medicine (www.nlm.nih.gov).

■ All three of these sites provide access to Medline, a highly respected database of medical literature, with abstracts and article summaries from *The New England Journal of Medicine, Journal of the American Medical Association*, and elsewhere.

OTHER SEARCH TOOLS FROM A TO Z

www.shareware.com

CNET Shareware.com

CNET Shareware.com is a "virtual software library" that let's you search a catalog of 250,000 shareware programs of all types—games, utilities, screensavers, word-processor add-ons, fonts, and so forth. (Shareware is "software on the honor system." Try the program for a designated period—usually 30 days—and then register and pay for it if you decide to keep it on your system.) The programs themselves are located in shareware archives and corporate sites throughout the Internet, but they can be downloaded directly from Shareware.com (`www.shareware.com`).

A related CNET search service called Download.com is also offered on the Shareware.com home page. The names are confusing at first, since, as we've said, you can both search for and download shareware from Shareware.com. So what's Download.com? It's a searchable catalog of demos, drivers, and patches offered by the creators of *commercial* (rather than shareware) programs.

✔ Tips

■ For best results, use Shareware.com's drop-down menu to specify your computer platform (Windows 95/98, Windows NT, Macintosh, etc.).

■ You can use double quotes to search for phrases (`"download accelerator"`), and plus and minus signs to include (+) or exclude (-) search terms.

■ Searching Shareware.com and downloading software are the easy parts. The hard part is identifying the really good stuff. (We know, because we've been evaluating and writing about shareware for almost two decades.) For our recommendations on the best tools and utilities for Web searchers, see Appendix D.

consumerworld.org

Consumer World

Consumer World (`consumerworld.org`) is a master site for consumer-related information. Created in 1995 by consumer advocate and educator Edgar Dworsky, the site provides links to over 2,000 consumer resources available on the Internet (categorized for easy browsing), as well as a search form you can use to zero in on a specific topic.

Consumer agencies, product reviews and buyer's guides from *Consumer Reports* and other sources, travel bargains and airline farefinders, the best credit card deals, health insurance options, tips for reducing junk mail and getting off telemarketing lists—you'll find information on these and more with a Consumer World search.

✔ Tips

■ Searching online for product reviews and buyer's guides is a lot easier than storing all those back issues of *Consumer Reports* and paging through them when you're ready to make a purchase decision.

■ If you're a *Consumer Reports* subscriber, you might want to consider signing up for the searchable online version of the magazine, which gives you access to the current issue and four years of back issues. The annual fee is $19 for magazine subscribers ($24 for non-subscribers). For more information, go to Consumer Reports Online at `www.consumerreports.org`.

www.cuisinenet.com

CuisineNet Menus Online

How's this for a neat idea: collect reviews, menus, and prices for hundreds of the best restaurants all over the United States and make them available (and searchable) on the Web? That's what CuisineNet Menus Online (www.cuisinenet.com) offers for these major metropolitan areas:

Atlanta	New Orleans
Boston	New York
Chicago	Philadelphia
Dallas	Portland
Houston	San Diego
Kansas City	San Francisco
Los Angeles	Seattle
Miami	Washington, DC

You can search for restaurants in a given area by location, type of cuisine, price, or "amenities" (things like wheelchair access, parking, special menus, smoking rules, entertainment, outdoor dining, and so forth). You can also specify that you only want to see listings for restaurants whose write-ups include menus.

✔ Tips

- To display the menus for a specific restaurant, click on the Menus link that appears right below the ratings section in the write-up. (If you don't see a Menus link, that particular restaurant hasn't yet made its menus available online.)

- For a second opinion on a restaurant's food, decor, service, and price, consult the popular *Zagat Surveys*, available online at Zagat.com (www.zagat.com). Both the Web site and the familiar pocket-sized burgundy guides are the creation of Nina and Tim Zagat—whose name, the Web site helpfully explains, is pronounced "za-GAT" (rhymes with "the cat").

www.edmunds.com

Edmund's Automobile Buyer's Guides

Edmund's Guides are required reading for anyone in the market for a new or used car. This Web site (www.edmunds.com) lets you search online for the following information and more, whenever you need it:

- Reviews by make and model
- Road test reports
- Dealer prices
- Used car and truck prices
- Loan and lease quotes

It's actually a directory rather than a search engine, but the site is so well designed and organized that you really won't mind.

www.elibrary.com

Electric Library

Electric Library (www.elibrary.com) is an incredible research tool. It gives you access to a searchable database of more than 150 full-text newspapers, 800 magazines, 2,000 classic books, two international news wires, and countless maps, photographs, and TV and radio transcripts.

You can pose a question in plain English and launch a search of the entire Electric Library database, or focus on one or more types of sources (newspapers, magazines, books, pictures, maps, or transcripts). This is a subscription service, but at $10 a month or $60 a year, it's a real bargain. You can sign up for a 30-day free trial at the Electric Library Web site.

✔ Tips

- For search tips and details on the specific sources that are included in an Electric Library search, go to the home page and click on Customer Service and then on Where Can I Find Help About.

- Infonautics, the company behind Electric Library, also offers a free service called NewsDirectory. Located on the Web at www.newsdirectory.com, this site organizes more than 14,500 news sources (magazines, newspapers, TV stations, government agencies, etc.) into a searchable directory.

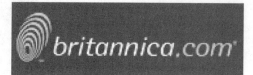

www.britannica.com

Encyclopedia Britannica

If you own a musty, outdated, 32-volume set of the *Encyclopedia Britannica*, you'll be pleased to know that the full text of this venerable reference work is now available—and searchable—online. In fact, there are two services, one free and one requiring a subscription:

◆ **Britannica.com**, located on the Web at www.britannica.com, is a free service, supported by advertising. It gives you complete access to the *Britannica* database, along with original commentary, special multimedia presentations, and a searchable and browsable directory of outstanding Web sites, selected by *Britannica* editors to supplement your database searches.

◆ **Encyclopedia Britannica Online** (www.eb.com), the subscription service, gives you faster access to the *Britannica* database, plus all the other features associated with the free service, but without the advertising. You can also format articles for printing and set up a personal workspace for storing articles associated with a particular research project. And you can tap into *Britannica Intermediate*, designed for students in elementary and high school. The annual subscription fee is $50.

✔ Tips

■ You can use plus and minus signs in your *Encyclopedia Britannica* queries to include (+) or exclude (-) words and phrases. To search for a phrase, enclose the words in double quotes.

■ Both sites also support the use of the Boolean operators AND, OR, NOT, and ADJ (to look for two words adjacent to each other).

www.epicurious.com

www.expedia.com

Epicurious Food

Created by Condé Nast, the publisher of *Gourmet* and *Bon Appétit* magazines, Epicurious (`www.epicurious.com`) is a cook's and food-lover's delight. You'll find complete menus, practical cooking tips and techniques, and cookbook reviews and recommendations. But the best part about the site is its Recipe File, a searchable database of more than 11,000 recipes that have appeared in *Gourmet* and *Bon Appétit.*

If you're a subscriber to one or both magazines, you'll appreciate not having to root through the recycle pile to find a recipe you forgot to clip out. Just search the database, using one or two keywords to identify the type of recipe and a unique ingredient: `eggplant` and `appetizer`, for example. Chances are, you'll find it.

✔ Tip

- Recipes from Martha Stewart's magazine and television show are also available online at `www.marthastewart.com`. As Martha herself would say, "It's a good thing!"

Expedia Travel Information

When we're going on a trip that involves air travel, we prefer using a travel agency to actually book our flights and issue the tickets. After all, they're the pros and are much more likely to know about the best fares and any special deals that might be available. But we often use the Net prior to calling our travel agent to get an idea of airline schedules and fares. And one of the fastest and most reliable places to do that is Microsoft's Expedia travel Web site (`www.expedia.com`).

You can also use Expedia to check the status of a specific flight, search for hotels and "specialty lodgings" (apartments, country inns, and bed-and-breakfast accommodations), and locate the best car-rental deals. There's also a handy currency converter so that you can check the exchange rate just prior to leaving for a foreign country.

✔ Tips

- Sign up for Expedia's Fare Tracker service and they'll send you an e-mail message each week alerting you to the best fares for up to three travel destinations.

- Travelocity (`www.travelocity.com`) is another good choice for travel information. It's quite similar to Expedia and offers most of the same services, including airline fare-finder and fare-tracker features.

www.fedex.com

FedEx Package Tracking

If you use overnight courier services on a regular basis, the FedEx Web site (www.fedex.com) is one you should definitely get to know. It can be a real time-saver when the FedEx phone lines are jammed up, or any time you want to get a question answered quickly.

With FedEx Package Tracking, you can search the company's shipping database by airbill number to find out exactly when your shipment was delivered and who signed for it. The Drop-off Locator, another searchable database, will help you identify the nearest self-service and staffed FedEx locations and the cutoff times for dropping off your package.

FindLaw

www.findlaw.com

FindLaw Legal Resources

FindLaw (www.findlaw.com) is one of the premier sites for doing legal research on the Web. You can browse the site's legal resources directory, which is organized by topic. Or use one of several FindLaw search services:

◆ **LawCrawler**, to find cases, codes, and regulations at legal sites throughout the Internet.

◆ **Supreme Court Center**, for Supreme Court decisions dating back to 1893.

◆ **Find a Lawyer**, to locate a lawyer or law firm by name, practice, or city/state.

◆ **Forms**, for over 8,000 Federal and State Court forms and sample agreements for small businesses.

◆ **Legal News**, for current news articles on a specific subject.

◆ **Library**, for background information in articles written by top attorneys, bar associations, and government agencies.

✔ Tips

■ To display FindLaw resources geared to your particular interests, click on the appropriate link in the navigation bar at the top of the home page (Legal Professionals, Students, Business, or Public).

■ For best results, be sure to click on Help & Information at the bottom of the home page and get to know the material presented there. The search tips and advice provided in FindLaw Help and LawCrawler Information are likely to prove especially useful.

firstgov.gov

FirstGov

An official Web site of the United States government, FirstGov (firstgov.gov) is designed to give you one-stop access to all local, state, and federal government resources that are available online. The site offers three ways for locating information:

◆ Search by keyword using the FirstGov search form.

◆ Browse the FirstGov subject directory, which is organized into topics like "Agriculture and Food," "Federal Benefits and Grants," and "Money and Taxes."

◆ Click on the link for a specific branch of the U. S. Government (Executive, Legislative, or Judicial).

✔ Tips

■ FirstGov doesn't currently offer much in the way of search tips and help information, except to say that, in choosing your search terms, you should "try to be as exact as possible."

■ Give the search form a try, but if you don't find what you're look for after a couple of queries, use the subject directory or the links for branches of government.

■ If it's Congressional activities you're interested in, for example, click on Legislative Branch and you'll find information about the United States Senate and House of Representatives, the Congressional Budget Office, and the Library of Congress.

Then click on Library of Congress and you'll find a link for Thomas Legislative Information. Named in honor of Thomas Jefferson, this site (thomas.loc.gov) gives you access to the full text of the *Congressional Record*, all legislation currently under consideration by Congress, and historical documents like the Declaration of Independence and the Constitution.

OTHER SEARCH TOOLS FROM A TO Z

www.infoplease.com

Information Please Almanacs

Sometimes all you need is a quick fact or a bit of trivia—the latest population figures from the United States Census, for example, or Oprah Winfrey's birthday. When that's the case, visit Infoplease (www.infoplease.com), a free online reference site that gives you access to data from the various *Information Please* almanacs as well as material from *The Columbia Electronic Encyclopedia*, a dictionary provided by Random House, and a database of biographical information.

✔ Tip

- There's also a special kids' version of Infoplease called Fact Monster (www.factmonster.com), where school students can not only search but also ask questions and get help with homework assignments.

imdb.com

Internet Movie Database

"Where have I seen that character before?" If you've ever left a movie theater puzzling over that question, you need the Internet Movie Database (IMDb). With information on over 150,000 movies and hundreds of thousands of actors, actresses, and crew members, IMDb (imdb.com) is the single best film resource we've encountered on the Web.

You can search IMDb for a specific actor or actress (or crew member) for a brief biography and a complete list of other movie credits. Or you can search by movie title to find out when a particular film was made and who was involved in the production—director, cast, and crew.

There's lots more besides, and the site is now owned by online bookseller Amazon.com, so it's sure to get better and better.

✔ Tip

- For Advanced Search options, like finding the names of all the movies in which, say, Lauren Bacall and Humphrey Bogart appear together, click on More searches on the IMDb home page and then on people working together.

www.mapquest.com

MapQuest

MapQuest (www.mapquest.com) specializes in worldwide maps and driving directions between any two places in the United States. The maps won't replace your trusted road atlas or the large, fold-out variety you keep in the glove compartment of your car. But the point-to-point driving directions, including estimated mileage, are a neat feature.

Based on our experience, you'll still want to consult your favorite map or road atlas to verify the suggested route, but in general, MapQuest is pretty reliable. Give it a try before your next road trip.

✔ Tip

- If you want to *buy* an atlas, road map, or wall map, go to Mapquest's MapStore Web site (www.mapstore.com). The site offers maps of all types from more than 100 publishers.

support.microsoft.com/directory

Microsoft Product Support Services

If you've ever tried calling a major software company for technical support, you know how frustrating it can be to get even the simplest question answered. You either get a busy signal right from the start, or you work your way intently through the company's voice-mail menu system, only to be put on hold.

Microsoft does a better job than most at handling technical support calls, but they also supplement their phone operation with an outstanding product-support Web site, located at support.microsoft.com/directory.

The site gives you access to the Microsoft Knowledge Base—the place to look for answers to questions about any Microsoft product. Other searchable databases offered at the site include Frequently Asked Questions, Download Center (for service releases, patches, and updates), and Microsoft Newsgroups.

✔ Tip

- If all else fails and you simply have to talk to a real person, click on Phone Numbers to access a directory of Microsoft technical support numbers and service options, organized by product.

content.monster.com

Monster Career Center

Originally known as the Monster Board, Monster.com is the Internet's most popular job-hunting site. But in addition to its gigantic searchable database of job openings and resume postings, the site's Career Center (`content.monster.com`) offers one of the best collections of job-hunting and career-development resources on the Net.

You'll find sound advice on writing cover letters and resumes, the latest salary surveys from the U. S. Department of Labor's Bureau of Labor Statistics and other sources, relocation tools and calculators, and a searchable database of company information.

✔ Tip

- The Bureau of Labor Statistics Web site (`www.bls.gov`) is another excellent place to look for career information and salary data. Among other things, you can search the latest edition of *The Occupational Outlook Handbook*, one of the most comprehensive sources of information on a wide range of occupations. Updated every two years, *Handbook* entries for specific occupations typically include descriptions of job activities, working conditions, education and training requirements, projected earnings, and job prospects.

The New York Times ON THE WEB **Books**

nytimes.com/books

New York Times Book Reviews

One of several "*New York Times* on the Web" features, the Book Review site (`nytimes.com/books`) gives you access to all the book reviews, book news, and author interviews that have appeared in *The New York Times* since 1980, searchable by title, author, or keyword. You can also browse the current issue of *The New York Times Book Review*, which is supplemented by Web-only features like author interviews, complete first chapters of selected books, and expanded versions of the hardcover and paperback bestseller lists (30 titles instead of 15).

✔ Tips

- For best results when looking for a book title or an author's name at the *New York Times* Web site, enclose the words in double quotes: `"Ship of Gold"` or `"Gary Kinder."`

- Another good source of book reviews and first chapters is Steve Brill's Contentville (`www.contentville.com`).

www.parentsoup.com

Parent Soup

Whether you're awaiting the birth of your first child or packing the last one off to college, you're sure to have questions and concerns, and iVillage's Parent Soup Web site (www.parentsoup.com) may just have the answers.

Parent Soup's database includes thousands of articles on all aspects of parenting, from very specific concerns (like how to deal with the current body-piercing craze) to more general issues like baby-proofing your house and financing your child's college education.

Other popular features at the site include:

◆ The Baby Name Finder

◆ Pregnancy and First Year Calendars

◆ Child and Senior Care Directories

www.petersons.com

Peterson's Education & Career Center

Brought to you by the publishers of *Peterson's Guide to Four-Year Colleges* and dozens of other well-known education and career guides, the Peterson's site (www.petersons.com) makes much of that same information available online in searchable form.

There are separate databases for private secondary schools, colleges and universities, graduate programs, studying abroad, camps and summer programs, and executive education and training.

✔ Tip

■ If you've found the right school but need help figuring out how to pay for it, visit the FinAid Web site (www.finaid.org), where you can search for scholarships, fellowships, and loans.

www.gutenberg.net

Project Gutenberg E-Texts

Project Gutenberg was started 30 years ago by Michael Hart at the University of Illinois. His objective was to make all of the world's great works of literature available online so that students and researchers could study them at no cost. Volunteers from all over the world do the typing, and the project survives solely on donations.

Today, the Project Gutenberg archive (www.gutenberg.net) includes more than 3,000 works, all of which are in the public domain, so no laws are being broken. You can search the archive for the complete text of *Aesop's Fables*, *Alice in Wonderland*, the Bill of Rights, the Book of Mormon, and the King James Bible, to name just a few examples. The project is also slowly expanding to include musical scores and important images (like the original Tenniel illustrations for *Alice in Wonderland* and an MPEG file of the moon landing).

Of course, only the most dedicated and under-funded scholars would choose to read *Moby Dick* on their computer screens. The real advantage to having great works of literature available online is that they can be down-loaded to your computer and then *searched* using any word processor.

✔ Tip

■ For those occasions when all you need is a quick quote (rather than the full text) from one of the literary classics, try Bartleby.com (www.bartleby.com).

www.1040.com

Tax Forms and Information

Have you ever sat down to work on your taxes, only to find that you're missing one vital form? It's probably an obscure one, too—one that's not likely to be available at the post office or library, even if they're still open when you make your discovery.

Thanks to 1040.com (www.1040.com), a service of Drake Software, you need never face this problem again. You can download federal and state tax forms, along with all the relevant instructions and publications, at any time of the day or night.

✔ Tips

■ You'll need a program called Adobe Acrobat Reader to view and print the forms that you get from 1040.com. If you don't have that program on your system already, you can download it for free at many Web sites, including 1040.com.

■ The Internal Revenue Service Web site (www.irs.gov) offers tax forms, too, of course. But 1040.com is easier to use and often faster than the official government site.

www.tvguide.com

TV Guide Online

Television listings and the Internet were simply made for each other, so we're happy to report that *TV Guide* has done an excellent job with its Web site (www.tvguide.com). Suppose you like to tape reruns of "The Practice" to watch while doing your NordicTracking. Or maybe you want to know when a PBS show will be aired again. With the magazine, the only way to find the channels and times is to laboriously page through each day's listings. But with the *TV Guide* Web site, it's a snap!

The first time you visit the site and click on TV Listings, you'll be asked to enter your Zip code and type of service (cable, broadcast, or satellite). From then on, whenever you visit the site and use any of the search functions, your local area listings will be presented automatically.

✔ Tip

■ The *TV Guide* Web site uses *cookies* to remember your zip code information. If you've disabled cookies in your Web browser, you'll have to enter your zip code information each time you visit the site.

www.ups.com

UPS Package Tracking

Not to be outdone by FedEx, rival United Parcel Service (UPS) also offers Package Tracking and Drop-off Locator features at its Web site (www.ups.com).

For Package Tracking, you simply key in the UPS tracking number and you'll be presented with a detailed report on the status of your shipment. The Drop-off Locator helps you find the nearest place (often your neighborhood grocery or office-supply store) that will accept packages for shipping by UPS.

✔ Tip

■ UPS tracking numbers are typically quite long, and it's easy to make a mistake when typing them into the search form. If you were sent the tracking number in an e-mail message, use your program's Copy and Paste features to enter the number in the UPS search form instead of typing it yourself.

THE WALL STREET JOURNAL.

wsj.com

Wall Street Journal Online

Don't cancel your subscription to the traditional paper version of *The Wall Street Journal* that's delivered in time to enjoy with your morning coffee or carry with you on the train for your commute to work. But if you'd like to be able to search for articles that have appeared in the *Journal* during the past 30 days, spring for an extra $29 per year ($59 for non-subscribers) for access to the online edition, available on the Net at `wsj.com`.

✔ Tip

■ Subscribers to the online edition of *The Wall Street Journal* are also given access to the Dow Jones News/Retrieval Publications Library—more than 6,000 newspapers, news wires, magazines, trade and business journals, transcripts, and newsletters going back 20 years. Searching this database is provided as part of your online subscription, but any articles you choose to view and print (or save to disk) are billed at $2.95 each.

www.zdnet.com

ZDNet Computer Information

ZDNet (`www.zdnet.com`) is the online home for *PC Magazine*, *Macworld*, and more than a dozen other Ziff-Davis computer publications. It's one of the best technology sites on the Internet, and a great place to search for hardware and software reviews, shareware and public domain software, and information on high-tech companies.

For best results, click on `Power Search` to access ZDNet's search options for these areas:

◆ **Product Information**. Use the Articles search form to find articles, reviews, buyer's guides, and company information in Ziff-Davis computer magazines and newspapers.

◆ **PC Downloads**. Use the Downloads search form to locate shareware and public domain software for Windows and DOS.

◆ **Mac Downloads**. Click on the `Mac Downloads` link to search for shareware and public domain software for the Macintosh.

✔ Tip

■ The next time you're considering a hardware or software purchase or struggling with a computing problem of some sort, check here first. You won't be disappointed.

www.usps.com

Zip Code Lookups

The United States Postal Service (USPS) is the target of lots of criticism and jokes, but here's an example of something they're really doing right: a convenient, easy to use, zip code locator. Just go to the Web site (www.usps.com), click on Find ZIP Codes, and key in a street address, city, and state. Almost instantly, the system tells you the nine-digit ZIP+4 code for that location.

When you think about the time and effort required to travel to the Post Office and thumb through that big fat Zip code directory they keep there, this is a wonderful innovation. And a great example to leave you with as we end this chapter (and this part of the book) on special-purpose search engines.

✔ Tips

- To save keystrokes when you want to visit the USPS Web site, you can just type usps in your Web browser's Address or Location box.

- In addition to Zip codes, you can also get postal-rate information, order stamps, and track packages at the USPS Web site.

Search Engines Quick Reference

A

For each search engine covered in this book, we've assembled the most important commands and other essential information into one or more Quick Reference guides. How do you do an AND search with AltaVista or Google? Are Yahoo queries case-sensitive? What Boolean operators are allowed with Lycos? This is the information *we* have always wanted to have at hand for our own online searches but could never find all in one place.

The Quick Reference guides appear throughout the book in the individual search engine chapters. But we've collected all of them into this appendix, arranged in alphabetical order by search engine name, to make them easier to find. If you're like us, you'll be turning to these pages often as you explore the Web with your favorite search engines.

AltaVista   www.altavista.com

AltaVista Basic Search Quick Reference		
FOR THIS TYPE OF SEARCH:	**DO THIS:**	**EXAMPLE:**
Plain-English Question	Simply type the question in the search form text box. Use as many words as necessary.	What is the date of the Battle of Trafalgar?
Phrase Search	Type the phrase as a sequence of words surrounded by **double quotes.**	`"Battle of Trafalgar"`
AND Search (multiple words and phrases, each of which *must* be present)	Use a **plus sign (+)** in front of each word or phrase that must appear in the results.	`+London + "art museum"`
OR Search (multiple words and phrases, any one of which may be present)	Type words or phrases separated by spaces, without any special notation.	`Stratford Shakespeare`
NOT Search (to exclude a word or phrase)	Use a **minus sign (–)** in front of a word or phrase you want to exclude from the results.	`+python –monty`
Case-Sensitive Search	Use lowercase to find any *combination* of uppercase and lowercase. Use capital letters (initial caps or a combination of uppercase and lowercase) to force an exact match of your search term. The first example would match *Bath* (but not *bath* or *BATH*). The second example would match *BATH* only.	`Bath` `BATH`
Date Search	Not available on the Basic Search form. Use Advanced Search or Power Search.	

Field Search	Type field-search keyword in lowercase, followed by a colon and your search word or phrase. (See page 292 for a complete list of field-search keywords.)	`title:"Victoria and Albert Museum"`
		`host:cambridge.edu`
		`domain:com`

Nested Search	Not available on the Basic Search form. Use Advanced Search or Power Search.	
Proximity Search	Not available on the Basic Search form. Use Advanced Search or Power Search.	
Wildcard Search	Use an **asterisk (*)** at the end of or within a word, along with at least three letters at the beginning of the search term.	`Brit*` `col*r`

AltaVista www.altavista.com

AltaVista Advanced Search Quick Reference		
FOR THIS TYPE OF SEARCH:	DO THIS:	EXAMPLES:
Plain-English Question	Not recommended on Advanced Search form. Use Basic Search instead.	
Phrase Search	Just type the phrase in the search box (*without* quotation marks). AltaVista interprets as a phrase any words that appear together without a search operator between them.	Tower of London
AND Search (multiple words and phrases, each of which *must* be present)	Use AND between words or phrases to specify that both must be present in the results.	Oxford AND Cambridge
OR Search (multiple words and phrases, any one of which may be present)	Use OR between words or phrases to specify that you want to find references to either or both terms.	Oxford OR Cambridge
NOT Search (to exclude a word or phrase)	Use AND NOT in front of the word or phrase you want to exclude from the query.	Oxford AND NOT Cambridge
Case-Sensitive Search	Use lowercase to find any *combination* of uppercase and lowercase. Use capital letters (initial caps or a combination of uppercase and lowercase) to force an *exact match* of your search term, as shown in the example.	Round Table
Date Search	Type the range of dates you want to search in the From and To boxes, using the form DD/MM/YY. The example would search for dates between January 1, 2001, and December 3, 2001 (not March 12, 2001).	From: 01/01/01 To: 03/12/01
Field Search	Type field-search keyword in lowercase, immediately followed by a colon and your search word or phrase. (See page 292 for a complete list of field-search keywords.)	title:Castle Howard domain:com host:cambridge.edu
Nested Search	Use **parentheses** to group search expressions into more complex queries. The example would find *Queen Mother* as well as *Queen Mum*.	Queen (Mother OR Mum)
Proximity Search	Use NEAR to find words or phrases that appear within 10 words of each other. The example would find *bed and breakfast* as well as *bed & breakfast* and *breakfast in bed*.	bed NEAR breakfast
Wildcard Search	Use an **asterisk (*)** at the end of or within a word with at least three letters at the beginning of the search term.	bicycl* col*r

SEARCH ENGINES QUICK REFERENCE

AltaVista www.altavista.com

AltaVista Field Search Quick Reference

SEARCH TERM	DESCRIPTION	EXAMPLES
anchor:	Searches for Web pages that contain the specified hyperlink.	anchor:"free product samples"
applet:	Searches for Java applets. If you don't know the name of the applet, try combining an applet wildcard search with some other search term.	applet:beeper +applet:* +Java
domain:	Searches Web addresses for a specific domain (**com, edu, gov, net, org**, etc.) or two-letter Internet country code. (See Appendix B for a complete list.)	domain:edu domain:uk
host:	Searches just the *host name* portion of Web addresses.	host:beatlefest.com host:oxford.edu host:BBC
image:	Searches Web pages for the filenames of images matching your search term.	image:ringo.gif image:*.gif
like:	Searches for Web pages similar (or related in some way) to the specified URL.	like:www.beatle.net
link:	Searches for hypertext links (URLs) embedded in a Web page.	link:www.songlyrics.com
text:	Searches for text in the body of the Web page.	text:"Strawberry Fields"
title:	Limits search to the part of the Web page that the author labeled as the title.	title:"John Lennon"
url:	Searches for text in complete Web addresses (URLs).	url:beatles.html

AOL Search search.aol.com

AOL Search Quick Reference

FOR THIS TYPE OF SEARCH:	DO THIS:	EXAMPLES:
Plain-English Question	Type a question that expresses the idea or concept, using as many words as necessary. Don't include a question mark, because it may be interpreted as a wildcard character.	Does Norm Abram have a Web site
Phrase Search	Type the phrase enclosed in **double quotes**.	"New Yankee Workshop"
AND Search (multiple words and phrases, each of which *must* be present)	Type words or phrases separated by a space. You can also use the Boolean operator AND (uppercase or lowercase) to connect two or more search terms, or put plus signs (+) directly in front of required search terms. All three examples will produce the same results.	"paint shaver" clapboard "paint shaver" AND clapboard +"paint shaver" +clapboard
OR Search (multiple words and phrases, any one of which may be present)	Use the Boolean operator **OR** (uppercase or lowercase) to combine words and phrases.	woodworking OR cabinetry
NOT Search (to exclude a word or phrase)	Use the Boolean operator **NOT** (uppercase or lowercase) to exclude a word or phrase.	"custom windows" NOT software
Case-Sensitive Search	Not available.	
Date Search	Not available.	
Field Search	Not available.	
Nested Search	Use **parentheses** to group search expressions into more complex queries.	hardware AND (antique OR reproduction)
Proximity Search	AOL Search offers three different proximity operators, which you can type in uppercase or lowercase:	
	ADJ to find words next to each other. The example would find *paint stripping* and *stripping paint*.	paint ADJ stripping
	NEAR or **NEAR/**n to find one search term within a specified distance (*n* is number of words) from another. The example would find *moss* within five words of *roof*.	moss NEAR/5 roof
	W/n to find one search term within a specified distance (*n* is number of words) *after* another. The example would find *roof* within three words after *moss*.	moss W/3 roof
Wildcard Search	Use an **asterisk (*)** to match *multiple* characters anywhere in a word (beginning, middle, or end). The example would find *cabinetmaker*, *cabinetry*, and *cabinets*.	cabinet*
	Use a **question mark (?)** to match a *single* character.	"anders?n windows"

Argus Clearinghouse www.clearinghouse.net

Argus Clearinghouse Quick Reference*

FOR THIS TYPE OF SEARCH:	DO THIS:	EXAMPLES:
Word or Phrase Search	Type the word or phrase without any special punctuation.	news media
AND Search (multiple words and phrases, each of which *must* be present)	Use AND to connect two or more words or phrases. The example would find guides whose titles or keywords include both words.	Asia AND business
OR Search (multiple words and phrases, any one of which may be present)	Use OR to connect two or more words or phrases, either one of which may appear in the guide's title or keywords.	justice OR judicial
Wildcard Search	Use an **asterisk (*)** to search for wildcard characters at the end of a word. The example would find *biology* as well as *biological* and *biologist*.	biolog*
Nested Search	Use **parentheses** to group search expressions into more complex queries. The example would find references to *art museum*, *art gallery*, and *art galleries*.	art AND (museum OR galler*)

*Note: *Argus Clearinghouse searches are not case-sensitive. Also, punctuation marks (apostrophes, dashes, hyphens, etc.) are ignored, so it's recommended that you leave them out when searching.*

Deja www.deja.com

Deja Quick Reference

FOR THIS TYPE OF SEARCH:	DO THIS:	EXAMPLES:
Plain-English Question	Not recommended. Use a phrase or AND search instead.	
Phrase Search	Type the phrase as a sequence of words surrounded by **double quotes**.	"forensic medicine"
	Restrictions: Phrases must contain at least two words that are not Deja stopwords. For a list of *stopwords*, see **Figure 15.15**.	
AND Search (multiple words and phrases, each of which must be present)	Use AND or & to connect two or more words or phrases. Or simply type the words or phrases separated by a space. All three of the examples would produce the same results.	cholesterol AND exercise cholesterol & exercise cholesterol exercise
OR Search (multiple words and phrases, any one of which may be present)	Use OR or | (**pipe symbol**) to connect two or more words or phrases. Both examples would find newsgroup postings that mention either *fitness* or *nutrition*.	fitness OR nutrition fitness | nutrition
NOT Search (to exclude a word or phrase)	Use AND NOT or &! in front of a word or phrase you want to exclude from your results. To look for postings about vitamins but not multi-level marketing deals, for example, you might want to exclude *mlm*.	vitamins AND NOT mlm vitamins &! mlm
Case-Sensitive Search	Not available.	
Date Search	Use the Power Search form and specify a range of dates in the fill-in-the-blanks form. Use the format MMM D YYYY (for single-digit days of the week) or MMM DD YYYY (for double-digit days).	Oct 1 2000 Apr 15 2001
	Alternatively, you can use the date-search operator ~dc (for *date created*) right on the search form, in which case the date format must be YYYY/MM/DD.	~dc 2001/03/24
Field Search	Use the Power Search form for fill-in-the blank searching of newsgroup Author, Subject, and Forum (i.e., newsgroup name) fields.	
	Alternatively, you can use the following field-search operators on the search form itself:	
	Author: ~a Subject: ~s Group name: ~g	~a bjones@nih.edu ~s "lyme disease" ~g sci.med.diseases.*
Nested Search	Use **parentheses** to group search expressions into more complex queries. The example would find postings that mention *clinical study* or *clinical trial*.	clinical AND (study OR trial)
Proximity Search	Use NEAR or ^ (**carat symbol**) to find words that appear in close proximity to each other. The default distance is 5 characters, but you can change that by including a number along with the carat symbol.	infertility NEAR treatment
	The second example would look for the two words within 30 characters of each other.	infertility ^ treatment
	Restrictions: Phrases aren't allowed with Deja proximity searches. Also, neither search term can be on the Deja stopwords list. (See **Figure 15.15** for stopwords.)	infertility ^30 treatment
Wildcard Search	Use an **asterisk (*)** to search for wildcard characters. The example would find *therapeutic, therapist,* and *therapy*.	therap*
	You can also use **braces** ({ }) to search for a range of words. The example would find all words that fall alphabetically between *therapeutic* and *therapy*.	{therapeutic therapy}
	Restrictions: Wildcards cannot be used in phrases.	

Excite www.excite.com

Excite Quick Reference		
FOR THIS TYPE OF SEARCH:	DO THIS:	EXAMPLES:
Plain-English Question	Simply type a phrase or question that expresses the idea or concept. Use as many words as necessary.	thoroughbred racing in Kentucky
		Where can I find information about thoroughbred racing in Kentucky?
Phrase Search	Type the phrase enclosed in **double quotes**.	"Kentucky Derby"
AND Search (multiple words and phrases, each of which *must* be present)	Use a **plus sign (+)** in front of each word or phrase that *must* appear in the results.	+racing +"Churchill Downs"
	Alternatively, you can use **AND** (full caps required) between the words or phrases.	racing AND "Churchill Downs"
OR Search (multiple words and phrases, any one of which may be present)	Type words or phrases separated by a space.	Derby Preakness
	Alternatively, you can use **OR** (full caps required) between each word or phrase.	Derby OR Preakness
NOT Search (to exclude a word or phrase)	Use a **minus sign (-)** directly in front of the word or phrase you want to exclude from your results. (Note that there's no space between the minus sign and the search word.)	"horse race" –Derby
	Or use NOT or AND NOT (all caps) in front of the word or phrase you want to exclude.	"horse race" NOT Derby "horse race" AND NOT Derby
Case-Sensitive Search	Not available.	
Date Search	Not available.	
Field Search	Not available.	
Nested Search	Use **parentheses** to group Boolean expressions into more complex queries.	racing AND (horse OR thoroughbred)
Proximity Search	Not available.	
Wildcard Search	Not available.	

Google www.google.com

Google Quick Reference		
FOR THIS TYPE OF SEARCH:	**DO THIS:**	**EXAMPLES:**
Plain-English Question	Simply type a phrase or question that expresses the idea or concept, using as many words as necessary.	Who invented the steam engine?
Phrase Search	Type the phrase surrounded by **double quotes**. (Common words will be ignored, even with quotes.)	"industrial revolution"
AND Search (multiple words and phrases, each of which must be present)	Type the words (or phrases in quotes) separated by a space, without any special punctuation.	Edison "light bulb"
	Use a **plus sign (+)** only if one of the words in your query is a very common word (or *stopword*). The second example would help you find guides at the popular About.com Web site dealing with history.	+about guides history
OR Search (multiple words and phrases, any one of which may be present)	Type words or phrases (no quotes allowed) separated by **OR** (full caps required).	phonograph OR speaking machine
NOT Search (to exclude a word or phrase)	Use a **minus sign (–)** directly in front of the word or phrase you want to exclude.	Lincoln –"town car"
Case-Sensitive Search	Not available.	
Date Search	Not available.	
Field Search	Type the field-search term followed by a colon and the search word or phrase. Note that there is no space after the colon. (For fill-in-the-blanks field searching, use Advanced Search.)	
	Titles: Use `allintitle:` or `intitle:` with one or more search words. The first example would look for *both* words in page titles, the second *either* word.	`allintitle:inventions inventors` `intitle:inventions inventors`
	URLs. Use `allinurl:` or `inurl:` with one or more words you want to find in the URL. The first example would look for *both* words, the second *either* word.	`allinurl:pdf 1099` `inurl:patents trademarks`
	Domains. Use `site:` followed by a domain name or type (com, edu, gov, etc.), along with the search word or phrase you want to find at that site or domain type.	`site:nationalgeographic.com inventions` `site:gov patents`
	The first example would find pages at the National Geographic Web site that include the word *inventions*. The second would find government (gov) Web sites that include the word *patents*.	
	Links. Use `link:` with a specific Web address to find all pages that link to that address. The example would find pages that link to the U.S. Patent and Trademark Office (`www.uspto.gov`).	`link:www.uspto.gov`
	Note: You *cannot* combine a `link:` search term with another search word or phrase.	
Nested Search	Not available.	
Proximity Search	Not available.	
Wildcard Search	Not available.	

HotBot www.hotbot.com

HotBot Quick Reference	
FOR THIS TYPE OF SEARCH:	**DO THIS:**
Plain-English Question	Simply type the question in the search form and select `all the words` from the search form's Look For menu.
Phrase Search	Type the phrase with or without quotes and select `exact phrase` on the Look For menu.
	To look for multiple phrases, or a phrase and a single word, put the phrase in quotes and select `all the words` from the Look For menu.
AND Search (multiple words and phrases, each of which *must* be present)	Type words and/or phrases and select `all the words` from the Look For menu. You can use a **plus sign (+)** in front of each word or phrase, but it's not really necessary with an `all the words` search.
	You can also combine words and phrases with **AND** and select `Boolean phrase` from the menu.
OR Search (multiple words and phrases, any one of which may be present)	Type words or phrases separated by spaces and select `any of the words` from the menu. Alternatively, combine words and phrases with **OR** and choose `Boolean phrase` from the menu.
NOT Search (to exclude a word or phrase)	Use a **minus sign (-)** in front of a word or phrase you want to exclude from the results. Or use **NOT** in front of the word or phrase and specify `Boolean phrase`.
Case-Sensitive Search	Use lowercase to find *any combination* of uppercase and lowercase. Use capital letters (initial caps or a combination of uppercase and lowercase) to force an *exact match* of your search term.
Date Search	Use the Date menu on the HotBot home page to select a timeframe (one week to two years).
	Alternatively, you can use the Date meta words `after:`, `before:`, or `within:` in your query. For examples, see the HotBot Meta Words Quick Reference (page 299).
	For point-and-click date searching, use `Advanced Search`.
Field Search (Web page titles)	Use the Look For menu on the HotBot home page to specify that you want to search the page title.
	Or you can use the HotBot meta word `title:` in your query. (See page 299 for examples.)
Field Search (geography, domain, or domain type)	Use the HotBot meta word `domain:`. For example, use `domain:jp` to look for sites in Japan. Use `domain:com` to look for commercial sites in North America. (For more examples, see page 299.)
	Alternatively, you can click on `Advanced Search` and use the Location/Domain section to focus your search on a particular geographic region, country, domain, or domain type (com, edu, gov, etc.).
Field Search (multimedia)	Use the Pages Must Include section on the HotBot home page to look for image, video, MP3, or JavaScript files. For an expanded list of multimedia options, click on `Advanced Search`.
	Alternatively, you can use `feature:` meta words in your queries on the HotBot home page to find plug-ins, embedded scripts, Java applets, audio and video files, etc. (See page 299 for a complete list.)
Nested Search	Combine search terms with parentheses and select `Boolean phrase` from the Look For menu.
Proximity Search	Not available.
Wildcard Search	Use an **asterisk (*)** with at least two adjacent characters to search for zero or more characters anywhere in a word or string of characters (beginning, middle, or end).
	Use a **question mark (?)** with at least two adjacent characters to search for a single character.
	For example, `car*` would match *cars*, *cart*, *carrot*, and *cardiovascular*. But `car?` would only match *cars*, *cart*, and other four-letter words.

HotBot www.hotbot.com

HotBot Meta Words Quick Reference*	
META WORD FORMAT	WHAT IT DOES
title: *word* or *phrase*	Searches Web page titles for the word or phrase you specify. For example, title:Edmund's or title:"car guides".
domain: *name*	Restricts search to the domain name selected. Domains can be specified up to three levels: domain:com, domain:ford.com, domain:www.ford.com.
linkdomain: *name*	Restricts search to pages containing links to the domain you specify. For example, linkdomain:edmunds.com finds pages that point to the Edmund's Car Guides Web site.
outgoingurlext: *extension*	Restricts search to pages containing embedded files with a particular extension. For example, outgoingurlext:ra finds pages containing RealAudio (RA) files.
depth: *number*	Limits how deep within a Web site your search goes. To go three pages deep, use depth:3.
feature: acrobat	Detects Acrobat files.
feature: applet	Detects embedded Java applets.
feature: activex	Detects ActiveX controls or layouts.
feature: audio	Detects audio formats.
feature: embed	Detects plug-ins.
feature: flash	Detects Flash plug-in HTML.
feature: form	Detects forms in HTML documents.
feature: frame	Detects frames in HTML documents.
feature: image	Detects image files (GIF, JPEG, etc.).
feature: script	Detects embedded scripts.
feature: shockwave	Detects Shockwave files.
feature: table	Detects tables in HTML documents.
feature: video	Detects video formats.
feature: vrml	Detects VRML files
scriptlanguage: javascript	Allows you to search for pages containing JavaScript. (Note that lowercase is required for javascript.)
scriptlanguage: vbscript	Allows you to search for pages containing VBScript. (Note that lowercase is required for vbscript.)
after: *dd/mm/yy*	Use in a Boolean expression to restrict search to pages created or modified *after* the specified date: Explorer AND after:31/12/00. (Note that date format is day/month/year.)
before: *dd/mm/yy*	Use in a Boolean expression to restrict search to pages created or modified *before* the specified date: Corvette AND before:30/6/99. (Note that date format is day/month/year).
within: *number/unit*	Use in a Boolean expression to search for pages created or modified within a specified time period. Units can be expressed in days, months, or years: (Jeep Cherokee OR "Grand Cherokee") AND within:3/months.

*Note: The words shown in italics are variables. You'll find examples of the terms you can use for each of these variables in the column labeled "What It Does."

InfoSpace www.infospace.com

InfoSpace Quick Reference	
FOR THIS TYPE OF SEARCH:	DO THIS:
E-mail Address Search (worldwide)	Click on Email in the White Pages section of the InfoSpace home page to display the search form. Start by completing just the Last Name and First Name fields.
	To narrow a search, complete additional fields one at a time, in this order: Country, State/Province, City.
	To broaden a search, try a partial entry in the First Name field. Searching for A in the First Name field and Fletcher in the Last Name field would find listings for *Albert, Al,* and *A. S. Fletcher.*
Phone Number and Address Search (U.S., Canada, and Europe)	Click on Phone & Address in the White Pages section of the InfoSpace home page to display the search form. Start by completing the Last Name, First Name, and State/Province fields.
	To narrow a search, complete the City field.
	To broaden a search, try a partial entry in the First Name field. Searching for Jo Anderson would find listings for *Joe Anderson* as well as *Joseph Anderson.*
	Another way to broaden a search that includes a City field is to select the Including Surrounding Region option.
Reverse Lookup (phone and fax numbers, street addresses, e-mail addresses, and area codes)	Click on Reverse Lookup in the White Pages section of the InfoSpace home page.

Lycos www.lycos.com

Lycos Basic Search Quick Reference*

FOR THIS TYPE OF SEARCH:	DO THIS:	EXAMPLES:
Plain-English Question	Simply type a phrase or question that expresses the idea or concept, using as many words as necessary.	Are oyster mushrooms poisonous?
Phrase Search	Enclose the phrase in **double quotes**.	"edible mushrooms"
AND Search (multiple words and phrases, each of which *must* be present)	Type words or phrases separated by a space, without any special punctuation. By default, Lycos searches for *all* the words in your query, so even though **plus signs (+)** are allowed, you'll get the same results without them. The two examples shown here would return identical results: Web pages that contain both the phrase *oyster mushrooms* and the word *recipes*.	"oyster mushrooms" recipes +"oyster mushrooms" +recipes
OR Search (multiple words and phrases, any one of which may be present)	Enclose the words or phrases in **parentheses**. The example would find Web pages that include references to either *edible mushrooms* or *mycology*.	("edible mushrooms" mycology)
NOT Search (to exclude a word or phrase)	Use a **minus sign (-)** in front of a word or phrase you want to exclude from your results.	mushrooms -recipes
Case-Sensitive Search	Not available.	
Date Search	Not available.	
Field Search	To search titles of Web page documents, use `title:` directly in front of a word or phrase. (Note that there's no space between the colon and the search term.) For URL and Host/Domain, and Link Referral field searches, use Advanced Search.	`title:mushrooms` `title:"mushroom gardening"`
Nested Search	Not available.	
Proximity Search	Not available.	
Wildcard Search	Not available.	

Note: This table applies to searches using the form on the Lycos home page. For Advanced Search, see page 302.

Lycos www.lycos.com

Lycos Advanced Search Quick Reference		
FOR THIS TYPE OF SEARCH:	DO THIS:	EXAMPLES:
Plain-English Question	Simply type a phrase or question that expresses the idea or concept, using as many words as necessary. Leave the drop-down menu set to all words (AND match).	What are the best French table wines?
Phrase Search	Type the phrase without any special punctuation and choose exact phrase (quoted query) from the drop-down menu.	French table wines
	Alternatively, you can type the phrase in **double quotes** and leave the drop-down menu set to all words (AND match).	"French table wines"
AND Search (multiple words and phrases, each of which *must* be present)	Type the words (or phrases in quotes) in the search form and leave the drop-down menu set to all words (AND match).	California "Cabernet Sauvignon"
OR Search (multiple words and phrases, any one of which may be present)	Type the words (or phrases in quotes) in the search form and choose any words (OR match) from the drop-down menu.	"sparkling wine" Champagne
NOT Search (to exclude a word or phrase)	Use a **minus sign (-)** in front of a word or phrase you want to exclude from the results.	Chardonnay -California
Case-Sensitive Search	Not available.	
Date Search	Not available.	
Field Search	Click Page Field and use the fill-in-the-blanks form to search Web page Title, URL, and Host/Domain fields. (For best results, avoid using quotation marks and other punctuation when using the Page Field option.)	
	Click Link Referrals and use the fill-in-the-blanks form to look for links to a specific Web page.	
	For examples, see "Using Advanced Search" on pages 130–133.	
Nested Search	Not available.	
Proximity Search	Not available.	
Wildcard Search	Not available.	

MSN Search `search.msn.com`

MSN Search Basic Search Quick Reference*

FOR THIS TYPE OF SEARCH:	DO THIS:	EXAMPLES:
Plain-English Question	Simply type a question that expresses the idea or concept, using as many words as necessary.	What's the best place for cross-country skiing in Minnesota?
Phrase Search	Type the phrase enclosed in **double quotes**.	"Gunflint Lodge"
AND Search (multiple words and phrases, each of which *must* be present)	Type words or phrases separated by a space. MSN Search automatically searches for *all* the words, so **plus signs (+)** aren't necessary.	skiing snowboarding
OR Search (multiple words and phrases, any one of which may be present)	Not available. Use Advanced Search.	
NOT Search (to exclude a word or phrase)	Use a **minus sign (-)** directly in front of the word or phrase you want to exclude from your results. (Note that there's no space between the minus sign and the search word.)	skiing -downhill
Case-Sensitive Search	Not available.	
Date Search	Not available. Use Advanced Search.	
Field Search	Not available. Use Advanced Search.	
Nested Search	Not available. Use Advanced Search.	
Proximity Search	Not available.	
Wildcard Search	Not available. Use Advanced Search.	

Note: This table applies to searches using the form on the MSN Search home page. For Advanced Search, see page 304.

MSN Search `search.msn.com`

MSN Search Advanced Search Quick Reference*		
FOR THIS TYPE OF SEARCH:	DO THIS:	EXAMPLES:
Plain-English Question	Type a question that expresses the idea or concept and choose `all the words` on the Find menu.	When was the Mir space station launched"?
Phrase Search	Type the phrase without any special punctuation and choose `the exact phrase` on the Find menu.	Hubble space telescope
AND Search (multiple words and phrases, each of which *must* be present)	Type words or phrases separated by a space and choose `all the words` on the Find menu.	"space camp" scholarships
	Alternatively, you can combine words and phrases with the Boolean operator **AND** (full caps required) and choose `Boolean phrase` on the Find menu.	"space camp" AND scholarships
OR Search (multiple words and phrases, any one of which may be present)	Type words or phrases separated by a space and choose `any of the words` on Find menu.	NASA "space program"
	Alternatively, you can combine words and phrases with the Boolean operator **OR** (full caps required) and choose `Boolean phrase` on the Find menu.	NASA OR "space program"
NOT Search (to exclude a word or phrase)	Use the Boolean operator **AND NOT** (full caps required) with the word or phrase you want to exclude and choose `Boolean phrase` on Find menu.	shuttle AND NOT challenger
Case-Sensitive Search	Not available.	
Date Search	Specify range of dates in the **Modified between** section of the search form, using the format dd/mm/yyyy.	Modified between: 01/01/2001 and: 30/06/2001
Field Search	Three types of field searches are possible:	
	Titles. Type search words or phrases in the search box and choose `words in title` on Find menu.	astronaut hall of fame
	Links. Type complete URL (including `http://`) in search box and choose `links to URL` on Find menu.	http://www.astronaut.org
	Domain. Use Domain section of form to limit your search by domain type (com, edu, gov, org, etc.) or to a specific domain.	Domain: com Domain: nasa.gov
Nested Search	Combine search terms with **Boolean operators** and **parentheses**, and choose `Boolean phrase` from the Find menu.	(NASA OR "space program") AND budget AND 2001
Proximity Search	Not available.	
Wildcard Search	Use **Enable stemming** option to automatically search for both *root* words and *variations*. With stemming enabled, a search for budget would also find references to *budgets*, *budgetary*, and *budgeting*.	budget

*Note: This table applies to searches using MSN Search's Advanced Search form. For searches using the form on the MSN Search home page, see page 303.

Netscape Search search.netscape.com

Netscape Search Quick Reference		
FOR THIS TYPE OF SEARCH:	DO THIS:	EXAMPLES:
Plain-English Question	Simply type a question that expresses the idea or concept, using as many words as necessary.	Where can I buy accessories for my IBM Thinkpad?
Phrase Search	Type the phrase enclosed in **double quotes**.	"thinkpad accessories"
AND Search (multiple words and phrases, each of which *must* be present)	Type words or phrases separated by a space, or use the Boolean operator AND (uppercase or lowercase) to connect two or more search terms. Both examples would produce the same results.	IBM thinkpad IBM AND thinkpad
	You can also put **plus signs (+)** directly in front of required search terms, in which case your results will be limited to Partner Search Results (paid listings from GoTo) and Web pages from Google.	+IBM +thinkpad
OR Search (multiple words and phrases, any one of which may be present)	Use the Boolean operator **OR** (uppercase or lowercase) to combine words and phrases.	notebook OR laptop
NOT Search (to exclude a word or phrase)	Use a **minus sign (-)** directly in front of the word or phrase you want to exclude from your results. (Note that there's no space between the minus sign and the search word.)	notebook -thinkpad
	Alternatively, you can use the Boolean operator **ANDNOT** (one word, uppercase or lowercase) followed by the word you want to exclude.	notebook ANDNOT thinkpad
Case-Sensitive Search	Not available.	
Date Search	Not available.	
Field Search	Not available.	
Nested Search	Not available.	
Proximity Search	Not available.	
Wildcard Search	Use an **asterisk (*)** to search for multiple characters at the end of a word only. The example would find references to *technological*, *technologies*, and *technology*.	technolog*

SEARCH ENGINES QUICK REFERENCE

Northern Light `www.northernlight.com`

<table>
<tr><td colspan="3">Northern Light Quick Reference</td></tr>
<tr><td>For this type of search:</td><td>Do this:</td><td>Examples:</td></tr>
<tr><td>Plain-English Question</td><td>Simply type a phrase or question that expresses the idea or concept, using as many words as necessary.</td><td>Where can I find information about study abroad programs in France?</td></tr>
<tr><td>Phrase Search</td><td>Type phrase surrounded by double quotes.</td><td>"youth hostel"</td></tr>
<tr><td>AND Search
(multiple words and phrases, each of which must be present)</td><td>Type words (or phrases in quotes) separated by a space. You can also use plus signs (+) or AND operator if you're accustomed to doing so. All three examples would produce the same results.</td><td>Princeton "financial aid"
+Princeton +"financial aid"
Princeton AND "financial aid"</td></tr>
<tr><td>OR Search
(multiple words and phrases, any one of which may be present)</td><td>Type words or phrases separated by OR (in uppercase or lowercase).</td><td>scholarship OR
"student loan" OR grant</td></tr>
<tr><td>NOT Search
(to exclude a word or phrase)</td><td>Use a minus sign (-) directly in front of the word or phrase you want to exclude. Alternatively, you can use NOT (uppercase or lowercase).</td><td>booksellers -Amazon.com
booksellers NOT Amazon.com</td></tr>
<tr><td>Case-Sensitive Search</td><td>Strictly speaking, not available. Northern Light returns the same set of results regardless of case. But if you use mixed case, hits that make an exact case match will appear higher on the results list.</td><td>"Scholastic Aptitude Test"</td></tr>
<tr><td>Date Search</td><td>Not available with Simple Search form. Use Power Search or Business Search.</td><td></td></tr>
<tr><td>Field Search</td><td>Type field-search term followed by a colon and the search word or phrase.

For Web pages and Special Collection documents:
title: (to look for words in Web page or document titles)
url: (to look for words in Web page URLs)
link: (to find Web pages or documents that include links to a specific site)
text: (used with another field-search term to look for words in the text of Web pages or documents)

For Special Collection documents only:
company: (to find documents by company name)
ticker: (to find documents by ticker symbol)
pub: (to find documents in specific publication)
recid: (to find document based on ID number from Northern Light article summary page)
Note: For fill-in-the-blanks field searching, use Power, Business, or Investext search forms.</td><td>

title:"Favorite Poem Project"

url:booktv
link:abouttheauthor.com

url:npr.org text:"Car Talk"

company:ebay
ticker:MSO
pub:business week
recid:AA20010207020001236</td></tr>
<tr><td>Nested Search</td><td>Use parentheses to group Boolean expressions into more complex queries.</td><td>SAT AND ("sample test" OR "prep course")</td></tr>
<tr><td>Proximity Search</td><td>Not available.</td><td></td></tr>
<tr><td>Wildcard Search</td><td>Use an asterisk (*) to search for multiple characters at the end of (or within) a word, or a percent sign (%) to look for a single character. Wildcard must be preceded by at least four other characters.</td><td>GRE test prep*
gene%logy</td></tr>
</table>

Topica www.topica.com

Topica Quick Reference		
FOR THIS TYPE OF SEARCH:	DO THIS:	EXAMPLES:
Phrase Search	Type the phrase as a sequence of words enclosed in **double quotes**.	"book reviews"
AND Search (multiple words and phrases, each of which *must* be present)	Use AND to connect two or more words and phrases.	authors AND mystery
OR Search (multiple words and phrases, any one of which may be present)	Use OR to connect two or more words and phrases.	grisham OR turow
NOT Search (to exclude a word or phrase)	Use NOT in front of a word or phrase you want to exclude from your results.	"genre fiction" NOT romance
Nested Search	Use **parentheses** to group words and phrases into more complex queries.	(fantasy OR SF) AND writers
Wildcard Search	Use an **asterisk (*)** to search for wildcard characters. The example would find references to *literacy, literature,* and *literary.*	litera*

Yahoo www.yahoo.com

Yahoo Quick Reference		
FOR THIS TYPE OF SEARCH:	DO THIS:	EXAMPLES:
Plain-English Question	Not recommended.	
Phrase Search	Type the phrase as a sequence of words surrounded by **double quotes.**	"Russian lacquer boxes"
AND Search (multiple words and phrases, each of which must be present)	Use a **plus sign (+)** in front of a word or phrase that *must* appear in the results.	+antiques +Victorian
OR Search (multiple words and phrases, any one of which may be present)	Type words or phrases separated by a space, without any special notation.	eggs "Carl Faberge"
NOT Search (to exclude a word or phrase)	Use a **minus sign (-)** in front of a word or phrase you want to exclude from your results. To find software Easter eggs, for example, you might want to exclude the word *Fabergé*.	"Easter eggs" -Faberge
Case-Sensitive Search	Not available.	
Date Search	Not available. However, you *can* search for categories and Web sites that have been added to the Yahoo directory within a certain time frame.	
	To do that, click on *advanced search* on the Yahoo home page and use the drop-down menu to select a timeframe (1 day to 4 years).	
Field Search	To search titles of Web page documents, use t: directly in front of a word or phrase.	t:"oriental rugs"
	To search Web page URLs, use u: directly in front of the word you want to find. To search for multiple words, use multiple u: search terms with **plus signs (+)**.	u:carpeting +u:oriental +u:rug
Nested Search	Not available.	
Proximity Search	Not available.	
Wildcard Search	Use an **asterisk (*)** with at least the first three letters of your search term. The example would find references to *lacquer* as well as *lacquered* and *lacquerware*.	lacq*
	(Note: You *cannot* search for wildcard characters at the beginning or in the middle of a word.)	

Zip2 www.zip2.com

Zip2 Quick Reference*	
FOR THIS TYPE OF SEARCH:	DO THIS:
Business Name Search	To search for a specific business, enter its name (or one or two unique words) in the search form text box.
	Click on the radio button to specify whether you want to search Near You or City & State. If you select Near You, make sure the drop-down menu is set to Near My Home, Near My Work, or whatever location you want to use as a starting point.
Business Category Search	To search for all the businesses in a particular category, type one or two unique words in the search form text box.
	Be sure to specify the area you want to search (Near You or City & State), as described above.
Point-to-Point Driving Directions and Maps	Click on the Get Directions icon that appears next to every listing in your Zip2 search results. (The Get Directions icon will be either a car in a circle or a double-pointing arrow in a square.)
	To get maps and driving directions without searching, use the Get a Map section of the Zip2 home page.

*Note: Zip2 always performs an AND search, looking for all the words in your query. (There's no way to do an OR search.) Also, Zip2 ignores case.

Internet Domains and Country Codes

B

Top-Level Domains (TLDs)

Common Domains (in use now)

DOMAIN	TYPE
com	Commercial establishments/businesses
edu	Educational institutions
gov	Government agencies
int	International organizations
mil	U.S. military facilities
net	Networks like AT&T and MCI
org	Non-profit organizations

New Domains (to be introduced in 2001)

DOMAIN	TYPE
aero	Airports, airlines, and related companies
biz	Commercial establishments/businesses
coop	Non-profit cooperatives
info	Unrestricted use
museum	Museums
name	Individuals
pro	Accountants, lawyers, and physicians

Domain Name Update

For the latest information on the availability of the new Internet top-level domains, visit the ICANN Web site at www.icann.org. ICANN, short for Internet Corporation for Assigned Names and Numbers, is the organization responsible for approving the new domains.

Many search engines let you look for Web sites based on Internet *domains* and *country* codes. Searching by domain allows you to focus your search on a particular *type* of organization: commercial, education, government, etc. Searching by country code makes it possible to zero in on (or avoid) sites that originate in a specific country.

To help you take full advantage of domain and country-code search options, this appendix includes three tables:

♦ **Top-Level Domains (TLDs)**
 Includes the seven TLDs currently in use as well as seven new ones that are expected to be introduced in 2001.

♦ **Country Codes (Alphabetical by Country)**

♦ **Country Codes (Alphabetical by Code)**

Even if you never have occasion to do a country-code or domain search, this information may come in handy from time to time, simply for deciphering an e-mail or Web site address. Internet domains are pretty obvious, but you'll find that country codes aren't always easy to guess: AU, for example, is Australia (not Austria, which is AT).

Country Codes (Alphabetical by Country)

COUNTRY	CODE	COUNTRY	CODE	COUNTRY	CODE
Afghanistan	AF	Chile	CL	Greenland	GL
Albania	AL	China	CN	Grenada	GD
Algeria	DZ	Christmas Island	CX	Guadeloupe	GP
American Samoa	AS	Cocos (Keeling) Islands	CC	Guam	GU
Andorra	AD	Colombia	CO	Guatemala	GT
Angola	AO	Comoros	KM	Guinea	GN
Anguilla	AI	Congo	CG	Guinea-Bissau	GW
Antarctica	AQ	Congo, Dem. Republic of	CD	Guyana	GY
Antigua/Barbuda	AG	Cook Islands	CK	Haiti	HT
Argentina	AR	Costa Rica	CR	Heard Island/ McDonald Islands	HM
Armenia	AM	Cote D'Ivoire	CI	Holy See (Vatican)	VA
Aruba	AW	Croatia	HR	Honduras	HN
Australia	AU	Cuba	CU	Hong Kong	HK
Austria	AT	Cyprus	CY	Hungary	HU
Azerbaijan	AZ	Czech Republic	CZ	Iceland	IS
Bahamas	BS	Denmark	DK	India	IN
Bahrain	BH	Djibouti	DJ	Indonesia	ID
Bangladesh	BD	Dominica	DM	Iran	IR
Barbados	BB	Dominican Republic	DO	Iraq	IQ
Belarus	BY	East Timor	TP	Ireland	IE
Belgium	BE	Ecuador	EC	Israel	IL
Belize	BZ	Egypt	EG	Italy	IT
Benin	BJ	El Salvador	SV	Ivory Coast	CI
Bermuda	BM	Equatorial Guinea	GQ	Jamaica	JM
Bhutan	BT	Eritrea	ER	Japan	JP
Bolivia	BO	Estonia	EE	Jordan	JO
Bosnia-Herzegovina	BA	Ethiopia	ET	Kazakstan	KZ
Botswana	BW	Falkland Islands (Malvinas)	FK	Kenya	KE
Bouvet Island	BV	Faroe Islands	FO	Kiribati	KI
Brazil	BR	Fiji	FJ	Korea (North)	KP
British Indian Ocean Territory	IO	Finland	FI	Korea (South)	KR
Brunei Darussalam	BN	France	FR	Kuwait	KW
Bulgaria	BG	French Guiana	GF	Kyrgyzstan	KG
Burkina Faso	BF	French Polynesia	PF	Laos	LA
Burundi	BI	French Southern Territories	TF	Latvia	LV
Cambodia	KH	Gabon	GA	Lebanon	LB
Cameroon	CM	Gambia	GM	Lesotho	LS
Canada	CA	Georgia	GE	Liberia	LR
Cape Verde	CV	Germany	DE	Libyan Arab Jamahiriya	LY
Cayman Islands	KY	Ghana	GH	Liechtenstein	LI
Central African Republic	CF	Gibraltar	GI	Lithuania	LT
Chad	TD	Greece	GR	Luxembourg	LU

Country Codes (Alphabetical by Country)

COUNTRY	CODE	COUNTRY	CODE	COUNTRY	CODE
Macau	MO	Paraguay	PY	Tajikistan	TJ
Macedonia	MK	Peru	PE	Tanzania	TZ
Madagascar	MG	Philippines	PH	Thailand	TH
Malawi	MW	Pitcairn	PN	Togo	TG
Malaysia	MY	Poland	PL	Tokelau	TK
Maldives	MV	Portugal	PT	Tonga	TO
Mali	ML	Puerto Rico	PR	Trinidad and Tobago	TT
Malta	MT	Qatar	QA	Tunisia	TN
Marshall Islands	MH	Reunion	RE	Turkey	TR
Martinique	MQ	Romania	RO	Turkmenistan	TM
Mauritania	MR	Russian Federation	RU	Turks and Caicos Islands	TC
Mauritius	MU	Rwanda	RW	Tuvalu	TV
Mayotte	YT	Saint Helena	SH	Uganda	UG
Mexico	MX	Saint Kitts and Nevis	KN	Ukraine	UA
Micronesia	FM	Saint Lucia	LC	United Arab Emirates	AE
Moldova	MD	Saint Pierre and Miquelon	PM	United Kingdom	GB
Monaco	MC	Saint Vincent and Grenadines	VC	United States	US
Mongolia	MN			U.S. Minor Outlying Islands	UM
Montserrat	MS	Samoa	WS	
Morocco	MA	San Marino	SM	Uruguay	UY
Mozambique	MZ	Sao Tome and Principe	ST	Uzbekistan	UZ
Myanmar	MM	Saudi Arabia	SA	Vanuatu	VU
Namibia	NA	Senegal	SN	Vatican City State	VA
Nauru	NR	Seychelles	SC	Venezuela	VE
Nepal	NP	Sierra Leone	SL	Viet Nam	VN
Netherlands	NL	Singapore	SG	Virgin Islands (British)	VG
Netherlands Antilles	AN	Slovakia	SK	Virgin Islands (U.S.)	VI
New Caledonia	NC	Slovenia	SI	Wallis and Futuna	WF
New Zealand	NZ	Solomon Islands	SB	Western Sahara	EH
Nicaragua	NI	Somalia	SO	Yemen	YE
Niger	NE	South Africa	ZA	Yugoslavia	YU
Nigeria	NG	South Georgia/ Sandwich Islands	GS	Zambia	ZM
Niue	NU			Zimbabwe	ZW
Norfolk Island	NF	Spain	ES	
Northern Mariana Islands	MP	Sri Lanka	LK	
Norway	NO	Sudan	SD	
Oman	OM	Suriname	SR	
Pakistan	PK	Svalbard and Jan Mayen	SJ	
Palau	PW	Swaziland	SZ	
Palestinian Territory	PS	Sweden	SE	
Panama	PA	Switzerland	CH	
Papua New Guinea	PG	Syrian Arab Republic	SY	
		Taiwan	TW	

Country Codes (Alphabetical by Code)

CODE	COUNTRY	CODE	COUNTRY	CODE	COUNTRY
AD	Andorra	CK	Cook Islands	GR	Greece
AE	United Arab Emirates	CL	Chile	GS	South Georgia/ Sandwich Islands
AF	Afghanistan	CM	Cameroon		
AG	Antigua/Barbuda	CN	China	GT	Guatemala
AI	Anguilla	CO	Colombia	GU	Guam
AL	Albania	CR	Costa Rica	GW	Guinea-Bissau
AM	Armenia	CU	Cuba	GY	Guyana
AN	Netherlands Antilles	CV	Cape Verde	HK	Hong Kong
AO	Angola	CX	Christmas Island	HM	Heard Island/ McDonald Islands
AQ	Antarctica	CY	Cyprus		
AR	Argentina	CZ	Czech Republic	HN	Honduras
AS	American Samoa	DE	Germany	HR	Croatia
AT	Austria	DJ	Djibouti	HT	Haiti
AU	Australia	DK	Denmark	HU	Hungary
AW	Aruba	DM	Dominica	ID	Indonesia
AZ	Azerbaijan	DO	Dominican Republic	IE	Ireland
BA	Bosnia-Herzegovina	DZ	Algeria	IL	Israel
BB	Barbados	EC	Ecuador	IN	India
BD	Bangladesh	EE	Estonia	IO	British Indian Ocean Territory
BE	Belgium	EG	Egypt	IQ	Iraq
BF	Burkina Faso	EH	Western Sahara	IR	Iran
BG	Bulgaria	ER	Eritrea	IS	Iceland
BH	Bahrain	ES	Spain	IT	Italy
BI	Burundi	ET	Ethiopia	JM	Jamaica
BJ	Benin	FI	Finland	JO	Jordan
BM	Bermuda	FJ	Fiji	JP	Japan
BN	Brunei Darussalam	FK	Falkland Islands (Malvinas)	KE	Kenya
BO	Bolivia	FM	Micronesia	KG	Kyrgyzstan
BR	Brazil	FO	Faroe Islands	KH	Cambodia
BS	Bahamas	FR	France	KI	Kiribati
BT	Bhutan	GA	Gabon	KM	Comoros
BV	Bouvet Island	GB	United Kingdom	KN	Saint Kitts and Nevis
BW	Botswana	GD	Grenada	KP	Korea (North)
BY	Belarus	GE	Georgia	KR	Korea (South)
BZ	Belize	GF	French Guiana	KW	Kuwait
CA	Canada	GH	Ghana	KY	Cayman Islands
CC	Cocos (Keeling) Islands	GI	Gibraltar	KZ	Kazakstan
CD	Congo, Dem. Republic of	GL	Greenland	LA	Laos
CF	Central African Republic	GM	Gambia	LB	Lebanon
CG	Congo	GN	Guinea	LC	Saint Lucia
CH	Switzerland	GP	Guadeloupe	LI	Liechtenstein
CI	Cote D'Ivoire (Ivory Coast)	GQ	Equatorial Guinea	LK	Sri Lanka
				LR	Liberia

Country Codes (Alphabetical by Code)

CODE	COUNTRY	CODE	COUNTRY	CODE	COUNTRY
LS	Lesotho	PG	Papua New Guinea	TM	Turkmenistan
LT	Lithuania	PH	Philippines	TN	Tunisia
LU	Luxembourg	PK	Pakistan	TO	Tonga
LV	Latvia	PL	Poland	TP	East Timor
LY	Libyan Arab Jamahiriya	PM	Saint Pierre and Miquelon	TR	Turkey
MA	Morocco	PN	Pitcairn	TT	Trinidad and Tobago
MC	Monaco	PR	Puerto Rico	TV	Tuvalu
MD	Moldova	PS	Palestinian Territory	TW	Taiwan
MG	Madagascar	PT	Portugal	TZ	Tanzania
MH	Marshall Islands	PW	Palau	UA	Ukraine
MK	Macedonia	PY	Paraguay	UG	Uganda
ML	Mali	QA	Qatar	UM	U.S. Minor Outlying Islands
MM	Myanmar	RE	Reunion	US	United States
MN	Mongolia	RO	Romania	UY	Uruguay
MO	Macau	RU	Russian Federation	UZ	Uzbekistan
MP	Northern Mariana Islands	RW	Rwanda	VA	Vatican (Holy See)
MQ	Martinique	SA	Saudi Arabia	VC	Saint Vincent and Grenadines
MR	Mauritania	SB	Solomon Islands	VE	Venezuela
MS	Montserrat	SC	Seychelles	VG	Virgin Islands (British)
MT	Malta	SD	Sudan	VI	Virgin Islands (U.S.)
MU	Mauritius	SE	Sweden	VN	Viet Nam
MV	Maldives	SG	Singapore	VU	Vanuatu
MW	Malawi	SH	Saint Helena	WF	Wallis and Futuna
MX	Mexico	SI	Slovenia	WS	Samoa
MY	Malaysia	SJ	Svalbard and Jan Mayen	YE	Yemen
MZ	Mozambique	SK	Slovakia	YT	Mayotte
NA	Namibia	SL	Sierra Leone	YU	Yugoslavia
NC	New Caledonia	SM	San Marino	ZA	South Africa
NE	Niger	SN	Senegal	ZM	Zambia
NF	Norfolk Island	SO	Somalia	ZW	Zimbabwe
NG	Nigeria	SR	Suriname		
NI	Nicaragua	ST	Sao Tome and Principe		
NL	Netherlands	SV	El Salvador		
NO	Norway	SY	Syrian Arab Republic		
NP	Nepal	SZ	Swaziland		
NR	Nauru	TC	Turks and Caicos Islands		
NU	Niue	TD	Chad		
NZ	New Zealand	TF	French Southern Territories		
OM	Oman	TG	Togo		
PA	Panama	TH	Thailand		
PE	Peru	TJ	Tajikistan		
PF	French Polynesia	TK	Tokelau		

INTERNET DOMAINS AND COUNTRY CODES

USENET NEWSGROUP HIERARCHIES

Deja (www.deja.com) and several of the leading general-purpose search engines greatly simplify the process of finding information in Usenet newsgroups. It's no longer necessary to know exactly which newsgroup deals with a particular topic. Just tell Deja (or a search engine like HotBot or Yahoo that offers newsgroup searching) that you want to direct your query to newsgroups instead of the Web and let it take care of the details.

Eventually, though, you may want to employ the power-searching technique of limiting your newsgroup queries to *specific* newsgroups. Or you may simply want to know what those "alt-dot-something" names mean and how they get assigned. The key concept is newsgroup *hierarchies*.

The first part of a newsgroup name is the major topic or *top-level* hierarchy—alt for the wildly popular "alternative" newsgroups, biz for business-related groups, comp for computer hardware and software, sci for science, and so forth. Each of these major topics is then broken down into subtopics, and those are broken down again and again as additional groups are created for discussions of greater and greater specificity.

For example, in the alt hierarchy, a group called alt.music might be formed to discuss music in general. Over time, some participants may decide they want to focus on a specific *type* of music, like jazz, while others prefer to discuss bluegrass. So two new groups are formed: alt.music.jazz and alt.music.bluegrass. Things can get even more specific as people decide to focus on a favorite jazz or bluegrass musician. The newsgroup name gets longer and longer as the topic of discussion becomes more and more specific.

Of the hundreds of top-level newsgroup hierarchies, the ones you are most like to encounter are presented in **Table C.1**, along with a brief description.

✔ Tips

- For advice on searching Usenet newsgroups with Deja, see Chapter 16.

- Although Deja's specialty is newsgroup searches, it isn't the best place to look for a comprehensive list of newsgroup hierarchies. Instead, try one of these sites:

  Liszt's Usenet Newsgroups Directory
  www.liszt.com/news

  Master List of Newsgroup Hierarchies
  www.magma.ca/~leisen/mlnh

  Tile.Net Newsgroup Hierarchy List
  tile.net/news

Table C.1

Popular Usenet Newsgroup Hierarchies	
TOPIC	DESCRIPTION
alt	Alternative newsgroups—everything from sexually oriented topics to the truly offbeat. They're called "alternative" because they don't fit neatly anywhere else. Many Usenet servers don't carry these groups.
bionet	Biology network.
bit	Articles from Bitnet LISTSERV mailing lists, used mainly by the academic community.
biz	Business-related newsgroups. This is the place for advertisements, marketing, and other commercial postings (product announcements, product reviews, demo software, etc.).
cern	Discussions relating to CERN, the European Particle Physics Lab located in Geneva, Switzerland. It was at CERN that Tim Berners-Lee developed the World Wide Web to enhance collaboration on research documents.
clari	ClariNet News, a commercial service providing UPI wire news, newspaper columns like Dave Barry, and lots more to sites that subscribe.
comp	Computer-related newsgroups. Topics of interest to computer professionals and hobbyists, including computer science, software source code, and information on hardware and software systems.
gnu	Discussions about the GNU (Gnu's Not Unix) project and the Free Software Foundation.
hepnet	Higher Energy Physics network.
humanities	Discussions of humanities and the arts.
info	Creators of Internet mailing lists often place their messages automatically into Usenet. This is where you'll find them.
k12	Topics of interest to teachers of kindergarten through grade 12 (curriculum, language exchanges with native speakers, and classroom-to-classroom projects designed by teachers).
linux	Discussions about Linux, a version of the UNIX operating system that's distributed as freeware for use on personal computers. Linux is a system for the very technical professional—not for casual PC users.
microsoft	Newsgroups devoted to discussions of Microsoft products and services.
misc	A catch-all category for groups that address topics not easily classified anywhere else. Two of the most popular are misc.jobs and misc.forsale.
news	Groups concerned with the Usenet network (*not* current affairs, as you might think). The newsgroups news.announce.newusers, news.newusers.questions, and news.answers are the places to check for information aimed at first-time Internet and newsgroup users.
rec	Groups focusing on recreational activities and hobbies of all sorts—arts and crafts, games, music, sports, etc.
schl	Resources for elementary and secondary school teachers (similar to k12).
sci	Discussions of scientific research and applied sciences.
soc	Groups devoted to social issues, often related to a particular culture.
talk	Debates and long-winded discussions without resolution and with very little useful information.
vmsnet	Virtual Memory System Net, a place where people talk about VAX/VMS issues.

WEB SEARCHER'S TOOLKIT

Toolkit at a Glance

Categories of tools for Windows users:

- Screen and Web site capture
- Download tools
- File compression and extraction
- Fast browser and tools
- Convenience tools
- Multimedia players, editors, and tools
- Sound-related tools
- Image-related tools
- Security and encryption

Categories of tools for Mac users:

- Screen and Web site capture
- Download tools
- File compression and extraction
- Sherlock companions
- Sound-related tools
- Image-related tools
- Security and encryption

Whether it's an article, a file, or an image, getting the information you want online can be a major challenge. Fortunately, there are many software tools that can either make the task easier or help you work with the information once you've saved it to disk.

For example, a program like Download Accelerator Plus (DAP) can boost your download speed by as much as 300 percent. How? By cleverly searching the Net for copies of the target file and then downloading pieces of it simultaneously from several different sites.

Another program called Webforia lets you "clip" and save complete Web pages with fully functional hyperlinks. You can then organize them into a "library" that you can search by keyword. You can also assemble the Web pages into a report, add content of your own, and send the results as a single file to colleagues and co-workers for viewing with their Web browsers. No need for them to go online.

Good news, bad news

Perhaps best of all, tens of thousands of tools like these can be downloaded from the Net and used *free of charge*. (As you may recall from our discussion of specialty search sites in Chapter 20, CNET Shareware.com (www.shareware.com) and ZDNet (www.zdnet.com) both offer excellent searchable software libraries.)

That's the good news. The bad news is that there are so *many* programs that it is very difficult for most people to know which are worth the time and trouble involved in downloading and installing them.

That's where this appendix can help.

We have been writing books and articles alerting people to the wonders of "free software" since the days when the only way to connect a computer to a phone line was to place foam cups around the mouth- and earpieces of a telephone handset. (If you were lucky enough to get a good connection, you might be able to communicate at the "blazing" speed of 300 bits per second.)

We know how to find the really good stuff— the best of which is not only equal to the top-rated commercial programs, it is often superior.

That's because most freely available programs are works of art that embody the vision of a single individual. Commercial software, in contrast, tends to be written by a committee guided by input from marketing focus groups.

Shareware, freeware, and public domain software

In this appendix, we've identified and provided brief descriptions of specific programs that, in our opinion, rank as the "best of breed" in their respective categories. *Public domain* and *freeware* programs may be used completely free of charge.

Shareware programs may also be used that way. But shareware is "software on the honor system." If you like and regularly use a shareware program, you are honor-bound to pay the requested *registration fee*. The cost is usually between $15 and $40, and registering the program may even entitle you to technical support from the programmer who created it (not something one should expect anytime soon from Microsoft or Apple!).

To encourage you to do the right thing, many shareware programs delay their startups with a "nag screen" that reminds you to register. Some are set to operate for 30 days and will then refuse to load until you pay the requested fee. Still others can be used forever, but with certain features disabled.

Shareware registration options

Our advice: If you find that one of these programs saves you time or aggravation, pay the fee and become a registered user. Often you can handle the transaction online, using your credit card and a secure server, and download the product directly. (The download may take a while, and you'll want to be sure to copy the downloaded file to a backup location.)

In some cases, you may simply receive a numerical code via e-mail and thus be able to unlock your copy of the program without downloading a separate registered version.

Getting the programs

Windows Users. All of the Windows programs described in this appendix are available from Web sites like CNET Shareware.com and ZDNet. (For a truly extensive list of sites, go to Yahoo and do a search using the keyword *shareware*.)

Alternatively, if you'd prefer to save yourself the time and trouble of downloading the programs, you can order them all on a CD-ROM that we've put together for the convenience of our Windows readers. The cost is $15, including shipping. To place an order, and to find out about other programs that may have come to our attention since the book was published, visit our Web site at www.trulyuseful.com.

Macintosh Users. The shareware situation for Macintosh users is a bit different. Because the audience is substantially smaller, and the Mac has traditionally been viewed as such a complete, user-friendly system, there simply isn't as much free software out there.

In addition, you don't have to do very many searches at the major shareware sites to realize that they aren't making Mac programs a priority. Even the top-rated programs that are available are often several years old.

So you have to be clever. Instead of one-stop shopping at a site like CNET Shareware.com, you may have to visit the Web site of the program's creator and download a copy from there.

You might also try MacUpdate, MacShare.com, or The Shareware Place, all of which specialize in Macintosh information and software. Another good choice is The Ultimate Macintosh, where you'll find a page of links to the major Mac software archives as well as Sherlock news, set managers, and plug-ins.

Where to Look for Shareware

Windows and Macintosh

- CNET Shareware.com
  www.shareware.com

- ZDNet
  www.zdnet.com

Macintosh Only

- MacShare.com
  www.macshare.com

- MacUpdate
  www.macupdate.com

- The Shareware Place
  www.sharewareplace.com

- The Ultimate Macintosh
  www.ultimatemac.com

Essential Tools for Windows Users

Our recommended toolkit for Windows users includes 35 programs organized into nine different categories. Some of the programs are designed to save you time. Others make up for shortcomings and annoyances in Web browser software. Still others handle tasks that you may not have even known were possible.

One thing's for sure, with this collection of tools, you'll be equipped to handle a great majority of the search-related and computing challenges that come your way.

Screen and Web site capture

◆ **Collage Complete**. Have you ever wondered how people who write about computers—book authors, journalists, trainers, etc.—create the screen images that illustrate their work? Many of them use this sophisticated screen capture and image processing program. It lets you capture, crop, convert, magnify, dither, and manipulate images in every conceivable way and in all the most popular image file formats. No wonder it's the book publishers' choice.

◆ **HyperSnap**. While Collage captures just what you see on your computer screen, Hypersnap can take a picture of an entire Web page—even those portions that you have to scroll down to in order to read. It also can clip out screens from games, MS Direct X and 3Dfx GLIDE applications, and DVD movies. In general, it offers an excellent combination of power and ease of use.

◆ **Webforia**. This program captures Web screens as HTML files with all the images and links intact (and active if you are logged onto the Net while viewing them). As part of the process, it creates a document summary, a list of keywords, and several index entries. You can then organize your stored documents into libraries that can be searched or exported as a single file to be shared with others. You can also use the saved Web pages to produce an impressive report.

◆ **Offline Explorer Pro**. This is the program to use to download a *complete* Web site and store it to disk for offline viewing. You simply key in the address of the target site and Offline Explorer goes out to the Net, downloads all the files, and fixes their internal links to point to a location on your hard drive. If you like, you can even export the entire collection of files to CD-ROM or some other location, from which it can be viewed using any browser.

Download tools

◆ **Cute FTP**. The Internet's File Transfer Protocol (FTP) is designed to make it as fast and easy as possible to copy—upload and download—files between your computer and a Web server. It's a task that comes up frequently if you need to put updated files on a Web site or if you do a lot of downloading. This program's claim to fame is that it makes the file transfer process as easy as copying files from one of your local disk directories to another.

◆ **WS-FTP Pro**. Although its interface is quite user-friendly, this really is a program for FTP power users. Feature-rich, with a solid history, this is *the* program for frequent FTPers.

- **Download Accelerator Plus (DAP)**. This is one of those programs you fall in love with because of what it does for you and the way it works. Like GoZilla, its worthy competitor, it is ad-sponsored. But if you want to download a file as quickly as possible, and be able to resume where you left off should you be knocked offline (a frequent occurrence, especially with very large files), you want DAP on your disk.

- **Picture Agent**. Usenet newsgroups were started to facilitate discussion of the UNIX operating system. But the discussion topics soon expanded to cover nearly every aspect of life. There are tens of thousands of newsgroups, and many of them (`alt.binaries.clip-art`, for example) allow users to post images and other binary files as part of their messages. Picture Agent will comb the list of newsgroups you specify and download and save to disk whatever image postings those groups contain.

File compression and extraction

- **WinZip**. From the beginning of the online world, programmers have developed techniques for compressing files or groups of files so that they can be transmitted faster. Once downloaded, the files can be extracted from the compressed archive file and restored to their original form.

  The Zip compression format has become the standard, but you will still encounter archives on the Net that use formats like TAR, GZIP, and BinHex. This program can handle them all. And it will let you create archive files that are *self-extracting*, so the person using the file doesn't need a compression program in order to open it.

- **Aladdin StuffIt/Expander**. StuffIt, from Aladdin Systems, occupies the same position in the Mac world as Zip does among Windows users. This pair of programs lets Windows users compress and extract files or groups of files in the Macintosh format. Expander also handles Zip, GZIP, ARC, ARJ, uuencode, BinHex, MacBinary, MIME/Base64, and self-extracting StuffIt archives.

Fast browser and tools

- **Opera Browser**. Here's a full-featured browser written from the ground up to be both fast and frugal with your hard-drive space, memory, and system resources. Yet it has plenty of unique features.

  For example, you can specify both a search engine and a keyword or phrase in your browser's Address or Location box (where you normally enter Web addresses). So typing g Peachpit Press would take you to Google and perform a search on the name of our publisher.

  Opera also provides the ability to resume failed file downloads. And it allows keyboard (as opposed to mouse) access in all levels of the program—one of several features designed to help people with visual and mobility impairments.

- **Cache Explorer**. Browsers store the contents of the Web pages you visit in a cache directory on your hard disk. That way, the second time you visit a page, it will be displayed much faster because the elements are coming from your hard disk instead of from the Internet.

  Cache Explorer organizes these files and presents them with easily understandable names. A search function lets you find the Web pages you've visited on the basis of the keywords you specify. So if you've forgotten a site's address but remember a keyword or two, chances are that everything you need is in the cache—and Cache Explorer will help you find it.

◆ **Bookmark Magic**. This program will convert Internet Explorer Favorites into Netscape Bookmarks and vice versa. It will also sort Favorites/Bookmarks by their descriptions, find and delete duplicates, and allow you to make descriptions bold and/or italicized. You can also save your Favorites or Bookmarks list in a single HTML file that can be used with any browser or even posted to a Web site.

◆ **Internet Watcher Ad Blocker**. Banner ads at Web sites are like TV commercials—most people ignore them. But now there's a way to prevent them from even making their way to your screen. This program can also be used to prevent pop-ups from appearing and to stop animations (or "dancing baloney," as they are sometimes called). And it can prevent children or employees from accessing the Web sites you specify. It works its magic by setting itself up as a *proxy server* and can be used as such on any network.

Convenience tools

◆ **Magellan Explorer**. If you find the Windows built-in file explorer a pain to use, you'll love the double-window approach to file management offered by Magellan. Highly customizable, it places all the tools you need right at your fingertips.

◆ **ClipMate**. Here's another tool we couldn't live without. It remembers every piece of data (both text and graphics) that you cut or copy. Once your data is saved in ClipMate, you can select an item and it is automatically placed *back* on the Clipboard or directly into an application.

◆ **PC Data Finder**. This program goes far beyond the file searching function offered by Windows to let you use AND, OR, NOT and NEAR operators, wildcards, and phrases. You can also search by document title and author. It's like having a search engine dedicated to your own computer's contents.

◆ **12 Ghosts**. This is a collection of utility programs (there are actually 21 of them), each of which uses a different color PacMan-style ghost icon. Included are a timer that can run programs or pop up reminders, a shredder that wipes out any trace of a given file, and a text-replacement program. Best of all, one of ghosts lets you shut down Windows with a single click.

◆ **EZ Macros**. A *macro* is a script of the things you want your computer (or a specific program) to do when you strike a single hotkey combination. For example, you might hit `Ctrl` `E` and your system would load Internet Explorer, go to AltaVista, and conduct a search that you want to do on a regular basis. Perform this action once with EZ Macros in Record mode, and it will create the macro for you.

◆ **AutoMate**. This powerful program will do macros as well. But its main focus is true automation. Actions can be scheduled for specific times or intervals (daily, weekly, only on weekends, etc.), but they can also be triggered by the appearance of certain dialog boxes, certain windows, system startup or shutdown, and more. So if you want to get daily sports scores, or pick up a newspaper Op-Ed piece by a columnist who appears only on Wednesdays and Sundays, this is the program to use to automate the task.

- **Quick View Plus**. From the creators of Paint Shop Pro, this program can correctly display over 200 Windows, DOS, Macintosh, and Internet file types. Files created by both old and current word processors, spreadsheets, and database programs are included. As is nearly every graphics file type ever created.

Multimedia players, editors, and tools

- **MultiMedia Xplorer**. Unlike the Windows Media Player or RealPlayer, this program is designed to not only *play* the multimedia files you find on the Net but to help you *manage* them as well. It can display all major image formats and convert among them (including a mass convert that handles any number of files at the same time). It handles sound and video files, of course, and includes a Multimedia Detective that scans your disks for sound, image, icon, and graphics files.

Sound-related tools

- **MP Convert**. This is a compact little *CD-ripper* that will pull tracks off an audio CD and convert them into one of three formats: WAV, WMA (Windows Media Audio), or MP3.

- **DMC Audio Converter and CD Ripper**. Designed for the more advanced audio user, this program will "rip" audio files from CDs and convert them into not only WAV format but also MP3 (Blade), MP3 (Lame), Ogg Vorbis, and WMA. The program will also let you convert LP record tracks into digital format for recording on a CD disk.

- **5-Star MP3 Finder**. Key in a musical artist, group, or song title and this program will search the leading MP3 music sites for you. You can then download and play the files it has found.

- **Nullsoft WinAmp**. Billed as the "ultimate high-fidelity music player" for Windows, this is a superb sound-file player, with a built-in graphic equalizer. It's considered the emerging standard.

- **Aladdin Tuner**. Brought to you by the folks who do StuffIt and Expander, this is the slickest, most user-friendly Internet radio tuner available. You can select states or countries on the map or search for stations by location, format (rock, classical, NPR, etc.), media type (Real Audio, MP3, etc.), or keyword. When you run Aladdin Tuner the first time, it will have to go out to the Net to download the current database of stations.

- **Gold Wave Sound Editor**. On a par with Sonic Foundry and other top commercial programs, Gold Wave displays sound files as a waveform that you can cut, paste, and manipulate like a graphic image. We've used it to cut together music and sound effects for holiday slide-show sound tracks. The program includes lots of built-in effects and other powerful tools, including a filter to remove pops and clicks from files recorded from your old vinyl LPs.

Image-related tools

- **Graphic Workshop Professional**. The ultimate viewer and converter for image files, Graphic Workshop will display, scale, alter, and convert files in nearly 30 major graphics and animation formats— GIF, TIF, JPEG, PCX, MAC, IMG, EPS, and many others. You can also use it to display thumbnail images showing quick renditions of each graphic file on your disk.

continues on next page

◆ **PrintStation**. Getting multiple images to print on a single sheet of paper is a real hassle with a conventional paint program. With PrintStation, you simply select the files and specify how many rows and columns you want. The program will automatically size the images to fit. You can even enlarge one or more images on the page and the surrounding images will be adjusted accordingly. Once you have the images arranged, you can add labels and borders.

◆ **Slide Show to Go**. This program helps you turn all those images you've found online or elsewhere into a really snazzy slide show, complete with captions and a sound track. Best of all, when you're finished, you can export the show to a single EXE file and send it to friends. When the recipient double clicks on the file, the show will run automatically.

Security and encryption

◆ **Surf Secret**. In the interests of efficiency and convenience, Windows, AOL, and all browsers, chat, and instant messaging programs record the addresses of the Web sites you visit and keep copies of the text and images that come in. This program knows where all those tracks are hidden and methodically wipes them out. You can set it to run automatically in hidden mode, so that no one will know you're using it.

◆ **Neocrypt**. This easy-to-use program gives you strong encryption capability and a file "shredder"—point, click, encrypt. It can even handle files on removable media like Zip and CD-R disks.

◆ **CS Enigma**. With this smooth, powerful encryption program, you can place many different files into a single encrypted archive. The encrypted file can then be sent via e-mail, and the recipient can extract the contents by simply entering the correct password—no need to have the CS Enigma program installed.

◆ **Zone Alarm**. If you have an always-on cable or DSL connection to the Net, you are as vulnerable to hackers as any company. Zone Alarm sets up a firewall on your computer to prevent outsiders from getting in. It was ZDNet's most popular download for the year 2000.

Windows Toolkit on CD-ROM

In response to requests from readers who would like to try a number of these programs but prefer not to spend their time finding and downloading them, we've put the entire collection of Windows tools on a single CD-ROM. The cost is $15 including shipping. For more information or to place an order, visit our Web site at www.trulyuseful.com.

Essential Tools for Macintosh Users

We've identified 19 programs for Mac users in seven different categories, including one for Sherlock companions. For the programs that aren't widely available from several sources, we've included the Web addresses for their creators.

Screen and Web site capture

◆ **Screen Catcher**. This program from St. Clair Software will take snapshots of screen images and save them in image formats that include PICT, GIF, JPEG, TIFF, BMP, PNG, Photoshop, SGI, MacPaint, TGA, and QuickTime. Its Catch-All feature will automatically scroll a window to capture images that are longer than your screen. Once captured, you can resize, dither, and otherwise manipulate the image file.

◆ **WebWhacker**. From Blue Squirrel comes a program that lets you download Web pages, including text and images, at the click of a single button. Once downloaded, you can view and surf the site offline, or incorporate it into a presentation.

Download tools

◆ **Interarchy**. Formerly known as Anarchie, this FTP client is among the most popular of all Mac shareware programs. It lets you upload and download files via the Net with an interface that makes the process as easy as transferring files from one folder to another on your local hard drive. Compatible with both MacTCP and Open Transport, the program also lets you do a "Mac file search" to quickly search the Net for Macintosh software.

◆ **Download Deputy**. This is a batch download utility that lets you use a Finder-like interface to create a list of the files you want to get and then download them in sequence. You can schedule the download to occur at any hour of the day or night. It can even be set to quit and shut down your system when it's finished.

File compression and extraction

◆ **StuffIt Lite**. As its name implies, this is a very basic program for creating StuffIt (SIT) archives. Sending a single compressed StuffIt file over the Net is far faster and more convenient than sending several uncompressed files one at a time.

◆ **StuffIt Expander**. You'll need OS 8.1 or higher, but if that's what you've got, then this program can easily decompress or extract any archive you're likely to encounter—including Zip files, LHA, TAR, MIME/Base64, ARC, RAR, and more.

Sherlock companions

◆ **Sherlock 2 Banner Ad Remover**. This patch for the OS 9 version of Sherlock 2 will remove the banner ads that appear when you search the Web. Available at CNET Shareware.com and elsewhere, the actual filename to look for is `sherlock-2-no-ads-90.hqx`.

◆ **Sherlock 2 Mod Patch**. Also for OS 9 users, this patch removes the default "brushed metal" surface of Sherlock 2 and adds new 3-D Copeland-style icons. Also removes white channel windows and replaces them with Mac buttons. The file is called `sherlock-2-mod-patch.hqx`.

continues on next page

- **Sigerson Sets Manager for Sherlock**
"Sigerson" was the name Sherlock
Holmes traveled under after sending
Moriarty to his death over the Richenback
Falls. The program is designed to help
users cope with the fact that there are
now over 300 Sherlock plug-ins. It really
puts you in control!

Sound-related tools

- **SoundJam**. Here is what has been called
the first "full-featured, all-in-one MP3
Player and Encoder for the Macintosh."
SoundJam can rip audio CDs and read
and convert AIFF, QuickTime, and WAV
formats into high-quality MP3s. No need
to use separate programs to convert and
play. A good place to get this and other
audio programs is www.macradio.com.

- **Aladdin Tuner**. Another winner from
Aladdin Systems, this media tuner and
player (formerly known as MacTuner)
uses a comprehensive database of available
Internet radio and TV broadcasts to let
you listen to radio stations all over the
world. You can search for stations by
name, location, or type of programming
(including police and fire scanners!).
You can also play MP3 and CD Audio
files and customize the program's look
and feel with your choice of "skins." The
program and skins are available for
download at www.aladdinsys.com.

Image-related tools

- **Picture Snooper**. Usenet newsgroups
provide an incredible way to find and
exchange information with others around
the world on any topic you can imagine.
Long ago, a technique was developed for
converting binary files (images, sound,
animations, and programs) into text
characters that Usenet would accept.
Picture Snooper automatically searches
for, downloads, decodes, and saves to

disk the images and other binary files
that have been posted to newsgroups you
select. It's available from QSys Software
(www.qsyssoft.com).

- **Graphic Converter**. You can use this
powerful program to import nearly 145
kinds of graphic files and convert them
to nearly 45 different formats. Batch
conversion of multiple files at once, a
slide show feature, AppleScript support,
and both basic and advanced image
manipulation features are all part of this
terrific package. The author's Web site
is www.graphicconverter.net.

- **Picture Archive**. This program lets you
store your images in a searchable database organized into up to five categories
of your own choosing. You can establish
filters to control which images will be
displayed, create a series of images, produce a simple slide show, and more.
The program will also take a "fingerprint"
of a given image and compare it to the
fingerprints of other images in your database to alert you to duplicate images
stored under different names.

Security and encryption

- **Web Confidential**. With this handy
program, you can organize and save all
your passwords, account names, user
IDs, software keys, and other codes in a
single convenient—strongly encrypted—
file. Get it from www.web-confidential.com.

- **Window Washer**. This program from
SiegeSoft protects your privacy and erases
any traces of your Web browsing sessions.
Compatible with Internet Explorer,
Netscape, and AOL, it automatically
removes tracking information stored in
your browser's cache, cookie collection,
and history files. And it "bleaches"
(shreds) the files to be deleted beyond all
prospect of recovery.

◆ **NetShred**. A simpler alternative to Window Washer, this program will shred your browser's cache and history files and your e-mail trash file. You can activate the program manually by double-clicking on the NetShred icon, or set it to run automatically each time you close your browser or shut down your system. The same company also offers ShredIt, a program you can use to shred any file. For details, visit www.arccom.bc.ca.

◆ **SafeMail**. This is one of several Macintosh encryption programs available at www.highware.com. The others encrypt ("password protect") individual files or complete hard disk drives. But this one focuses on e-mail messages.

SafeMail is compatible with the OpenPGP (Open Pretty Good Privacy) standard, so anyone using a similar program on any platform will be able to decrypt the messages you send. The program uses the recipient's public key code to encrypt the message, which can then be decoded only with the recipient's private key code. (Each person's public and private key codes are mathematically connected.)

◆ **QuickEncrypt**. This program offers a quick and easy way to encrypt files and e-mail messages. As long as your recipients know the password (which you send separately), they will be able to decrypt your message or file, even if QuickEncrypt is not installed on their own machines.

INDEX

INDEX

and Netscape Search, 217, 218, 219
overview, 79–80
PDF search, 79, 86
Quick Reference, 89, 297
refining a search, 88
SafeSearch filter, 96
search forms
    Advanced Search, 82, 90
    home page, 81, 82
search results, 86–87, 92, 95–96
specialized search tools, 82, 94
statistics bar, 87
stopwords, 84, 85
strengths, 37, 79–80
Web directory, 83
and Yahoo, 157–158
Googlebot, 79
GoTo, 10, 224
Gourmet, 277
government search, 57, 279
Graphic Converter, 330
Graphic Workshop Professional, 327–328
guides
    About.com, 15, 150, 248
    Argus Clearinghouse, 247–251

H

habits, search, 35–42
Hanover Hacker, 4
Hart, Michael, 284
Health A to Z, 271
Healthfinder, 271
help information, 7, 38
    AltaVista, 65, 72
    AOL Search, 190
    Deja, 238
    Excite, 202
    Google, 88
    HotBot, 103
    Lycos, 129
    MSN Search, 215
    Netscape Search, 227
    Northern Light, 145, 150
    Topica, 246
    Yahoo, 165, 169
    Zip2, 267
hierarchies, newsgroup, 234–235, 317–319
hit, 5
Home button, Web browser, 43
host search, AltaVista, 68

HotBot, 97–116
    Advanced Search option, 101, 110–111
    Boolean operators, 100, 104, 105
    case-sensitive search, 105
    company history, 97
    contact information, 98
    customizing, 101, 114–116
    date search, 110, 112
    entering search terms, 104–106
    field search, 110–113
    help information, 103
    home page, 99–103
    improving results, 110–113
    language options, 114
    meta words, 110, 111–113, 299
    multimedia search, 110, 111, 112
    newsgroup search, 103
    overview, 97–98
    pay-for-submission service, 10
    Quick Reference, 109, 113, 298–299
    refining a search, 107
    saving a search, 116
    search form, 100
    search results, 100, 106–108, 108
    specialized search tools, 102
    strengths, 37, 97–98
    Web directory, 101
    wildcard search, 106
http://, in Web address, 8, 46
human-compiled directories, 150. *See also* Web
    directories
Human Internet Guide. *See* About.com
HyperSnap, 324

I

ICANN, 311
IE. *See* Microsoft Internet Explorer
Illinois, University of, 284
image-related tools, 327–328, 330
images. *See* multimedia search
IMDb, 280
index, search engine, 9
InFind, 39
Infonautics, 275
information brokers, 42
Information Broker's Handbook, The, 42
Information Please, 280
InfoSpace, 253–260
    alternatives to, 253
    Celebrity Search feature, 257
    contact information, 253
    home page, 255

Y

Yahoo, 157–175
 Boolean operators, 163
 case-sensitivity, 164
 company history, 157, 158
 contact information, 158
 customizing, 162, 173–175
 entering search terms, 163–165, 167
 "express" submission service, 10
 field search, 165
 help information, 165, 169
 home page, 159–162
 News Clipper feature, 173, 174
 newsgroup search, 169
 overview, 157–158
 Quick Reference, 166, 308
 relationship with Google, 157–158
 Saved Searches feature, 173, 174
 search forms
  home page, 160, 163
  Search Options page, 167
 search results, 163–164, 167, 168
 specialized search tools, 161
 strengths, 37, 157–158, 170
 Web directory, 161–162
  browsing, 171–172
  contrasted with other directories, 170
  searching, 167–168
 Web Site Tracker feature, 173, 175
 wildcard search, 165
Yahoo! People Search, 253, 254
Yahoo! Yellow Pages, 262
Yahooligans, 161
Yang, Jerry, 158
yellow pages directories, 261–262, 267. *See also* Zip2

Z

Zagat.com, 274
ZDNet, 286, 322, 323
Ziff-Davis, 286
Zip2, 261–267
 alternatives to, 262
 case-sensitivity, 266
 contact information, 261
 Get a Map feature, 264
 help information, 267
 home page, 264
 Quick Reference, 267, 309
 search profile, 262
 searching for businesses with, 265–267
 what you can search, 261
Zip code locator, 287
Zone Alarm, 328

Features Comparison — Big Six Search Engines

SEARCH ENGINE	ALTAVISTA	GOOGLE	HOTBOT	LYCOS	NORTHERN LIGHT	YAHOO
Number of Web Pages in Database*	350 million	1.2 billion	500 million	575 million	330 million	1.2 billion
Powered By	AltaVista	Google	Inktomi (GEN3)	FAST	Northern Light	Google
Web Directory	LookSmart	Open Directory	Open Directory	Open Directory	Northern Light	Yahoo
Default Search	OR	AND	AND	AND	AND	OR
Require/Exclude Search Terms	+/- (Basic Search) AND/AND NOT (Advanced Search)	+/- (Use + for stopwords only)	+/-	+/-	+/- AND/NOT	+/-
Phrase Search	Double Quotes	Double Quotes	Use exact phrase menu option.	Double Quotes	Double Quotes	Double Quotes
Boolean Search	✔		✔		✔	
Nested Search	✔		✔		✔	
Case-Sensitive Search	✔		✔			
Date Search	✔		✔		✔	
Field Search	✔	✔	✔	✔	✔	✔
Multimedia Search	✔		✔	✔		
Proximity Search	✔					
Wildcard Search	✔		✔		✔	✔
Search Customization	✔	✔	✔			
Strengths/ Unique Features	Full Boolean and case-sensitive searching. Field-search options. Search customization options.	Largest database of Web pages. Sophisticated relevancy ranking. PDF files included in search results.	Power searching with easy-to-use interface. Multimedia search options. Search customization options.	Multimedia search options. Ability to handle phrases with stopwords.	Searches include Web and "special collection" database. Organization of results into "custom search folders." Search Alert Service.	Best Web directory. Searches include both Yahoo directory and Google database.

*Note: For updates on database sizes and other search engine features, visit www.trulyuseful.com.